Home Office Research Study 185

Entry into the criminal justice system: a survey of police arrests and their outcomes

By Coretta Phillips and David Brown
with the assistance of Zoë James and Paul Goodrich

A Research and Statistics Directorate Report

Home Office
Research and
Statistics
Directorate

London: Home Office

Home Office Research Studies

The Home Office Research Studies are reports on research undertaken by or on behalf of the Home Office. They cover the range of subjects for which the Home Secretary has responsibility. Titles in the series are listed at the back of this report (copies are available from the address on the back cover). Other publications produced by the Research and Statistics Directorate include Research Findings, the Research Bulletin, Statistical Bulletins and Statistical Papers.

The Research and Statistics Directorate

The Directorate consists of Units which deal with research and statistics on Crime and Criminal Justice, Offenders and Corrections, Immigration and General Matters; the Programme Development Unit; the Economics Unit; and the Operational Research Unit.

The Research and Statistics Directorate is an integral part of the Home Office, serving the Ministers and the department itself, its services, Parliament and the public through research, development and statistics. Information and knowledge from these sources informs policy development and the management of programmes; their dissemination improves wider public understanding of matters of Home Office concern.

First published 1998

Application for reproduction should be made to the Information and Publications Group, Room 201, Home Office, 50 Queen Anne's Gate, London SW1H 9AT.

©Crown copyright 1998 ISBN 1 84082 138 8
ISSN 0072 6435

Fo reword

This report presents the findings of a survey of arrests which were made between late 1993 and early 1994. There were two main purposes behind the survey. The first was to examine the filtering process which follows arrest and determines which of those who come under suspicion are prosecuted or cautioned. The second was to compile a profile of persons in police custody, including not just those arrested but also those detained at police stations as a place of safety or for any other reason.

The importance of this information cannot be under-estimated. The period after arrest is crucial in deciding whether those suspected by the police of committing offences enter the criminal justice system. The way in which the police apply Home Office cautioning guidelines, for example, is a key determinant of the outcome of many cases. The study examines this and other factors, such as the circumstances of the arrest, exercise of the right of silence and the provision of legal advice, which play a part in shaping the outcome of each case. At the same time, the study fulfils the need for more information about the 1.75 million or more people arrested by the police annually. One aim here is to assist in identifying and avoiding any discrimination at this stage of the criminal process on grounds of race or sex, as required by s.95 of the Criminal Justice Act 1991. The information collected also meets other policy concerns: for example, in relation to domestic violence cases, suspects at risk through their youth or mental disorder, and offending on bail.

The criminal justice system does not, of course, stand still and since the research was conducted a range of initiatives has been introduced. These include: a new Home Office cautioning circular; provisions in the Criminal Justice and Public Order Act 1994 relating to inferences from silence and to bail; and CPS charging standards. The present study provides important information against which to assess the effects of these initiatives and any future changes.

The survey was carried out at ten police stations in seven forces. Home Office researchers collected information about 4,250 detainees, using a mix of direct observation, documentary sources and questionnaires. Information was also provided by the CPS about their decisions whether to proceed with prosecutions and, where cases were pursued, about the eventual court outcome.

DAVID MOXON
Head of Crime and Criminal Justice Unit
Research and Statistics Directorate
[8] 1998

Acknowledgements

We would like to thank the many officers in each force who were so helpful in answering our questions, completing our questionnaires and putting up with our presence in the custody areas of police stations. There were times when these officers were extremely busy and it cannot always have been a welcome experience to have to cope with our demands as well as performing their myriad of other tasks. We would also particularly like to thank the liaison officers in each force, who did much to ease the passage of the research, particularly in ensuring that officers at each station were aware of our coming and of the purpose of our presence. We are also very grateful to the CPS lawyers and support staff who assisted us by providing information about the outcome of cases which were put forward for prosecution. Like the police, CPS staff are invariably extremely busy and an additional burden of form-completion cannot have been entirely welcome.

We owe a great debt of gratitude to the observers who spent so many hours in police custody areas collecting data. While the task was eased by the good working relationships that they enjoyed with officers, it cannot be denied that custody areas were generally either too hot or too cold, sometimes cramped, often smelly and noisy, and that the language and behaviour of some prisoners sometimes shocked hardened researchers and even the police themselves. The observers (besides the authors) were: Debbie Archer, Jo Bartlett, Tamsen Courtenay, Nicola Dowds, Tim Edwards and Ian Hearnden. We would also like to thank Sharon Grace of the Home Office Research and Statistics Directorate, for her assistance in the preparation of the report on the CPS stage of the research, and Natalie Wood, for her help in preparing figures and charts for the report.

CORETTA PHILLIPS
DAVID BROWN
ZÖE JAMES
PAUL GOODRICH

Contents

Summary

Every year, around 1.75 million people suspected of committing offences are arrested by the police. The time spent at the police station is critical because key decisions are made at this point about any further action to be taken against the suspect. However, relatively little information has hitherto been available about the arrest and detention process. The study described in this report was designed to remedy this deficiency. Between September 1993 and March 1994 a survey was conducted of 4,250 people detained at ten police stations in England and Wales. The stations at which the survey was conducted were selected as far as possible to be representative of police stations generally. Thus: they were located in a range of different kinds of area (city centre, inner city, suburban and large town); varied considerably in the number of persons arrested; were distributed among forces with varying cautioning rates; and the ethnic mix of populations in the areas they covered varied considerably, some areas having relatively large ethnic minority populations.

The study was conducted in two parts. In **Part 1**, Home Office observers spent five weeks at each station, collecting information about all detainees and their detention and processing. They employed a mix of observation and direct questioning of custody, arresting and interviewing officers. The issues which it was possible to examine included: the use of stop and search powers; offending on bail; access to legal advice; the right of silence; arrests for domestic violence; cautioning; the processing of the mentally disordered; and the treatment of ethnic minorities. The observers also set in motion procedures for tracking cases after the suspect had left the station, where the outcome was charge, summons, bail for enquiries or a reference to a juvenile panel or bureau.

In **Part 2**, information was collected about CPS decision-making in cases forwarded for prosecution. Where proceedings were terminated, the reasons for this decision were recorded. For cases going to court, details of outcome and sentence were obtained.

The main findings of the research were as follows.

Part 1: The police station survey

Who is arrested?

- Those arrested were overwhelmingly male (85%). Fifteen per cent were juveniles (i.e. aged under 17). Fifty-four per cent were unemployed, 27 per cent were employed and 14 per cent were school pupils or students.

- Seventy-eight per cent were white, 13 per cent were black and seven per cent were Asian. Black people were more likely to be arrested than would be expected by their representation in local populations.

- Two per cent of detainees were treated by the police as mentally disordered. One-third of them were detained in police custody as a place of safety rather than for committing an offence.

- Just over 60 per cent of suspects had previous convictions. White suspects were more likely to have a prior record than members of ethnic minority groups. Ten per cent of suspects were currently subject to a court order (e.g. a probation order or conditional discharge).

Reasons for arrest

- Eighty-seven per cent were arrested on suspicion of committing offences, while most of the remainder were held on warrant, as a place of safety or in transit between prison and court. The pattern of offences was roughly similar between stations although particular local crime problems were evident in high arrest figures for specific offences at some stations.

- There were ethnic differences in the reasons for arrest. Compared to their presence in the general arrest population, there was an above average percentage of white suspects among those arrested for vehicle theft, criminal damage, public order offences and prostitution, of black people among those arrested for robbery and fraud and forgery, and of Asians amongst those arrested for thefts from vehicles and fraud and forgery.

Circumstances of the arrest

- 'Reactive' policing (for example, officers responding to a message from the force control room) accounted for nearly three-quarters of arrests. 'Proactive' policing led to 24 per cent of arrests, with 11 per cent following a stop/search and the remainder stemming from surveillance or enquiries. The percentage of arrests which resulted from a stop/search was higher for black than white suspects.

- Eyewitness evidence was the most common source of evidence available at the time of arrest. In over a quarter of cases this took the form of police observation of the offence. In 60 per cent of cases arresting officers considered that there was sufficient evidence to charge on arrest.

- Six per cent of suspects were arrested for offences arising from incidents of domestic violence.

- Less than one per cent of suspects were arrested for offences which allegedly had a racial motivation.

On arrival at the station

- Sixteen per cent of detainees appeared to be under the influence of alcohol or drugs on arrival, four per cent were injured, ill or acting in a bizarre manner, one per cent were violent and one per cent were very unco-operative.

- The police arranged the attendance of an appropriate adult (usually a parent or other relative) in 97 per cent of cases involving juveniles.

- The police generally arranged the attendance of a doctor and/or appropriate adult for mentally disordered detainees but 16 per cent saw neither.

- A foreign language interpreter was required in one per cent of cases.

Legal advice

- Thirty-eight per cent of suspects requested legal advice, although at individual stations the request rate ranged from 22 to 51 per cent.

- The more serious the offence the more likely were suspects to request legal advice. Males were more likely than females to request a lawyer and black suspects more likely than whites or Asians.

- Thirteen per cent of requests for advice were not met for various reasons, meaning that, overall, 33 per cent of suspects had a legal consultation. Over three-quarters of consultations were in person with an adviser at the station, but just under one-fifth were by telephone.

- Sixty-one per cent of consultations were with the suspect's own solicitor and the remainder with the duty solicitor.

Interviews

- About half of suspects admitted guilt when interviewed. Males, adults and black and Asian suspects were less likely than others to provide admissions; so too were those who had received legal advice, those held at particular stations and those arrested on evidence that was not initially sufficient to charge.

- Ten per cent of suspects refused to answer all questions during police interviews and 13 per cent refused selected questions. 'No comment' interviews were more frequent at Metropolitan Police stations than elsewhere.

Outcome of police custody

- Suspects were detained on average for nearly seven hours prior to charge or release.

- Overall, 52 per cent of suspects were charged, 20 per cent had no further action taken (NFA), 17 per cent were cautioned, and the remaining 13 per cent were dealt with in various other ways.

- Twenty-one per cent of suspects were initially bailed, either pending further enquiries or the outcome of consultation with a juvenile panel. In over a third of these cases NFA was ultimately taken. Black and Asian suspects were more likely to be bailed for enquiries than whites.

- NFA was most likely where: there was insufficient evidence to charge upon arrest; no admissions were made during interviews; or the suspect was black or Asian. Those who gave 'no comment' interviews or received legal advice were less likely to be NFAed.

- Where action by way of charge or caution was taken, the relative use of each varied according to the seriousness of the offence, with charge rather than caution being far more likely in serious cases. However, there was considerable variation between stations in charging and cautioning practice.

- Relative use of charge and caution also varied according to a range of other factors. Females rather than males, juveniles rather than adults, and those with no prior record rather than those with previous convictions were more likely to be cautioned. White suspects were more likely than black or Asian suspects to be cautioned.

- Custody officers' decisions to charge rather than caution were most influenced by the seriousness of the offence, the presence of previous convictions, the fact that the suspect was an adult and the view that a court sentence was necessary. In offences of violence the victim's support for prosecution was also very important.

- Where suspects were eligible for a caution because they had admitted guilt, the factors which most influenced the police decision to dispose of the case in this way were: lack of recent previous convictions or cautions; a display of remorse; and the agreement of the victim.

- Thirteen per cent of juvenile suspects were referred for inter-agency consultation. The predominant recommendation from inter-agency panels was to caution.

Bail

- Twenty-eight per cent of those charged were refused bail, although at individual stations the proportion ranged from 15 to 52 per cent.

- The risk of failure to appear at court was most often cited as a reason for refusing bail.

- Thirty per cent of those charged were on bail to appear at court or bail to return to a police station at the time of charge. Those charged with prostitution and theft and handling offences were the most likely to be on bail to appear at court.

Part 2: The CPS follow-up study

The sample

- Over 60 per cent of cases in which suspects were charged in Part 1 were successfully followed up. Due to the difficulties of keeping track of cases committed to the Crown Court, the follow-up rate for serious cases was lower than for less serious ones.

Initial CPS action

- In 94 per cent of cases, Crown Prosecutors reported that there was sufficient evidence on the file received from the police to determine whether it was appropriate to proceed both on evidential and public interest grounds.

- The police made a recommendation on bail to the CPS in only one-third of cases. In 85 per cent of these cases the CPS followed the police advice.

The decision to terminate or proceed

- In 14 per cent of cases all charges against the defendant were terminated. In 57 per cent of these cases termination was on evidential grounds and in 31 per cent on public interest grounds.

- Termination was three times more likely in domestic violence related offences than in others. Termination was also more likely where the defendant: was of ethnic minority origin; was charged as a co-defendant; denied the offence; had no previous convictions; and had been charged with moderately or very serious offences.

- Proceedings were halted prior to the accused's first court appearance in two per cent of all terminated cases. In the remainder, the case was dropped at court or between court appearances.

Magistrates' court

- Over 90 per cent of cases proceeded with were dealt with at the magistrates' court. In 82 per cent of these cases defendants pleaded guilty to the main charge and in a further 10 per cent were found guilty or the case was proven in their absence.

- Ten per cent of defendants found guilty were sentenced to immediate custody, while around one-quarter received a community sentence. Over one-third were fined or ordered to pay compensation. In just under a third of cases the defendant was conditionally discharged.

Crown Court

- In 9 per cent of cases proceeded with, the defendant was committed for Crown Court trial.

- Cases were significantly more likely to be committed where the defendant: was an adult; had been charged with more than one offence; was being dealt with for a serious offence; or had provided 'no comment' interviews. The committal rate also varied significantly between areas.

- There was a finding of guilt in 68 per cent of cases (52% guilty pleas and 16% after trial). Acquittals occurred in 28 per cent of cases (5% jury acquittals, 16% judge ordered and 7% judge directed).

- Of those sentenced, 62 per cent received immediate custody and 22 per cent were placed on probation. The strongest predictors of defendants receiving a custodial sentence were: having previous convictions; having received a previous custodial sentence; the seriousness of the offence; and having other cases outstanding.

Overview of the filtering process from arrest to conviction

- Of those arrested, 40 per cent were eventually convicted. The proportion was much lower for domestic violence cases (21%), but higher for those who had exercised their right of silence and made no admissions.

- In some kinds of offence, charges brought by the police were altered by the CPS in a signficant minority of cases. Fraud and forgery and assault charges were most often altered, usually to a less serious charge.

- Charges were most often altered to reflect the available evidence, to respond to the defendant's willingness to plead guilty to a lesser charge and to overcome problems in proving intent.

Part 3: Conclusions

The research reaches conclusions in four main areas.

The arrest population

It draws attention to the salient features of the arrest population at police stations, noting particularly that the bulk of arrests are for offences of intermediate seriousness, that relatively few occur because of proactive police tactics, and that those arrested are not representative of the general population in terms of age, sex or ethnic origin. The research also points out that a significant minority of those arrested are not being held on suspicion of committing offences but for various other reasons: for example, as a place of safety or pending a court appearance, having been arrested on warrant.

Groups raising particular concerns

The way in which the criminal justice system treats particular sub-groups of suspects has generated concern in recent years. The research concentrated on four. Members of *ethnic minority* groups – and black suspects in particular – appeared to be dealt with differently or responded differently from white suspects at a number of points between arrest and conviction. For example, they were on average: more likely to request legal advice; less likely to provide confessions; less likely to be cautioned and more likely to have no further action taken against them by the police; less likely to be bailed after charge; less likely (where the suspect was a juvenile) to have their case referred for inter-agency consultation; and much more likely to have their cases terminated by the CPS. While some of these differences (inasmuch as they relate to decisions about the suspect) are suggestive of discrimination, the research argues that variables not measured by the research may help explain them. It also notes that some differences reduce considerably when account is taken of other relevant factors. However, the research points out the need for managers, supervisors and policy makers to take note of these findings and examine specific areas of decision-making or other activity in the criminal justice system carefully.

Where suspects were arrested following a *stop and search*, the decision to arrest generally appeared to be well founded. Action by way of charge or caution was roughly as frequent as in other cases and fewer such cases were terminated by the CPS. However, there were two exceptions to this conclusion. Firstly, black suspects were less likely to be charged or cautioned when arrested following a stop/search and more likely to be NFAed. Secondly, those arrested following stop/searches for stolen property were significantly more likely to be NFAed. The research suggests that these findings need more detailed examination to see whether they show that stops and subsequent arrests in these circumstances are being made on less than reasonable suspicion or whether there are other explanations.

Turning to *mentally disordered suspects*, the research found that custody officers tended to seek the advice of police surgeons before calling an appropriate adult. The PACE Codes of Practice in fact require the latter to be called as soon as the custody officer has any suspicion that the suspect may be suffering from mental disorder. Where suspects were identified as mentally disordered by the police, they were much less likely to be charged and a significant minority were transferred to hospital. This suggests that the police are filtering out at an early stage cases in which it is not in the public interest to put offenders before the courts.

The fourth group considered were those arrested for *domestic violence*. The research found that the recent police moves towards a pro-arrest policy in such cases were backed up by a higher than average rate of charging domestic violence suspects. However, the termination rate of cases by the CPS was very high because complainants frequently withdrew their allegations or were reluctant to give evidence in court. The research notes the argument put forward by some commentators that a withdrawal does not necessarily represent "failure": for example, the threat of prosection may deter the abusing partner from further violence. However, some complainants withdraw through intimidation and it is not clear whether procedures for checking that withdrawals are genuine and unforced are always being implemented consistently by the CPS.

Recent criminal justice initiatives

The research draws attention to the value of the findings as baseline information at a time when a range of criminal justice initiatives have just been implemented and 'pre-information' is required in order to gauge their impact. One is the recent introduction of compulsory *ethnic monitoring in the police service*. Others stem from provisions of the CJPOA 1994. Thus, the Act's *inferences from silence provisons* have recently been shown to have led to a reduction in suspects' use of silence in police interviews, drawing on data from the present study by way of comparison with the current situation. The *bail* provisions of the same Act are intended to curb offending on bail. The research provides a measure of offending on bail which has been used to help gauge the impact of the new provisions. The most recent *Home Office cautioning circular* was implemented after the research was completed. The study provides information about the factors which decision-makers take into account in deciding whether to caution, which can be used to see how the criteria they consider may have been affected by the new circular.

The dynamics of the processing of suspects

The research concludes by drawing attention to the 'contingent' nature of the processing of suspects. At each key stage of the process, decisions made in relation to or by suspects are strongly related to a range of variables, some intrinsic to the individual (e.g. their age or ethnic origin) and others extrinsic (e.g. the evidence against them or the offence they are alleged to have committed). The conclusions also draw attention to various inter-relationships in the processing of suspects. Firstly, decisions made at one point may affect those made later on. Thus, the decision to seek legal advice, the provision of a confession and case outcome are all linked. Secondly, certain common factors crop up as related to decisions or events at a number of points in the system: for example, the suspect's ethnic origin or possession of previous convictions. The report concludes that understanding such connections in turn helps our broader understanding of the working of the criminal justice system and is essential for policy makers in helping them to plan new initiatives and to gauge their effect.

Introduction

Background to the study

Every year, around 1.75 million people suspected of committing offences are arrested by the police (Home Office, 1997a). Many more are detained in police custody for a variety of other reasons. These include arrests on warrant for failure to appear at court and the detention of persons believed to be mentally ill, who are held at police stations as a place of safety until more appropriate arrangements can be made for their care. Particularly for those arrested for offences, the time spent at the police station is critical, because it is during this period that key decisions are made about any further action that should be taken. In effect, for many suspects the question of whether they enter the formal criminal justice system is made during the few hours that they are held in police custody[1]. For some, the decision about what action to take is deferred, either because further enquiries need to be made or because, in relation to juveniles, other agencies need to be consulted. Nevertheless, for these suspects too the course of events during police detention undoubtedly plays a key role in the eventual outcome of the case.

Given the importance of the arrest and detention process, it is perhaps surprising that little systematic information is available about it, either from statistical or research sources. The only routinely collected statistical information is a total figure for all arrests, whether for notifiable or other offences[2]. Data are collected on recorded offences and how many are cleared up and by what means (Home Office, annually), but it is not possible to say what proportion are cleared up as the result of an arrest. Furthermore, these figures are offence-based; in fact, one offender may be responsible for a number of offences which are cleared up. Data are also collected on the numbers of offenders cautioned or proceeded against at court (Home Office, ibid). However, it is not possible to relate these figures to any prior arrest. Nor is it possible to determine how often cases in which an arrest is made do not result in a caution or prosecution.

---

1   Proceedings are also commenced against many persons by way of summons without any prior arrest. For the most part these are for motoring or regulatory offences.

2   See *Criminal Statistics England and Wales* (Home Office, annually). This information can be broken down by police force but not by offence. At the time at which the research was undertaken, figures on arrests in the Metropolitan Police were only collated for notifiable offences. Data for other offences are now available although it appears that these are limited to arrests where a crime record has been made.

In recent years, a range of policy concerns have pointed towards the need to collect more and better data on those arrested by the police. The following are among the significant policy issues:

- **Discrimination:** section 95(1)(b) of the Criminal Justice Act 1991 requires the Home Secretary to publish information that will aid those involved in the administration of justice in their duty to avoid discrimination on the basis of race, sex or any other improper ground. At the time at which this provision was introduced, relatively little information was available about the comparative treatment of different ethnic groups or of males and females at the post-arrest stage to help judge whether any unfair discrimination existed (see Home Office, 1992a; 1992b; FitzGerald, 1993)[3].

- **'At risk' groups:** the treatment of juveniles and the mentally disordered or mentally handicapped raises a number of concerns. For these groups of people the police are required by the Police and Criminal Evidence Act 1984 (PACE) to secure the attendance of an appropriate adult to safeguard the suspect's interests. However, doubts have been voiced, notably by the Royal Commission on Criminal Justice (RCCJ) (1993), about whether those who act as appropriate adults are always adequately equipped and briefed to fulfil this role. Another major issue is whether mentally disordered or mentally handicapped persons are always correctly identified by the police. Several studies have found that the police treat relatively few suspects as falling within these categories (see, for example, Brown, 1989; Brown, Ellis and Larcombe, 1992; Gudjunsson et al., 1993; Bean and Nemitz, 1994; Robertson, Pearson and Gibb, 1995) and that a far higher proportion of suspects may in fact need special help (Gudjunsson ibid. 1993).

- **Diversion from prosecution:** the avoidance of court proceedings in appropriate cases, particularly for juvenile and young offenders, remains an important strand of criminal justice policy, since diversion from the courts may well reduce the likelihood of reoffending. Police cautioning is the central plank of diversionary policy and relevant guidance is given to the police in Home Office circulars. There has been increasing concern in recent years over whether repeated cautioning of the same offenders or the issuing of cautions in serious cases is bringing this disposal into disrepute. Some information on cautioning practice is available from previous research (see, for example, Evans and Ferguson (1991) on the work of juvenile panels

---

3   Purely as a result of s. 95, but also prompted by other criminal justice developments, ethnic monitoring of four aspects of police activity (stop/searches, arrests, cautions and homicides) has been compulsory since 1996. See FitzGerald and Sibbitt (1997) for a full account of the background to and implementation of ethnic monitoring in police forces.

and bureaux and Evans (1992) on young adult diversion schemes). However, there is sparse information about the bulk of cautioning decision-making, which is carried out by the police themselves without the involvement of other agencies.

- **Offending on bail:** in recent years there has been increasing concern about the frequency with which those on bail to appear at court commit further offences while on bail. However, as Morgan (1992) has noted in a review of studies on this topic, there are various definitional and methodological problems associated with measuring offending on bail. It is therefore not clear to what extent any trends can be discerned from the available studies.

- **Domestic violence:** the extent of domestic violence and the way offences are dealt with by the criminal justice system have attracted considerable attention in the 1990s. The British Crime Survey (BCS) has pointed to a large increase in such incidents during this period – up from around 500,000 in 1991 to around one million in 1995 (Mayhew, Aye Maung and Mirrlees-Black, 1993; Mirrlees-Black, Mayhew and Percy, 1996). Home Office circular 60/1990 urged the police to take a more interventionist approach in domestic violence cases, with a presumption in favour of arrest (Home Office, 1990b). The Crown Prosecution Service also issued a policy statement on the handling of domestic violence cases (CPS, 1993). It recognised that, historically, such offences had been "under policed and under prosecuted" and stressed that, if sufficient evidence was available and the victim was willing to give evidence, it would be rare for the public interest not to require prosecution. In cases where victims wished to withdraw, the document advises that discontinuance of proceedings should only take place when all other options have been considered and found to be inappropriate. The Home Office has carried out an evaluation of the way in which the police have altered their policies and practices in response to the circular (Grace, 1995). However, little information is available about the way in which the pro-arrest policy is translating into charges and convictions.

These were among the specific issues which were the immediate driving forces behind the study described in this report. However, a number of more general considerations were also important in determining the need for the research. Foremost among these was a broad need for baseline information about one of the key stages in the criminal process. Establishing such information is important for a number of reasons.

First, it provides a yardstick against which to assess the impact of changes in policy or practice in the criminal justice system. In the past, the lack of such information was sorely missed in evaluating the impact of PACE. In the contemporary context, the information collected in the present study has already proved useful in monitoring the effect of Home Office cautioning circular 18/1994 (Home Office, 1994a), which was introduced shortly after the conclusion of the study. It has also proved valuable in evaluating the impact of certain of the provisions of the Criminal Justice and Public Order Act 1994, including those relating to the right of silence.

Secondly, there was felt to be a need for information on the consistency of application of policies at the post-arrest stage of the criminal process. Many studies have been confined to limited geographical areas, so limiting the extent to which an overview can be gained of the implementation of policies more broadly.

Lastly, there was considered to be a need for a resource which could be drawn upon in answering a range of official requests for information about the arrest process: for example in the form of Parliamentary Questions. However, given the costs of obtaining such information, these kinds of request would not in themselves have justified the undertaking of the research reported here.

The present study

The wide range of needs outlined above pointed to the need for a comprehensive data collection exercise. Three categories of data were identified as being required:

- **Socio-demographic information** about those arrested, in order to allow a profile to be compiled of those in police custody and to chart the treatment of different groups of suspects. The relevant information included: ethnic origin; age; gender; employment status; mental health; place of residence; and criminal history.

- **Contextual information** about the arrest and processing of the detainee. Among the items it was relevant to include here were: the circumstances leading to arrest; the nature of the offence; details of the evidence against the suspect; the condition of the suspect on arrest; whether the suspect was on police or court bail at the time of arrest; the provision of legal advice; and the suspect's exercise of the right of silence.

- **Criteria for decisions** about the processing of the suspect. The key decision is whether the suspect should be charged or cautioned. To a large extent this is a decision made by the police, typically by custody

4

officers. However, in relation to juveniles, inter-agency consultation arrangements are in place in many forces and it was considered important to examine the recommendations resulting from this process. It was also seen as vital, firstly, to examine the filtering process which occurs once cases are referred to the Crown Prosecution Service, since proceedings are terminated in a significant minority of cases, and, secondly, to capture the final outcome of cases at court.

Choosing the best way of tackling a data collection exercise of this order was not straightforward. Mounting a retrospective survey posed the difficulty that the information required in individual cases is located in records held in a number of different places and is not always readily accessible. Most importantly, existing information is not necessarily fit for the purpose and there are significant gaps in documentary and computer based records or inconsistencies between areas in what is collected. Another possibility considered was that of undertaking some form of 'snapshot' survey. This approach was used successfully to capture information about the various stages of Crown Court proceedings in Zander and Henderson's (1993) study for the RCCJ. The difficulty of this approach in relation to arrests is that the provision of the data required would have imposed an unacceptable burden on police officers. Doubts might also be raised about the reliability of data which was not collected by objective third parties. Furthermore, it was considered that this method would be unlikely to capture the filtering process as adequately as would tracking the progress of a group (or 'cohort') of suspects as they passed through the different stages of the pre-court process.

This last (i.e. cohort) approach was considered to be the most promising. A prospective study was mounted, in which samples of those arrested were tracked as they progressed through the criminal process. The research took place in seven police forces at a total of ten stations, which were selected to be representative as far as possible of police stations generally. Thus, the stations covered a range of areas – which might be broadly categorised as city centre, inner-city, large town and suburban – with a variety of policing problems. Also, bearing in mind that one aim of the research was to examine diversionary practice, the forces included ones with low, intermediate and high cautioning rates[4]. Furthermore, given that the study intended to monitor the way in which different ethnic groups are dealt with after arrest, the stations included some in areas containing appreciable numbers of people from the main ethnic minority groups. Whether the sample of arrests

---

4   At the time at which the selection of forces was made, the cautioning rate in England and Wales for indictable offences was 36 per cent but ranged from 20 per cent in South Wales to 44 per cent in Bedfordshire (Home Office, 1992a). Subsequently, the cautioning rate rose to 41 per cent in 1992 and stayed at that level until 1996, when it declined slightly to 40 per cent. Cautioning rates still vary considerably between forces: from 26 per cent in Dorset and Durham to 53 per cent in Surrey (Home Office, 1997a).

which was actually achieved was representative of arrests generally cannot be confirmed because data on arrests, broken down by key variables such as offence, are not collected at a national level[5].

Work on the study proceeded in two parts. In Part 1, fieldwork was carried out at the ten police stations; in Part 2, the CPS provided information about the eventual outcome of cases in which suspects had been charged. Fieldwork for the first phase of the study took place between September 1993 and March 1994. The following procedures for collecting data were adopted. Home Office research staff were present in the custody offices at each of the stations for an average of 25 days out of a five week period[6]. It was projected that this would yield samples of sufficient size to allow high-level comparisons to be made between stations and to provide adequate representation of small sub-groups of suspects (for example, those from ethnic minority groups, the mentally disordered and those arrested for domestic violence offences). In all, the sample comprised 4,250 of those arrested or detained[7], distributed between stations and forces as follows:

Force	Station	Sample size
Bedfordshire	Luton	602
GMP	Stretford	292
GMP	Rochdale	500
Leicestershire	Beaumont Leys (Leicester)	314
MPS	Croydon	555
MPS	Hackney	416
Northumbria	Gateshead	559
South Wales	Fairwater (Cardiff)	395
West Midlands	Birmingham Road (Wolverhampton)	354
West Midlands	Queen's Road (Birmingham)	263

---

5   However, data on arrests by ethnic group have been collected since 1996 as part of compulsory ethnic monitoring in the police service - see footnote 3 above.

6   An additional 5 days were spent at both Fairwater and Hackney, due to the lower number of prisoners detained at these stations. At all stations, research staff were normally present for around 20 hours per day, missing the period between 3 a.m. and 7 a.m. when, usually, little was happening. However, where custody offices were still busy at 3 a.m., researchers would stay on until a natural break in activity occurred.

7   The sample contained both those arrested on suspicion of committing offences and those detained for other reasons. The latter group included those held at police stations as a place of safety under s.136 of the Mental Health Act 1983, those detained on warrant for failure to appear at court and remand prisoners being transferred between prison and court. In this report, a distinction is made between the groups, where appropriate, by referring separately to those arrested and those detained. However, for the sake of brevity, the term 'detainee' is sometimes used to refer to all those in police custody, whether arrested or detained. Where this is done it is made clear in the text or in footnotes to tables.

Research staff were responsible for recording a range of data about those in custody and decisions made about their processing. They used a combination of direct observation, reference to documents (primarily the custody record), and questioning of arresting officers, custody officers and duty inspectors. Additionally, they were responsible for distributing a short questionnaire to arresting and interviewing officers. This elicited information about the circumstances of arrests and the nature of the evidence, previous cautions or convictions, and whether suspects admitted offences or exercised their right of silence.

For some detainees, no follow-up of their cases was required beyond the observation period, either because the police decided on no further action or an instant caution. Others who had been detained at the police station as a place of safety also passed out of the hands of the criminal justice system at this point, following an assessment by medical professionals that they should be committed to a psychiatric facility. In the remaining cases, procedures were put in place to track the suspect's future progress. The arrangements made varied according to the outcome of custody. The most straightforward situation was that in which the suspect was charged. In this instance, it was possible to proceed directly to Part 2 of the study – the monitoring of CPS decision-making and court outcomes. Arrangements were made with Administrative Support Units[8] (or their equivalent) at each station to include a monitoring form with the case file sent to the CPS. Lawyers would then record the appropriate details about the progress of the case. This phase of the research was lengthy, because some cases were not finalised at Crown Court until well over a year after the initial fieldwork at police stations was concluded.

Where the suspect was not charged, but a decision was deferred, arrangements were made to capture the eventual outcome of the case by forwarding a case tracking form to those responsible for decision-making. There were four situations in which decisions were deferred: to conduct further enquiries; to seek CPS advice; to consider whether to issue a summons; and to refer cases involving juveniles to inter-agency panels for a decision about the most appropriate action. Where the eventual decision was to prosecute, monitoring of the case's progress at the CPS and court stages was identical to that in other charged cases.

To some extent the study bears a resemblance to earlier work by McConville, Sanders and Leng (1991). They also mounted a prospective study, in which they charted the process of case construction against suspects. However, their initial data were collected from case files and there was no direct observation of charge room procedures. The bulk of their data was obtained from interviews with officers and CPS lawyers. The primary thrust of their

---

8   A main task of Administrative Support Units is to liaise with the CPS over the initial submission and, if appropriate, subsequent upgrading of prosecution files and to act as a quality control in relation to file content.

7

research was explanatory rather than statistical, and little information was provided about the nature of the arrest population or the custody process. The McConville study is now rather dated, since it was carried out very soon after the CPS was introduced (indeed some cases in their sample date from pre-CPS days) and prior to the introduction of the 1990 Cautioning Circular. Therefore, their research, while providing valuable insights into the principles underlying police and CPS case-building, should be seen as complementary to – but to some extent superseded by – the present study.

Structure of this report

The remainder of this report is in three parts. The findings from the police station phase of the research are presented in Part 1. Decision-making by the CPS and the outcome of cases at court is described in Part 2. The conclusions of the study are presented in Part 3.

Part I:The police station study

The first two chapters of this part of the report describe the arrest population and the context of arrests. Chapters 3 and 4 deal with some of the issues that arise on the detainee's arrival at the police station, including the requirement to obtain an appropriate adult in cases involving juveniles or the mentally disordered, and requests by suspects for legal advice. Chapter 5 looks at the interviewing of suspects and, specifically, at the frequency of admissions and use of the right of silence. Chapter 6 considers the factors which are important in determining whether suspects are charged, cautioned or released with no further action. Lastly, Chapter 7 is concerned partly with bail issues, including the extent of offending on bail and custody officers' decisions whether to grant police bail, but also presents information on the length of time detainees are held in police custody.

1 A profile of those arrested

This chapter provides details about those detained at each station by the police during the course of the research fieldwork. The sample consisted of a total of 4,250 people arrested for criminal offences or detained for other reasons.

Sex

Official statistics (Home Office, annually) and self-report research (see, for example, Mawby, 1980) have both noted that offenders are predominantly male. The present study's findings were no different: the sample consisted of 85 per cent men (n=3,610) and 15 per cent women (n=639)[1]. There was little variation between stations, with the exception of Birmingham Road (Wolverhampton), where 25 per cent of detainees were female. This reflected the high proportion of female prostitutes who were detained at this station (see Chapter 2). The ratio of male to female detainees was almost the same for white and black detainees (84:16 and 85:15 respectively), but almost all (96%) Asians arrested were male (see Appendix A, Table A.1).

Ethnic origin

Figure 1.1 gives information about the ethnic origin of the sample: 79 per cent were white, 13 per cent black, six per cent Asian and two per cent of other ethnic origin[2]. Whilst ethnic origin per se should not affect the decision to arrest (Brown, 1996), other research and official statistics have shown that black people are more likely to be arrested than whites (Stevens and Willis, 1979; Smith and Gray, 1985; Home Office, 1989; FitzGerald and Sibbitt, 1997; Home Office, 1997b; c.f. Jefferson and Walker, 1992). In the past, Asians have been variously reported as being as likely or less likely than

---

[1] The sex of the detainee was not recorded in one case.

[2] This four-point classification of ethnic origin is now the standard one in use throughout the criminal justice system for the production of ethnic monitoring data to meet the requirements of s.95 of the Criminal Justice Act 1991. Since 1996 it has been mandatory for the police to monitor stop/searches, arrests, cautions and homicides using these categories (FitzGerald and Sibbitt, 1997; Home Office, 1997b). At the time of the present research, those forces which recorded the ethnic origin of the suspect on the custody record still used a six-point system of 'IC' Codes. These codes remain in use for entering details on the Police National Computer. However, they have direct equivalents in the four-point classification (see FitzGerald and Sibbitt, 1997). Fieldwork staff either made a note of the 'IC' code recorded by the police and translated it into its four-point system equivalent or relied on direct observation. The 1991 Census used a more detailed nine-point system. However, this relies on self-identification and, as suspects were not interviewed by the researchers, it was not practical to use it in the present study.

white people to be arrested (Home Office, 1989; Walker, Jefferson and Seneviratne, 1990; Robertson, Pearson and Gibb, 1995). However, the most recent ethnic monitoring data on arrests (see footnote 2) show that in a number of police force areas Asians are more likely than white people to be arrested (Home Office, 1997b). The lack of agreement between these different sources of information suggests that the situation may well vary from area to area.

Figure 1.1   Ethnic origin of the sample

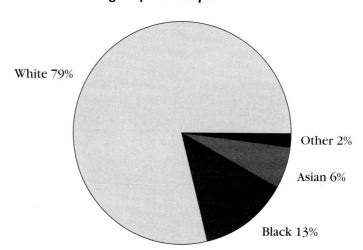

Notes:
1. N=4,231. Data were missing in 19 cases.
2. The table is based on all detainees.
3. 'Other' category includes those of Oriental and Arab appearance.

There are difficulties in estimating whether the number of ethnic minority suspects is higher than might be expected from their representation in local populations. One is that over 20 per cent of all suspects in the sample did not live in the area where the arrest occurred. The figures for the different ethnic groups were: whites – 20 per cent; black people – 29 per cent; and Asians - 33 per cent (see Appendix A, Table A.1). In London the proportion of transients was particularly high: 52 per cent at Croydon and 33 per cent at Hackney. Therefore, as others have noted, it may be misleading to compare the ethnic mix of the general arrest population at a specific station with that of the local community (FitzGerald and Sibbitt, 1997; FitzGerald, 1995; Brown and Ellis, 1994). It is more meaningful to treat separately those arrested who live locally and to consider to what extent they are representative of the ethnic mix in that area.

With these points in mind, Tables 1.1 and 1.2 show the proportion of black people and Asians among those arrested at each station, firstly for all those arrested and, secondly, for those who lived within the local police area. The third column shows the proportion of black people and Asians in the local population[3]. Looking first at Table 1.1, at almost all stations the proportion of black detainees was higher than the proportion in the local population. This was true both of areas with low black populations (Rochdale, Beaumont Leys, Stretford and Fairwater) and ones with higher numbers of black residents (Hackney, Croydon and Queen's Road). The disparity between the ethnic mix of the local population and that of the arrest population was usually slightly more pronounced when the comparison was restricted to detainees who lived locally[4]. This may be related both to features of the demographic distribution of black people and to the design of the research. In particular, members of black ethnic minority groups (and Asians) tend to cluster within closely circumscribed neighbourhoods (Ratcliffe, 1996). Some of the stations included in the research were specifically selected to include ones covering areas with significant ethnic minority populations. There was often a lower concentration of ethnic minorities in areas adjacent or close to those included in the research. It therefore follows that the proportion of ethnic minority suspects was likely to be lower among those arrested who travelled into the study areas to commit offences.

The reasons why black people were arrested more often than might be expected from their numbers in the local population are complex. Some studies have suggested that proactive police tactics – and particularly stop and search – impinge disproportionately upon black people (Stevens and Willis, 1979; Smith and Gray, 1985; Home Office, 1989; Walker, Jefferson and Seneviratne, 1990). The different age distribution of black people from that of the white population is also relevant (see further below).

---

3   Details of ethnic minority populations were obtained from local census data. While this was unavailable for police divisional areas, Census county reports provide a breakdown of the ethnic origin of residents for certain districts. It is important to note that the reports for the following areas are only a very general guide to the distribution of ethnic groups as they cover large city areas which may be dissimilar to the police divisional areas: Birmingham (Queens Road); Leicester (Beaumont Leys); and Cardiff (Fairwater).

4   The exceptions were Rochdale and Croydon. At the former, it is unsurprising that local black people did not feature in the arrest population because there were very few resident in the town. Most black suspects came from outside the town. Even so, they constituted only a relatively small proportion of the overall arrest population. Croydon was unusual in that over half of all those arrested here came from outside the town (see above).

Table 1.1 Proportion of black people in the sample and in the general population

Police station	Arrest sample (all detainees)		Arrest sample (local residents)		General population
	%	(n)	%	(n)	%
Stretford	15	(43)	16	(35)	2
Rochdale	1	(5)	<1	(1)	1
Luton	12	(74)	13	(66)	5
Queen's Road	22	(57)	24	(46)	6
Beaumont Leys	6	(19)	6	(15)	2
Birmingham Road	8	(29)	9	(26)	5
Fairwater	5	(19)	6	(19)	2
Gateshead	<1	(1)	<1	(1)	0
Hackney	46	(192)	48	(122)	22
Croydon	20	(103)	17	(40)	8

Notes:
1. Table based on all detainees: n=4,202. Data were missing in 48 cases.
2. General population data drawn from 1991 Census county reports.

Turning to Asians, Table 1.2 shows that, while there were some disparities between the proportions in the arrest population and in the local community, these tended to be less marked than those found for black people. Confining the analysis of the arrest population to those who lived locally made little difference to this conclusion. At some stations (Rochdale, Luton and Birmingham Road) the percentage of Asians among those arrested was slightly higher than the proportion in the local population; at others (Queen's Road and Fairwater) it was marginally lower. Some of the disparities picked up may have been chance variations and larger numbers of cases would be required to verify whether they reliably reflect a trend. This is particularly likely where either the number of Asians in the local population was low (as at Stretford) or there were few arrests of Asians (Hackney and Croydon). The large discrepancy at Beaumont Leys is probably explained by the lack of Census data for this precise area. The proportion of Asians in the local population of the area covered by this station was almost certainly lower than 24 per cent.

Table 1.2   Proportion of Asians in the sample and in the general population

Police station	Arrest sample (all detainees)		Arrest sample (local residents)		General population
	%	(n)	%	(n)	%
Stretford	5	(14)	6	(13)	2
Rochdale	10	(50)	10	(43)	7
Luton	17	(101)	18	(91)	13
Queen's Road	12	(31)	13	(25)	14
Beaumont Leys	6	(19)	6	(15)	24
Birmingham Road	17	(59)	17	(50)	12
Fairwater	2	(8)	2	(6)	3
Gateshead	<1	(2)	<1	(1)	<1
Hackney	2	(7)	2	(6)	6
Croydon	5	(24)	3	(7)	6

Notes:
1. Table based on all detainees: n=4,202. Data were missing in 48 cases.
2. General population data drawn from 1991 Census county reports.

Since the present research was completed, ethnic monitoring of arrests has become mandatory for the police[5]. Because the data are collected on a force-wide basis, it is possible to make comparisons between the arrest and local populations at this level, thereby reducing some of the problems noted above with small area analysis. The data for the first full year of monitoring (from April 1996 onwards) confirm that black people are more likely than white people to be arrested (Home Office, 1997b). The data are presented on a different basis from the present study but show that, depending on the police force, black people were between four and seven times more likely to be arrested than whites. The arrest rate for Asians was far lower than for black people but also varied between forces. Generally, they were more likely to be arrested than whites but arrest rates ranged from only marginally higher to nearly three times greater.

Age

Figures 1.2(a) and 1.2(b) provide details of the age distribution of suspects and other detainees. The main difference between the two groups was that a much higher proportion of suspects were juveniles, while a higher proportion of other detainees fell in the 21-29 age bracket. The youngest member of the sample was aged 7 and the oldest 75. There were some

---

5   See FitzGerald and Sibbitt (1997) for a full account of the background to the introduction of ethnic monitoring in police forces, its implementation and the problems surrounding the interpretation of the data it has produced.

marked differences between stations. The proportion of juvenile suspects[6] was particularly low at Birmingham Road (9%) and Hackney (13%). Other notable departures from the general pattern included a high proportion (40%) of 21 to 29-year-olds at Birmingham Road, which was related to the high number of prostitutes arrested there, a high percentage (32%) of young people aged 17 to 20 at Gateshead and an above average number (41%) of those in the 30 to 59 age bracket at Hackney.

Figure 1.2(a)   Age distribution of the sample (suspects)

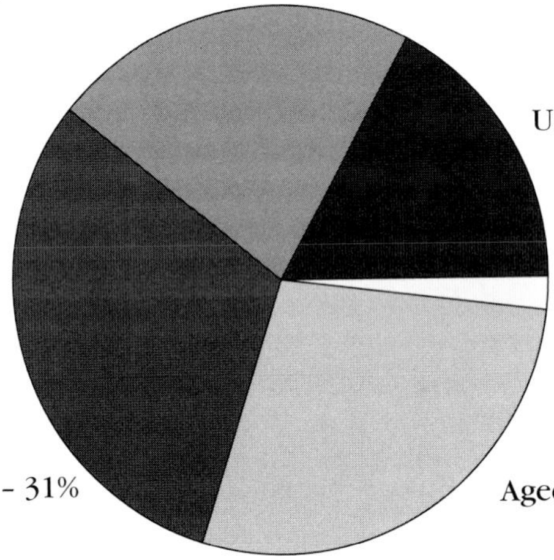

Aged 17 to 20 – 22%

Under 17 – 17%

Aged 60+ – 2%

Aged 21 to 29 – 31%

Aged 30 to 59 – 28%

Notes:
1. N suspects = 3,682.
2. Due to rounding, percentages do not sum to 100.

The age distribution for black people and Asians was examined to see whether it differed from that of white suspects (see Appendix A, Table A.1). One notable difference was that a far higher proportion of black than white suspects was aged under 17 (21% compared with 14%t). The figure for Asians – 17 per cent – was also higher than that for white suspects. Previous studies have drawn attention to the disproportionate number of young people in these two ethnic minority groups (FitzGerald, 1993; Brown and Ellis, 1994). The proportion of young Asians is particularly high, compared with both white and black populations. Since members of this age group are among those most prone to offend, irrespective of ethnic group, it would be expected that the presence in the general population of a higher than average number of young people from these ethnic minorities would boost

---

6   While those aged under 18 are now dealt with by the Youth Court, the provisions of PACE and the Codes of Practice only require the police to treat those who appear to be under the age of 17 as juveniles. In keeping with police

their numbers in the arrest population. The study provided some confirmation of this hypothesis in relation to young black males but not Asians[7]. Thus, where the available Census data were reasonably reliable at the local level (see footnote 3 above), as at Queen's Road police station, there were found to be relatively high proportions of young black males in both the local population and the arrest population. The same was true at Croydon and Hackney police stations. But, despite there being even higher proportions of young Asians in the local population, this was not reflected in their presence among those arrested. It should be noted that, even when account is taken of the different age distribution of black people, the proportion among those arrested was still considerably higher than the proportion in the local population. Home Office figures for the Metropolitan Police area confirm this picture. The most recent data for 1996 show that, while 9 per cent of the Greater London population aged 10 to 20 were black, this was true of 25 per cent of those arrested in this age group (FitzGerald and Sibbitt, 1997).

Figure 1.2(b)   Age distribution of the sample (other detainees)

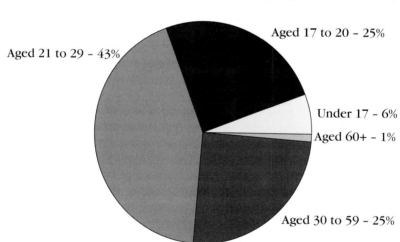

Aged 17 to 20 – 25%

Aged 21 to 29 – 43%

Under 17 – 6%

Aged 60+ – 1%

Aged 30 to 59 – 25%

Notes:
1. N other detainees = 568.
2. Other detainees included those held on warrant, place of safety detention under s136 MHA and those being transferred from court to prison

---

7   Because of the small numbers of ethnic minority females in the arrest population, they have been excluded from this analysis.

Employment status

Fifty-four per cent of the sample were unemployed, 27 per cent were in employment, and 14 per cent were school pupils or students. Three per cent were placed in the 'other' category (houseperson, housebound, retired, school non-attender, sick leave) and the employment status of two per cent was unknown. The proportion unemployed was higher among white (57 per cent) than black (50%) or Asian detainees (46%) (see Appendix A, Table A.1). There were particularly high rates of unemployment among 16- and 17-year-olds who had left school, rising to 75 per cent among those who were charged and appeared before the Youth Court. The present study was not designed to explore the links between unemployment and crime further[8], but it does provide striking evidence of the high level of unemployment among criminal suspects.

Previous convictions

Arresting officers and custody officers provided information about suspects' previous convictions either from the Police National Computer or their force's own computer system. Just over 60 per cent of suspects had previous convictions. Table 1.3 shows that there was some variation between stations. The lowest figure – 42 per cent at Croydon – is related to the fact that a high proportion of suspects there were juvenile shoplifters with no previous record of convictions (although some had prior cautions).

These figures can be compared with data from the Offenders Index (OI)[9]. The OI might be expected to show a higher proportion of offenders with previous convictions because it includes only convicted offenders. In contrast, the current study contained some suspects who did not go on to be convicted or recorded on the OI. This expectation was confirmed in relation to male offenders, although the difference was not great. A study of male offenders convicted in 1991, which used OI data, showed that 67 per cent of *offenders* had one previous conviction or more (Home Office, 1993). In the present research the figure for *suspects* was 64 per cent. For females there was only a very small difference. Thus, OI data from 1991 showed that 46 per cent of convicted females had one previous conviction or more, while the present study produced a figure of 45 per cent for suspects.

---

8   See Field (1990) for a discussion of the issues involved. Broadly, the debate revolves around the question of whether those who are unemployed turn to crime or whether those who commit crime either intentionally opt out of the labour market or find it difficult to obtain jobs because of their criminal records. A relevant consideration is that some of the characteristics associated with crime (such as low educational achievement) are also ones which make it hard for a person to get a job.

9   The Offenders Index contains information on the criminal histories of persons convicted of standard list offences, which are all indictable and triable either way offences, plus certain summary offences.

Table 1.3 Proportion of suspects with previous convictions by station

Station	Males %	Males (n)	Females %	Females (n)	Total %	Total (n)
Stretford	66	(146)	29	(9)	61	(155)
Rochdale	71	(242)	44	(25)	67	(267)
Luton	61	(267)	43	(37)	58	(304)
Queen's Road	63	(137)	60	(9)	63	(146)
Beaumont Leys	65	(160)	43	(18)	62	(178)
Birmingham Rd	64	(138)	82	(66)	69	(204)
Fairwater	72	(205)	54	(25)	70	(230)
Gateshead	70	(230)	39	(24)	65	(254)
Hackney	65	(205)	39	(18)	62	(223)
Croydon	47	(181)	22	(20)	42	(201)
All stations	**64**	**(1,911)**	**45**	**(251)**	**61**	**(2,162)**

Note:
1. Table based on suspects only: N=3,552. Data were missing in 130 cases.

Table 1.4 Proportion of suspects with previous convictions by offence

Offence	Total %	Total (n)
Violence against the person	61	(170)
Sexual offences	36	(19)
Burglary	71	(238)
Robbery	62	(45)
Theft and handling:		
Shoplifting	50	(158)
Theft of vehicle/TWOC	67	(245)
Theft from vehicle	65	(59)
Other theft and handling	54	(221)
Fraud and forgery	57	(75)
Criminal damage	49	(119)
Drugs	63	(78)
Public order	66	(314)
Motoring	57	(185)
Prostitution	97	(67)
Other offences	65	(169)

Note:
1. N=3,553. In a further 129 cases information on previous convictions was not available.
2. TWOC – unauthorised taking of a motor vehicle.

Whether suspects had a criminal history varied considerably according to the offence for which they had been arrested. OI data point to similar variation (although analysis is, of course, based on the offence for which offenders were convicted). Table 1.4 shows that higher than average proportions of those arrested for prostitution, burglary, vehicle related crime and public order offences had previous convictions. Those arrested for shoplifting, criminal damage, other theft and handling and sexual offences were the least likely to have previous convictions. It was not possible to check whether previous convictions were for similar offences. However, Tarling (1993) suggests that there is only a limited degree of 'specialisation' among offenders: those convicted of burglary or theft offences are the most likely to go on to commit further similar crimes.

The likelihood of suspects having previous convictions also varied according to their age, employment status and ethnic group. Figure 1.3(a) shows that juveniles were the least likely to have previous convictions. Juveniles are particularly likely to be cautioned (Evans and Ellis, 1997), especially for less serious offences, such as shoplifting and criminal damage. Since juveniles are disproportionately involved in such offences, this helps to explain the finding noted in the previous paragraph that those arrested for these offences were less likely than average to have a criminal record. Those in the 21 to 29 age bracket were most likely to have previous convictions (in over 70% of cases).

Figure 1.3(b) shows that unemployed suspects were significantly more likely than their employed counterparts to have previous convictions (in 76% of cases compared with 52%).

White suspects were more likely than those from other ethnic groups to have previous convictions (see Figure 1.3(c))[10]. In turn, more black than Asian suspects had previous convictions. The higher figure for whites was not simply a function of them being involved more frequently in the kinds of less serious offence which tend to be repeated (for example, public order and prostitution offences). Looking only at those arrested for notifiable offences, the proportion of white suspects with previous convictions remained at 63 per cent, while the figures for black and Asian suspects actually fell slightly to 57 per cent and 46 per cent respectively. There was a link with the different age structure of the black and Asian arrest populations. A higher proportion than their white counterparts were juveniles (see Appendix A, Table A.1), and juveniles stood a greater chance of being cautioned rather than being charged and, ultimately, convicted.

---

10   See Appendix A, Table A.1 for a breakdown of previous convictions by ethnic origin for for all detainees (i.e. suspects and those detained for other reasons).

Figure 1.3(a)   Proportion of suspects with previous convictions by age

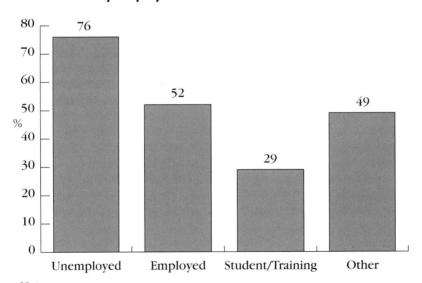

Note:
Data on previous convictions were not available in five per cent of cases.

Figure 1.3(b)   Proportion of suspects with previous convictions by employment status

Note:
Data on previous convictions were not available in five per cent of cases.

Figure 1.3(c) *Proportion of suspects with previous convictions by ethnic origin*

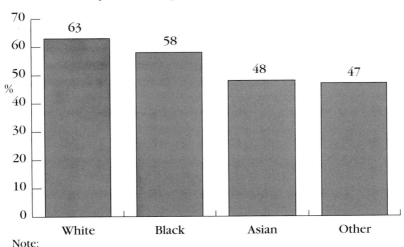

Note:
Data on previous convictions were not available in five per cent of cases.

Almost two-thirds of suspects who were mentally disordered had previous convictions. In the absence of any long-term intervention by appropriate agencies, many mentally disordered people repeatedly come to police attention as a result of their bizarre behaviour, which sometimes amounts to criminal conduct. This has been termed the 'revolving door' syndrome (Department of Health and Home Office, 1992).

Previous cautions

In some forces the study was also able to obtain information on suspects' previous cautions, using manual or computerised records. However, only five of the ten stations had reliable data[11]. Home Office cautioning circular 18/1994 (which had not come into effect at the time the research was undertaken) emphasises that the police should normally only issue a caution on one occasion, since multiple use may bring this disposal into disrepute. A second caution should only be considered where the later offence is trivial or where there has been a sufficient time lapse since the first caution to suggest that it had some effect (Home Office, 1994a). In the present study 41 per cent of suspects at the five stations had received a prior caution or cautions. This reflects the fact that cautioning has in the past been a relatively popular disposal for less serious matters, encouraged to some extent by previous Home Office circulars (see Home Office, 1985, 1990a).

11 Information on cautioning is not always updated as frequently as that relating to previous convictions. Where forces were able to provide information on cautioning, this related to practice within their own force. They were not at the time of the research able to check whether suspects had previously been cautioned in another force. This is increasingly becoming possible as information on cautioning is entered onto the 'Phoenix' Police National Computer database.

Figure 1.4 shows significant differences between stations in the proportion of suspects who had previous cautions. Slightly less than one-third of suspects at Stretford and Luton had been cautioned before, compared with nearly 40 per cent at Rochdale, and over half at Beaumont Leys and Birmingham Road. Previous research has also noted widespread variation in the cautioning of suspects by forces in England and Wales (Evans and Ferguson, 1991; Madison, 1994) as have official statistics (Home Office, 1997a). These variations are likely to be the result of differences in the interpretation and implementation of Home Office cautioning circulars, but may also reflect differences in local crime patterns.

Figure 1.4 Proportion of suspects with previous cautions by station

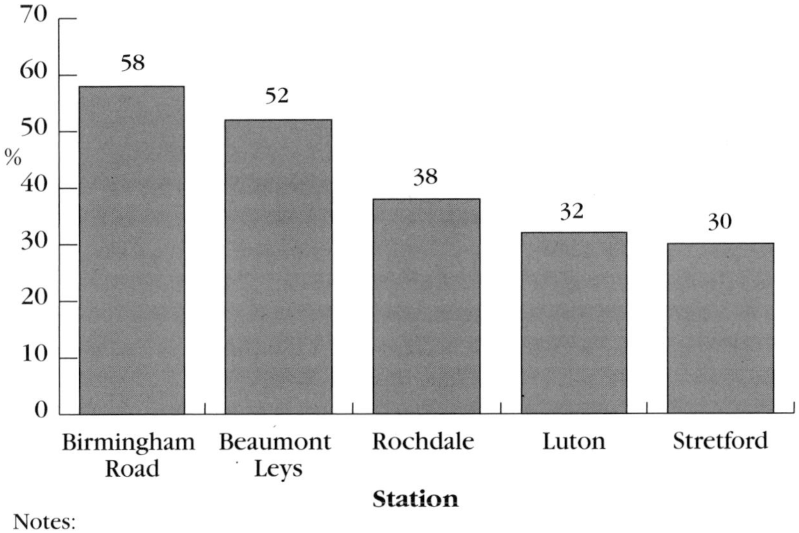

Notes:
1. N=1,716. Data on previous cautions were missing in 85 cases.
2. Data on previous cautions were missing in more than 15 per cent of cases at the following police stations, and they have therefore been excluded from the figure: Queen's Road (22%), Fairwater (36%), Gateshead (23%), Hackney (18%) and Croydon (36%).

Similar proportions of white and black suspects had previous cautions (45 and 42%, respectively), compared with 28 per cent of Asians[12]. More than 50 per cent of suspects aged 20 years and under had previously been cautioned. Those in older age groups were less likely to have been cautioned before: 40 per cent of 21- to 29-year-olds and one-quarter of those aged 30 and above. This reflects the fact that cautioning has only increased substantially relatively recently. It is also relevant to note that caution records are kept for only a limited period after the caution has been administered[13].

---

12   See Appendix A, Table A.1 for a breakdown of previous cautions by ethnic origin for all detainees (i.e. whether suspects or detained for other reasons).

13   At the time at which the present research was undertaken, details of cautions were retained on the Police National Computer ('Phoenix') for three years. However, since 1995 they have been kept for five years.

Court orders

Ten per cent of suspects were known to be subject to some form of court order at the time of their arrest. The most common ones were probation orders (27%). A further quarter were subject to a conditional discharge. Another one in ten were carrying out community service orders. The remaining 40 per cent were subject to a variety of other court orders, including combination and supervision orders, conditional discharges, suspended sentences, driving bans and bail conditions. The proportion of suspects who were under court orders varied between stations, with the highest proportions being at Stretford (16%) and Rochdale (23%). However, this may simply have been an artefact of more efficient recording of this information in the Greater Manchester force. Above average proportions of suspects arrested for burglary, robbery, vehicle crime and fraud and forgery were reported to be subject to a court order when they were arrested. Proportionately more males and suspects aged 17 to 20 years were subject to court orders.

Mental disorder

As Gudjunsson et al. (1993) have noted, identifying those suffering from mental disorder presents major difficulties for the police, although the evidence is that, by and large, they are accurate in their assessments in the more severe cases (Robertson, Pearson and Gibb, 1995). In the present study, just two per cent of detainees (n=67) were treated as mentally disordered by the police. The researchers observed a further 13 suspects whom they considered to be behaving in a bizarre or irrational way, but who were not treated as mentally disordered. There was some variation between stations in the proportion of detainees categorised as mentally disordered, ranging from less than one per cent at Stretford and Rochdale to four per cent at Beaumont Leys.

The proportion of mentally disordered detainees who were female was, at 22 per cent, higher than expected compared with the proportion of females in the sample as a whole (15%). Nearly half of the mentally disordered were aged between 30 and 59 and one third between 20 and 29.

While the figure of two per cent is a small proportion of all detainees, it is a slightly higher figure than that obtained by previous studies which have depended for their information on custody records. Studies by Brown (1989) and Brown, Ellis and Larcombe (1992), based on records from 32 and 12 police stations respectively, have suggested that around one per cent of detainees are treated as mentally disordered by the police. Bean and Nemitz (1994), who analysed nearly 20,000 custody records from Sheffield, Derby,

Grantham and Skegness police stations, reported that less than one per cent of records indicated that an appropriate adult had been called out to attend the police station on behalf of a mentally disordered detainee.

Brown (1996) and Dixon et al (1990) have argued that the numbers treated as mentally disordered by the police are much lower than might be expected, given the higher prevalence rates of mental disorder among the general population. They suggest that this may mean that the police are adopting a relatively robust stance to the way in which they interpret the provisions of the PACE Codes of Practice. Code C (para 1.4) stipulates that if an officer has any suspicion that a detainee may be mentally disordered or handicapped, he or she should be treated as such. This means that the custody officer should contact and secure the attendance of an 'appropriate adult' to advise and assist the detainee. In fact, custody officers often adopt a 'halfway house' of initally calling the police surgeon to examine the detainee. If the doctor pronounces the suspect fit and well, custody officers often do not take the additional step of calling an appropriate adult. This avoids the often lengthy and time-consuming process of contacting and awaiting the arrival of a suitably qualified person. Another factor tending to suppress the numbers of detainees categorised as mentally disordered may be deficiencies in the training of custody officers in identifying mental disorder, as a study by Evans and Rawstorne (1994) in Liverpool and Lancashire has indicated (see also Cherrett, 1995).

Further evidence that rather more than one or two per cent of detainees are mentally disordered comes from studies which have used trained observers to carry out assessments. A study for the RCCJ by Gudjunsson et al. (1993) found that 10 per cent of detainees could, in the view of psychiatrists who carried out screening interviews with detainees, be defined as mentally disordered or handicapped[14]. However, the study was confined to two London police stations and it would be unsafe to assume that quite such high levels of undetected mental disorder exist among detainees at police stations throughout London or elsewhere in the country.

A more recent study was carried out in London by Robertson, Pearson and Gibb (1995). Observers, who were all trained psychiatrists, were present in police custody areas and used a psychiatric inventory to assess detainees. Details of nearly 3,000 arrests were collected from seven police stations. The study concluded that 26 per cent of their sample were 'mentally disordered'. However, they used a very broad definition of mental disorder which included those who were drunk. Twenty-two per cent of their sample suffered from some degree of intoxication on arrival at the police station[15],

---

14 Their sample excluded juveniles, those not arrested for a criminal offence, and those who were intoxicated, disturbed or violent.

15 See Chapter 3 for information on the proportion of detainees in the current study who were intoxicated on arrival at the police station.

one per cent suffered psychotic symptoms or had a psychotic history, two per cent were suspected of having a possible mental illness, and one per cent appeared to have a mental handicap or other disorder. In addition, just under one per cent had been detained at police stations under s.136 Mental Health Act as a place of safety. If those who were drunk are excluded from the reckoning, this study points to levels of mental disorder or handicap rather higher than the present study, but not as high as Gudjunsson et al.'s study. Again, however, the study was London-based and may not typify the picture elsewhere.

Key points

- There were 4,250 detainees in the sample; 85 per cent were male and 15 per cent were female.

- In terms of ethnic origin, 78 per cent were white, 13 per cent were black and six per cent were Asian. Black people more likely to have been arrested than would be expected by their representation in local populations, although the situation as regards Asians showed no clear-cut pattern.

- Seventeen per cent of suspects were aged under 17.

- Fifty-four per cent were unemployed, 27 per cent were employed, and 14 per cent were school pupils or students.

- Around 60 per cent of suspects had previous convictions. White suspects were more likely to have previous convictions than those from other ethnic groups. Just over 40 per cent of suspects had at least one previous caution.

- Ten per cent of suspects were subject to a court order (e.g. a probation order or conditional discharge) at the time of their arrest.

- Two per cent of detainees were treated as mentally disordered or mentally handicapped.

2 Details of the arrest

Reasons for arrest

The great majority of the sample (87%) had been arrested on suspicion of committing offences. Table 2.1 provides a breakdown of the main categories of offence for which they had been arrested. Due to a lack of detailed statistics compiled on a national basis, it is not possible to comment on the extent to which the sample is typical of the pattern for the country as a whole. Most suspects (87%) had been arrested for a single offence. However, 11 per cent had been arrested for two offences, while two per cent had been arrested for three or more. Second or further offences were usually related to the first. For example, where the primary offence was one of violence, an additional offence might be one of assault on the police, committed during the course of the arrest. Again, where the primary offence was burglary, any additional offences were likely to be ones of handling stolen goods.

Thirteen per cent of those detained had not been arrested for offences. This group includes those held on warrant for failure to appear at court or for non-payment of fines, those detained at a police station as a place of safety and remand prisoners in transit from prison to court.

The pattern of arrests was generally similar between stations, although there were some noticeable differences, reflecting particular local crime problems or the nature of the areas policed. (An analysis by station is provided in Appendix Table A.2.) At Beaumont Leys in Leicester, for example, 11 per cent of arrests were for violent offences, compared with the study average of seven per cent. At Luton and Croydon, both city centre stations covering busy shopping areas, shoplifting was a major source of arrests: 13 per cent and 21 per cent respectively of suspects were held for this offence at these stations compared with the study average of eight per cent. Yet again, car crime was a particular problem in some areas: at Beaumont Leys, Rochdale and Gateshead rates of arrest for theft and unauthorised taking of vehicles were well above average.

Table 2.1   Reason for arrest or detention

Offence/reason for detention	%
Offences	
Violence	7
Sexual	1
Burglary	8
Robbery	2
Theft and handling:	
Shoplifting	8
Theft of vehicle/TWOC	9
Theft from vehicles	2
Other theft & handling	10
Fraud and forgery	3
Criminal damage	6
Drugs	3
Public order	12
Motoring	8
Prostitution	2
Other offences	7
Other detention	
Warrants, place of safety, transfers	
between prison and court	13
Total	**100**

Notes:
1.   N=4,250.
2.   'Other detention' also includes those committed to police detention by magistrates' courts under s.48 PACE for the purpose of enquiries into other offences.
3.   Where there were two or more offences, the table refers to the most serious. The relative seriousness of offences was assessed with reference to the maximum penalties available on conviction.
4.   TWOC – unauthorised taking of a motor vehicle.

Arrests for drug offences ran at double the study average at Hackney (6% compared with 3%), reflecting the drug problems affecting this and many inner-city areas. Public disorder was also a particular feature of arrests at Hackney and at the other London station, Croydon. At the former it was attributable to the presence locally of vagrants who were frequently to be found creating a public disturbance when the worse for drink. Thus, 64 per cent of those arrested for public order offences at this station were arrested for being drunk and disorderly or drunk and incapable. The public order problem at Croydon was rather different and associated more with the town's role as an entertainment centre containing numerous public houses and clubs. At both stations the provisions of the Public Order Act 1986 were used to make arrests in a significant minority of cases. In all, 13 per cent of public order arrests were made either under s.4 (causing fear or provocation of violence) or s.5 (causing harassment, alarm or distress). These figures are very similar to those found in London by Brown and Ellis (1994) in a previous study of arrests under the same Act.

Prostitution was a particular problem at Birmingham Road police station, which was situated in a 'red light' area. Sixteen per cent of the sample here were arrested for prostitution, compared with the study average of two per cent.

Certain other local differences are reflected in the figures. For example, Gateshead police station was connected directly to the local magistrates' court. It therefore housed a large number of remand prisoners each morning on their way from prison to appear at court, thus explaining why 27 per cent of prisoners at this station fell within the category of 'other detention'.

Socio-demographic differences

Gender

Chapter 1 noted that females were far less likely than males to be arrested: 85 per cent of the sample were male and 15 per cent female. As Table 2.2 shows, the ratio of male to female arrests followed this pattern for violence, drugs and public order offences. However, male suspects were more likely to be arrested for sexual offences, burglary, robbery, vehicle crime, criminal damage and motoring offences. In contrast, female suspects were more likely to be arrested for shoplifting, other theft and handling, fraud & forgery and prostitution. The imbalance in relation to theft and handling offences has also been noted by Hedderman and Hough (1994).

Table 2.2   Reason for arrest by gender of detainee

Offence/other reason	Male	Female
	%	%
Violence	84	16
Sexual	96	4
Burglary	94	6
Robbery	96	4
Theft and handling:	79	21
Shoplifting	55	45
Theft of vehicle/TWOC	95	5
Theft from vehicle	93	7
Other theft and handling	80	20
Fraud and forgery	73	27
Criminal damage	92	9
Drugs	85	15
Public order	88	12
Motoring	94	6
Prostitution	–	100
Other reasons (warrant, place of safety, transfers from prison to court)	89	11
% (n)	**85 (3,610)**	**15 (639)**

Notes:
1.   Data on gender were missing in one case.
2.   Percentages do not always sum to 100 due to rounding.
3.   TWOC – unauthorised taking of a motor vehicle.

Ethnic origin

In some offence categories, members of ethnic minority groups were markedly over-represented compared with their presence in the arrest population generally. Table 2.3 shows that this was particularly so in relation to black people and robbery offences: while they made up 13 per cent of all those arrested, they formed 46 per cent of those arrested for such offences. A similar over-representation has been observed in Metropolitan Police statistics (Home Office, 1989; FitzGerald and Sibbitt, 1997). The most recent MPS data for 1996 show that, of those arrested for robbery and other violent theft, 28 per cent were white, 58 per cent black and 6 per cent Asian[1]. (The ethnic origin of the remaining eight per cent was 'other' or unknown.) In the present study black people were also significantly more likely to be arrested for fraud and forgery, thefts from motor vehicles, violence against the person and drugs offences. The higher arrest rate for the above-

---

1   1991 Census data show that, in the area covered by the Metropolitan Police, 80 per cent of the population were white, eight per cent black, eight per cent Asian and four per cent of other ethnic origin.

mentioned offences appears to be driving the higher arrest rate overall of black people, which was noted in Chapter 1. For their part, Asians were more likely to be arrested for fraud and forgery and thefts from motor vehicles.

White people were also more likely to be arrested for certain offences. They featured most prominently among those arrested for criminal damage, theft or unauthorised taking of vehicles and prostitution. Significantly more white than either black or Asian suspects were arrested for public order offences. This finding contrasts with that of an earlier study of public order offences by Brown and Ellis (1994). In examining the use of s.5 Public Order Act 1986[2], they reported that black people were more likely to be arrested for this offence. The same study found that Asian suspects were less likely to be arrested – a finding which was confirmed in the present study.

Table 2.3 Reason for arrest by ethnic origin of detainee

Offence/other reason	White %	Black %	Asian %	Other %
Violence	70	18	7	5
Sexual	77	9	9	4
Burglary	80	11	6	2
Robbery	42	46	6	5
Theft and handling:	79	11	6	4
Shoplifting	76	16	3	6
Theft of vehicle/TWOC	84	6	8	3
Theft from vehicle	64	19	14	3
Other theft & handling	79	11	6	4
Fraud and forgery	61	27	10	2
Criminal damage	84	8	6	2
Drugs	76	18	4	2
Public order	86	7	4	2
Motoring	80	11	7	2
Prostitution	90	6	–	4
Other reason (warrant, place of safety, transfers from prison to court)	82	10	6	2
Total	**78 (3,284)**	**13 (533)**	**7 (274)**	**3 (140)**

Notes:
1. Data on ethnic origin were missing in 19 cases.
2. Percentages do not always sum to 100 due to rounding.
3. TWOC - unauthorised taking of a motor vehicle.

2 Under s.5(1) a person is guilty of an offence if he 'uses threatening, abusive or insulting words or behaviour, or disorderly behaviour .... within the hearing or sight of a person likely to be caused harassment, alarm or distress thereby'.

Age

Table 2.4 shows the age distribution of the sample according to the reason for arrest or detention. This demonstrates very clearly the variation in types of crime committed by different age groups. For example, those arrested for violent and sexual offences tended to fall into older age groups than those arrested for robbery. Juveniles were heavily over-represented amongst those arrested for burglary, robbery, shoplifting, vehicle crime and criminal damage, while those in the 17 to 20 age bracket were over-represented amongst those arrested for drugs offences and vehicle crime. Among older age groups, a disproportionate number of those arrested for fraud & forgery and prostitution were found in the 21 to 29 age group, while the same was true for the 30 to 59 age group in relation to sexual offences, fraud & forgery and motoring offences.

Employment status and place of residence

There were no systematic differences in the reasons for arrest according to whether suspects were or were not in employment or lived within or outside the police area in which they were arrested.

Mentally disordered detainees

Of the 67 detainees dealt with by the police as mentally disordered, one-third (n=23) were detained in police custody for reasons other than the suspected commission of an offence. Twenty-two were taken to the police station as a place of safety and one was arrested on warrant. Because of the small numbers of mentally disordered suspects (n=44), there is limited scope to look for patterns of offending. However, the offences which featured most regularly were violence against the person, sexual offences, burglary, theft and handling, criminal damage and public order offences.

Table 2.4 Reason for arrest or detention by age of detainee

Offence/reason	Juvenile %	17-20 %	21-29 %	30-59 %	60+ %
Violence	11	19	37	30	2
Sexual	15	6	19	47	13
Burglary	26	24	35	15	<1
Robbery	41	24	30	4	1
Theft and handling:	23	24	27	25	1
Shoplifting	31	16	19	31	4
Theft of vehicle/TWOC	24	39	26	12	-
Theft from vehicle	37	40	16	6	-
Other theft and handling	11	16	36	37	1
Fraud and forgery	2	7	45	45	1
Criminal damage	24	24	27	24	<1
Drugs	9	33	38	20	-
Public order	9	21	28	38	6
Motoring	4	13	34	46	2
Prostitution	-	23	68	9	-
Other reasons (warrants, place of safety, transfers from prison to court, etc.)	6	26	43	25	1
Total	15 (641)	22 (942)	33 (1,415)	28 (1,173)	2 (79)

Notes:
1. Table based on all detainees.
2. Percentages do not always sum to 100 due to rounding.
3. TWOC - unauthorised taking of a motor vehicle.

Circumstances surrounding the arrest

Relatively little information is available about the circumstances in which arrests take place. Most attention has probably been paid to the part played by stop and search in generating arrests (Skogan, 1990; 1994; Young, 1994; Painter et al., 1989; Crawford et al., 1990; Walker, Jefferson and Seneviratne, 1990; Dixon et al., 1989). This apart, a body of research has been more concerned with the slightly different question of how crimes which are cleared up come to police notice, rather than how the offenders themselves come to be arrested. While the same circumstances may lead on to an arrest, this is not invariably the case. The central theme of such research is that the majority of crime which is cleared up is brought to police attention by information from the public. Less often is the discovery of criminal offences the result of proactive policing. Mawby (1979), for example, looked at the reporting of standard list offences to the police in nine areas of Sheffield. In

75 per cent of cases the victim reported the crime. In a further six per cent the crime was notified to the police by a witness and in two per cent by security staff, while in five per cent the police learned of offences whilst on patrol. In nine per cent of cases the offence came to light during the course of questioning the suspect about another incident. Research by Bottomley and Coleman (1976) in a force in the North of England produced similar findings.

Another study carried out for the Royal Commission on Criminal Procedure by Steer (1980) examined how indictable offences in Oxford came to police attention. He also found that offences were most often reported by the victim (in over 70% of cases). Other eyewitness reports accounted for 11 per cent of cases. In most of the remaining cases (nearly one fifth), uniformed or CID officers discovered the offence either directly or indirectly. Those discovered indirectly included ones where the suspect admitted to further offences while in custody.

How incidents came to police attention

The present study differs from the research cited above in that it looked at incidents which culminated in an arrest. In some cases subsequent enquiries revealed that no offence had actually been committed and the suspect was released without any action being taken. The study also differs from the previous work in that it was concerned with offences of all kinds, not simply standard list ones, and therefore includes ones such as drunk and disorderly and motoring offences. Nevertheless, the previous research is useful in giving a broad indication of the way in which crime is discovered by the police and there are obvious parallels with the way in which arrests are made.

Information on how incidents leading to arrest came to police attention was available for 87 per cent of cases. Figure 2.1 shows that the bulk of arrests – nearly three-quarters – arose from what might loosely be termed reactive policing. Thus, 28 per cent of incidents were notified to arresting officers by their command and control room. This information, in turn, may often have come from members of the public (including victims) who had called the police to report an offence or suspicious occurrence. Slightly less than one-fifth were attended to by officers as a result of information received. This might include information from an anonymous caller, perhaps a helpful member of the public. Around one-quarter of incidents were brought to police attention either because police arrived as they were in progress, or as a result of a call from the public, presumably whilst the police were on routine patrol or attending another incident. Just under a quarter of arrests resulted from proactive police work. Over half of such arrests (amounting to 13% of all arrests) were made as a result of surveillance work or enquiries conducted by officers investigating offences, while the remainder (11% of all arrests) followed a stop/search[3].

Figure 2.1 How incident came to police attention

Reactive policing

Information received 19%

Command and control 28%

Other 5%

Incident in progress 16%

Stop/search 11%

Call from public 8%

Surveillance/enquiries 13%

Proactive policing

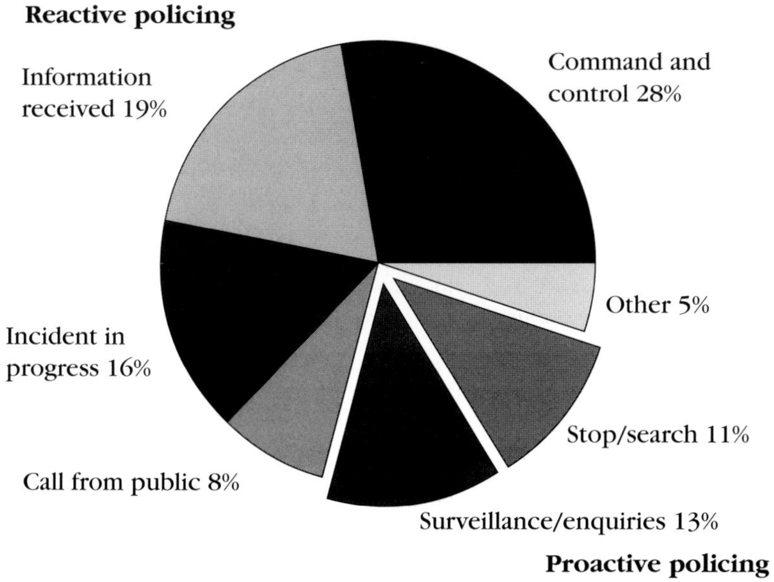

Note:
1. N=3,161 (suspects only). Data were missing in 31 cases.

The way in which offences came to police attention varied according to the offence (see Appendix Table A.3 for full details). Offences of violence against the person, theft, handling and criminal damage were most often notified to officers by their command and control rooms. Sexual offences, robbery, and fraud and forgery were typically notified to officers by other means. Thus, over half of arrests for sexual offences were made as a result of information received, while the remainder followed police surveillance or enquiries. Around a third of robbery and fraud & forgery arrests resulted from information received. Stop and search contributed disproportionately to arrests for drugs offences, accounting for nearly one-half. Almost all arrests for prostitution were the result of the police observing suspects soliciting potential clients. Public order offences were also most commonly brought to police attention as the incident was in progress (37%).

---

3   The most frequently used police stop and search powers are those contained in s.1 of PACE and s.23 of the Misuse of Drugs Act 1971 (Wilkins and Addicott, 1997). In addition, the police possess a range of other, less frequently used, statutory stop and search powers, such as those under the Firearms Act 1968. Since the present research was completed, new powers have been introduced for the police to stop persons and vehicles in anticipation of serious violence (s.60 CJPOA 1994) and to prevent acts of terrorism (s.81 CJPOA, inserting a new s.13A into the Prevention of Terorrism Act 1989). The police may also carry out a search, without calling upon their statutory powers, if the subject of the stop consents to be searched (see Bottomley et al., 1989, for a discussion of this issue). In the present research it was not possible to say which powers were drawn upon in carrying out stop/searches leading to arrest or whether some stop/searches were carried out with the suspect's consent.

Figure 2.2 How incident came to police attention

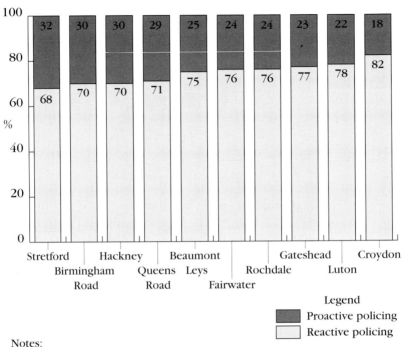

Legend

▨ Proactive policing

☐ Reactive policing

Notes:
1. N=3,010 (suspects only). In a further 641 cases no information was available either because questionnaires were not returned or were returned incomplete.

As Figure 2.2 shows, the split between reactive and proactive policing varied between stations. At the extremes, the reactive/proactive ratio was 68:32 at Stretford compared with 82:18 at Croydon. The differences between stations are related to variations in local crime patterns and to real differences in policing tactics. At Hackney, for example, police reaction to local disorder problems led to an above average level of arrests stemming from proactive policing. The higher than average proportion of incidents identified through proactive policing at Birmingham Road is accounted for by regular police crackdowns on the local prostitution problem. At the other end of the scale, the relatively low level of arrests at Croydon arising from proactive policing stems from the fact that an above average proportion of crime here is shop theft and the police can do little other than respond to reports of incidents from stores.

Since the present study was undertaken, police forces have shown increasing interest in a form of proactive policing which is generally referred to as 'intelligence-led'. The aim is to target prolific offenders, building up a sound body of evidence about their criminal activities prior to arrest. It is possible that this increased emphasis on proactive tactics may by now have led to some reduction in the preponderance of reactive arrests which characterised the present study.

Stop/search arrests

The Police and Criminal Evidence Act 1984 (PACE) laid down police powers to stop and search persons or vehicles for stolen or prohibited articles on reasonable suspicion, and an accompanying Code of Practice gave detailed guidance on the interpretation of these powers. Statistics published by the Home Office show that the number of recorded stops and searches has increased quite dramatically between 1986 and the present (Wilkins and Addicott, 1997). Research and official statistics have indicated that forces vary considerably in the extent to which they use these powers (Willis, 1983; FitzGerald, 1993; Wilkins and Addicott, 1997; FitzGerald and Sibbitt, 1997). The Metropolitan Police has been among the higher users of stop/search powers, which have played an important part in contributing to arrests and clear-ups in the capital (Willis, 1983; Smith and Gray, 1985). According to Home Office statistics, 11 per cent of searches lead to an arrest; again, there is wide variation between police forces and according to the reason for the search (Wilkins and Addicott, ibid). Figures from the 1994 BCS show a slightly lower proportion of searches leading to arrest – around 10 per cent (Bucke, 1995). This figure almost certainly includes some searches which have not been officially recorded by the police, as well as incidents perceived by members of the public as stops and searches, but not officially recognised as such. A study by Young (1994) in North London found that 18 per cent of stop/searches resulted in an arrest.

Figure 2.3   Reasons for stop/searches

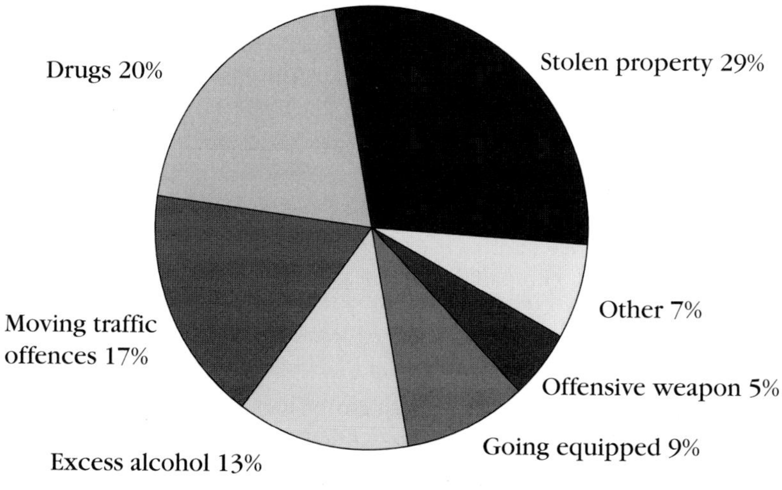

Drugs 20%

Stolen property 29%

Moving traffic offences 17%

Other 7%

Excess alcohol 13%

Offensive weapon 5%

Going equipped 9%

Note:
1. N=267. Data were missing in 71 cases.

In the present study 11 per cent (n=338) of all suspects in the sample were arrested as the result of a stop/search. This is not far removed from the figure of eight per cent reported by Young (1994) in his North London study. Figure 2.3 gives the reasons for stop/searches. In nearly one-half the purpose of the stop/search was to look for stolen property or drugs. The basis for stop/searches varied somewhat according to the age of the suspect. Juveniles and the 17 to 20 age group were most often searched for suspected stolen property and for going equipped. The latter were also often searched for controlled drugs. Among the older age groups (21 to 29 and 30 to 59) a significant minority of stops were made for motoring offences or driving with excess alcohol and it would appear that these led on to searches when police suspicions were aroused about other possible offences. Importantly, over a quarter of those stopped and searched did not live within the police division within which the stop was made. This further underlines the difficulty of relating stop rates for different ethnic minority groups to these groups' presence in local populations (FitzGerald and Sibbit, 1997 – and see Chapter 1).

Males were more likely than females to have been arrested following a stop/search: the ratio of males to females among those arrested following a stop/search was 92:8, compared with 85:15 for arrests generally.

The proportion of those arrested following a stop/search who were black was significantly higher than the proportion of black suspects in the sample as a whole. Thus, 18 per cent of stop/search arrests were of black people compared with 12 per cent of other arrests. No such disproportion was found for Asian suspects. The reason for the imbalance in relation to black people almost certainly rests with the disproportionate use of police stop and search powers against members of this ethnic minority group. Research pre-dating PACE (Willis, 1983; Smith and Gray, 1985) and since the Act came into force (Jones et al., 1986; Young, 1994; Skogan, 1990, 1994) has found that black people are more likely to be stopped than whites or Asians. The most recent figures, from the 1996 BCS, show that 23 per cent of black people recalled being stopped by the police during the previous year, compared with 16 per cent of whites and 15 per cent of Asians. Once stopped, higher percentages of black people were searched (20 per cent, compared with 15 per cent of Asians and eight per cent of whites) or arrested (12 per cent, compared with six per cent of Asians and three per cent of whites) (Bucke, 1997).

Skogan (1994) has pointed to particularly high use of stop and search powers against young black males. However, in the present research the above average number of black suspects among those arrested following a stop/search was not solely a function of the use of stop/search powers against young black people. In fact, there was a heavier over-representation of black people in the older age groups (21 and over) than among juveniles or those aged 17 to 20. For instance, black suspects comprised 12 per cent of all those arrested in the 30 to 59 age group, but 20 per cent of those in this age bracket who were arrested following a stop/search.

In attempting to explain the over-representation of black people among those arrested following stop/searches, Young (1994) has suggested that the police may discriminate on the basis of which groups are most likely to commit certain offences. Therefore, if as he suggests, young black men are significantly more likely than white people to be involved in street robbery and theft, stop/search arrests based on the suspicion that such offences have been committed may be legitimate[4]. In the current study it was certainly true that black suspects were more likely to be arrested for robbery offences than white suspects. However, where black suspects were arrested following a stop/search, the main reasons given for the stop/search were not just stolen property, but also traffic offences, drugs, carrying an offensive weapon and other reasons.

Domestic violence arrests

BCS estimates show that around 1.3 per cent of women reported that they had been the victim of one or more incidents of domestic violence in 1995; in total, there were estimated to be around one million incidents of such violence against women or men in that year (Mirrlees-Black, Mayhew and Percy, 1996). In 1990 the Home Office issued circular 60/1990, which was concerned with improving the police response to crimes involving domestic violence. One of the key recommendations was for police officers to arrest domestic violence offenders whenever appropriate (Home Office, 1990b). An evaluation of the police response to this circular by Grace (1995) found that 12 per cent of domestic violence incidents in the West Midlands and 14 per cent of those in Thames Valley led to an arrest.

The present study showed that six per cent of all arrests (n=217) were domestic violence related. There was some variation between stations, ranging from five per cent at Queen's Road to 11 per cent at Stretford. Figure 2.4 shows that the offences concerned were predominantly violence against the person (primarily actual bodily harm but also some cases of grievous bodily harm) and public disorder (particularly breach of the peace[5]). Together these accounted for almost three-quarters of domestic violence related offences. Similarly, in Grace's (1995) study of charges brought for domestic violence incidents in three forces, 43 per cent were for

---

4   Metropolitan Police statistics for the years 1980 to 1985 (the last year for which this information was compiled) record that victims of robbery reported that their assailant was 'non-white' in over 50 per cent of cases, although some doubts are expressed about the reliability of these figures in the Home Office Statistical Bulletin in which they are reported (Home Office, 1989)

5   Breach of the peace is not technically a criminal offence but for convenience's sake is included with offences here.

actual bodily harm, 25 per cent for breach of the peace, five per cent for grievous bodily harm, and seven per cent for criminal damage. In the current study, incidents involving domestic violence accounted for 27 per cent of all cases of violence against the person.

Figure 2.4 Offences for which suspects were arrested in domestic violence case

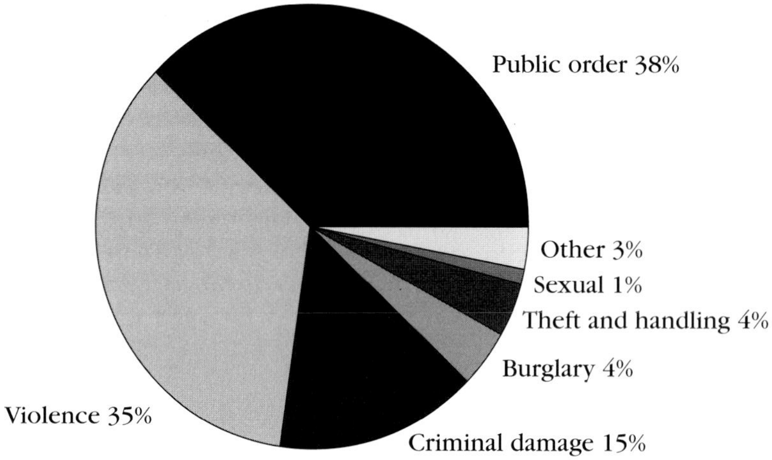

Public order 38%

Other 3%
Sexual 1%
Theft and handling 4%
Burglary 4%
Criminal damage 15%
Violence 35%

Note:
N=217.

There were some cases in which the offence for which the suspect was arrested was not of a type usually associated with domestic violence. A few suspects, for example, were arrested for burglary or theft. These cases usually involved a former partner in a relationship breaking into the other partner's home, followed by some form of confrontation. Grace (1995) also noted that some burglary and theft offences may be domestic violence related.

Those arrested for domestic violence related offences were predominantly in their 20s (42%) or 30s (30%). Only 13 per cent were in their 40s and seven per cent were aged 50 or over; eight per cent were under 20.

Racially motivated incidents

Guidance issued in 1985 by the Association of Chief Police Officers ¡states that an incident should be defined as racially motivated where the victim, investigating officer, or any person makes an allegation of racial motivation. The police are required to maintain a record of any such incidents. It has been alleged that the clear-up rate for incidents of racial harassment and violence is low (Home Affairs Committee, Third Report, 1994). Moreover, few arrests are made of those who perpetrate such attacks (Sampson and Phillips, 1992). In the present study only 14 arrests stemmed from incidents which arresting officers perceived as racially motivated. The arrests were made at six stations: Luton, Queens Road, Beaumont Leys, Birmingham Road, Gateshead and Hackney. Twelve of the 14 suspects were male and two were female. Nine suspects were white, three were black, one was Asian, and one was of Arab origin. Eight of those arrested were aged 20 or under, four were between 21 and 29 and two were 30 or over. The alleged offences were: violence against the person (4 cases), criminal damage (3 cases), violent disorder (3 cases), and other public order offences (4 cases).

Since the police are required to record incidents which are deemed to be racially motivated *by any person*, this may explain why the arrests included both white and ethnic minority suspects. Alternatively, as arresting officers were asked *Did the arrest arise from a racially motivated incident?*, it is possible that incidents where members of ethnic minority groups were arrested for retaliating against a racially motivated incident could also have been included by officers, although it must be emphasised that there is no firm evidence to suggest that this was the case.

Main grounds for suspicion

For each case, arresting officers were asked to list the main evidence or grounds for suspicion. In the majority of cases (71%) only one source of evidence was available. In a further 21 per cent, arresting officers reported that there were two sources of evidence and in eight per cent three or more. Figure 2.5 shows that, in 40 per cent of all offences, the main grounds for suspicion derived from police observation of the offence, whether from intercepting an incident in progress, building up evidence during a period of surveillance or uncovering a possible offence during the course of a stop/search. This contrasts with the findings of previous research by Mawby (1979), Bottomley and Coleman (1976) and Steer (1980) on the reporting and discovery of crime, which accorded a lower priority to evidence of this kind. The difference between the current study and earlier ones may partly be accounted for by its inclusion of all offences rather than standard list offences alone. Some kinds of offence, typically public order infringements, prostitution and motoring offences (including drink driving), only lead to arrest and prosecution because of the proactive role of the police. Consequently, police evidence forms the backbone of these cases. But it is also possible that there may have been a change over time in police tactics, with increased emphasis on proactive police work and the accumulation of key evidence prior to arrest.

Figure 2.5   Types of evidence available

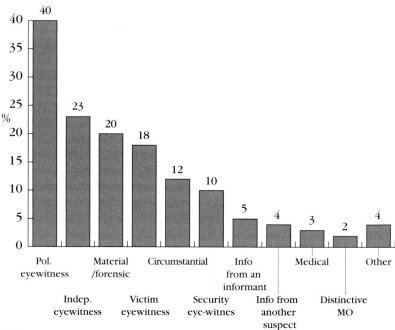

Notes:
1. N=3,169 (suspects only). In a further 513 cases no information was available, either because questionnaires were not returned or were returned incomplete.
2. Percentages sum to more than 100 because multiple responses could be provided.
3. 'Other' category includes police suspicion/experience, information from suspect and PNC checks.

Not surprisingly, for sexual and violent offences against the person, the eyewitness testimony of the victim was most frequently noted as the main source of evidence by arresting officers. For property offences, namely, burglary, theft and handling, and criminal damage, material or forensic evidence and independent eyewitnesses were often cited. In some types of offence (as might be expected from the observations in the previous paragraph) the eyewitness testimony of police officers was especially important: for example, prostitution (in all cases), public order offences (75% of cases), motoring offences (71% of cases), drugs offences (48% of cases), and thefts of vehicles (47% of cases). In contrast, in only one-third of arrests for burglary and thefts from vehicles was eyewitness testimony important.

Figure 2.5 also shows that, in almost a quarter of all cases, information from the public (i.e. independent eyewitnesses) provided the main grounds for suspicion. This was especially important in some types of crime, providing the grounds for suspicion in almost 50 per cent of robbery, theft from vehicle and criminal damage arrests, and in over one-third of burglary arrests. The latter finding agrees with that of Brown (1991) who, in a study of burglary investigation, observed that the public were often the primary means of detection. The public also provided evidence in around one-quarter of violence, theft of vehicle, other theft and handling, and fraud and forgery offences. The eyewitness testimony of security staff was most important in shoplifting cases (75%). Evidence provided by informants was especially important in drugs arrests (23% of cases) and robbery arrests (16% of cases).

Material or forensic evidence in the form of documents, fingerprints or other bodily samples was reported to be relevant in nearly 50 per cent of fraud & forgery and drugs cases, and in a quarter of burglary, other theft and handling, and motoring offences. Medical evidence was less commonly noted by officers, although it was reported in 19 per cent of violence against the person offences, presumably where the victim sought treatment. Circumstantial evidence was available in a minority of cases, but particularly in cases of intermediate seriousness, such as theft and handling, vehicle crime, burglary and criminal damage. (Appendix A, Table A.4 presents a full breakdown of the type of evidence by offence.)

The strength of evidence at arrest

Studies by Irving and McKenzie (1989), Bottomley et al. (1989) and Brown (1991), which have examined the evidential basis for arrest, have suggested that one effect of PACE has been to increase the standard of evidence on which arrests are based. It is possible that, out of fear of disciplinary action, custody officers are careful to ensure that the statutory criteria to justify detention at the police station are satisfied. However, both the work by Bottomley et al. (1989) and the present study cast doubt on how searchingly custody officers do enquire into the evidence. The reception of suspects into custody was often found to be a routine matter and arresting officers were not typically asked to provide much information about the offence. Bottomley et al. (ibid) also asked arresting officers how frequently arrests were made when the officer believed the suspect had committed an offence but reasonable grounds for suspicion did not exist. Thirty-four per cent of officers felt this occurred either frequently or sometimes.

The present research obtained a rough measure of the strength of the evidence by asking arresting officers *Did you consider the evidence on arrest was sufficient to charge?*. In conversation, some felt that the answer could only ever be 'yes', and that officers would not risk saying 'no' as it might suggest that an arrest was unwarranted. In fact, under PACE officers may arrest a person when they have reasonable grounds for suspicion that an offence has been committed. This standard is not necessarily as high as that required to charge. Despite their possible concerns about the implications of giving a negative answer, 30 per cent of arresting officers did say that they felt that there was insufficient evidence to charge the suspect at the time of arrest, while 60 per cent said that they felt that the evidence was sufficient[6]. Some of the latter may have responded positively because of their concerns about this question, which may suggest that the percentage of cases in which the evidence was deemed insufficient is an underestimate.

There was considerable variation between offences in the extent to which the evidence was felt to be sufficient to charge on arrest. Table 2.5 shows that the highest figures were for shoplifting, public order and prostitution. The proportion was also relatively high (around two-thirds) in cases of violence, theft from vehicles and criminal damage. This suggests that the grounds for suspicion cited in these kinds of case – usually eyewitness evidence of some kind (see previous section) – tended to be seen as providing strong evidence of guilt. The reason why the proportion of burglary and robbery cases in which there was felt to be sufficient evidence to charge was relatively low may also be related to the kind of evidence typically available in such cases. In particular, there may be problems with the quality of identification evidence from independent eyewitnesses. There may also be difficulties in linking suspects to offences where the evidence consists of the possession of items such as suspected stolen goods or tools for use in the course of burglary, for which there may be innocent explanations. The problems in such cases have implications for their eventual prosecution.

There were significant differences according to ethnic group in the proportion of cases in which the evidence on arrest was sufficient to charge. There was much more likely to be evidence of the required standard where the suspect was white (in 63% of cases) than where he or she was black (56%) or Asian (52%). The data were examined to see whether this finding was explicable on the basis of differences in the kinds of offence for which white and ethnic minority suspects were arrested. In other words, is it the case that ethnic minority and white suspects are generally arrested on the same standard of evidence, but that white suspects are more often arrested for the kinds of offence in which the evidence on arrest is likely to be strong, while ethnic minority suspects are typically arrested for the kinds of offence in which it is weaker? There was some support for this proposition in relation to robbery offences (where black people contribute nearly half of all arrests): the evidence on arrest was sufficient to charge in roughly the same proportion of cases for all ethnic groups. However, for most other

---

6   Seven per cent of officers answered that they did not know if there was sufficient evidence. It is possible that these questionnaires were completed by interviewing officers who did not make the initial arrest and were unaware of the details of the case leading up to the arrest. Data were not provided in the remaining two per cent (n=60) of cases. In 50 per cent of these cases the suspect was arrested for being drunk or for breaching the peace. A further 17 per cent involved those absconding from lawful custody or being held for immigration offences.

offence groups, the standard of evidence against black or Asian suspects was below that required to charge in a greater proportion of cases than for white suspects. In violent offences, for example, there was enough evidence to charge on arrest in 45 per cent of cases involving white suspects, but only 37 per cent and 17 per cent respectively of cases involving black and Asian suspects. And, in public order offences, the evidence to charge existed in 84 per cent of arrests of whites, compared with 65 per cent of arrests of black people and 64 per cent of arrests of Asians.

Table 2.5   Percentage of cases in which arresting officers said the evidence on arrest was sufficient to charge by offence

Offence	%	(n)
Violence	66	(175)
Sexual	49	(18)
Burglary	42	(125)
Robbery	32	(20)
Theft and handling:	58	(632)
Shoplifting	84	(256)
Theft of vehicle/TWOC	46	(154)
Theft from vehicle	61	(50)
Other theft and handling	47	(172)
Fraud and forgery	44	(51)
Criminal damage	62	(141)
Drugs	72	(77)
Public order	84	(369)
Motoring	55	(164)
Prostitution	100	(69)
Other offences	53	(81)
All offences	61	(1,922)

Note:
1.   Table based on suspects only (n=3,160). In 522 cases no data were available either because arresting officer questionnaires were not completed or were returned incomplete.
2.   TWOC – unauthorised taking of a motor vehicle.

It is not clear what is driving these differences. While it is possible that they may reflect discriminatory police action, there could be other explanations. It may be, for example, that grouping offences into broad categories – such as violence – for the purpose of analysis may conceal differences in offending between ethnic minority and white suspects. These different patterns of offending in turn could have implications for the level of evidence available on arrest. Much larger samples would be needed to pick up these differences. Another explanation draws upon evidence about the attitudes to each other of the police and ethnic minorities. Successive British Crime Surveys have noted higher levels of dissatisfaction with the police and the way encounters with them are handled among ethnic minorities (Skogan, 1990, 1994; Bucke, 1995, 1997). These attitudes may influence the way in which members of ethnic minorities react when they fall under police suspicion. For their part, the police sometimes view members of ethnic minority groups, and black people in particular, as 'problematic'. They tend to perceive them as being disproportionately involved in certain forms of crime and, correspondingly, have heightened notions about the 'suspiciousness' of their behaviour (FitzGerald and Sibbitt, 1997; Young, 1994). Taken together, these factors help explain how police encounters with ethnic minority suspects take shape. They may result in incidents being more likely to be formalised, which could in some instances result in an arrest on the basis of a lower standard of evidence than is the case for white suspects.

Whatever the explanation, the difference between the evidential standard in cases involving ethnic minority and white suspects has implications for the later stages of the criminal process. The police need to raise the evidence to the standard required to charge after arrest, and, if charges are laid on sub-standard evidence, this will affect the way in which the case is dealt with by the CPS. These issues are explored later in this report.

There was some variation between stations in the percentage of cases in which arresting officers thought that there was enough evidence to charge on arrest. The range was from 43 per cent at Beaumont Leys to 70 per cent at Croydon. The lower figure at Beaumont Leys is related to the nature of offences for which suspects were arrested at that station, especially burglary and theft of vehicles, where the evidence is less often sufficient to charge on arrest. The high figure at Croydon is accounted for by the large number of shoplifting and public order cases there. Typically, the evidence in such cases is straightforward and is derived from the direct observation of the offence by officers themselves or security staff.

Key points

- The mixture of offences for which suspects were detained varied relatively little between stations. There were high arrest figures for burglary, violence against the person, prostitution, shoplifting and public order offences at certain stations where these offences were a particular local problem.

- Those arrested on suspicion of committing an offence comprised 87 per cent of the sample. The remaining 13 per cent were detained: on warrant for failure to appear at court; for common law breach of the peace; as a place of safety; and on transfer from prison pending appearance in court.

- Males were far more likely than females to be arrested for almost all categories of offence (other than prostitution), with a particularly marked imbalance for burglary, robbery, car crime, sexual offences, criminal damage and motoring offences.

- The offences for which suspects were arrested varied according to ethnic group. White suspects were significantly more likely to be arrested for theft and taking of motor vehicles, shoplifting, criminal damage, public disorder and prostitution. Both black and Asian suspects were more likely than whites to be arrested for fraud and forgery and thefts from vehicles, while black people were more likely than either whites or Asians to be arrested for robbery and violence.

- One-third of those treated by the police as mentally disordered were detained in police custody as a place of safety rather than for committing an offence.

- Nearly three-quarters of arrests came about through reactive policing. Officers either responded to messages from force command and control (28%), attended the scene as a result of information received (19%), chanced upon an incident in progress (16%) or reacted directly to requests from members of the public (8%). Twenty-four per cent of arrests resulted from proactive policing, either in the form of surveillance work or police enquiries (13%) or use of stop/search powers (11%).

- In nearly a half of stop/search arrests, the purpose of the stop/search was to look for stolen property or drugs. Black suspects were more likely than whites to have been arrested following a stop/search.

- Six per cent of suspects were arrested following domestic violence incidents, typically for violence against the person or public order offences.

- Less than one per cent of suspects were arrested for incidents which were perceived by arresting officers to have arisen from a racially motivated incident.

- Eyewitness evidence of some kind was the most frequently cited source of evidence available at the time the suspect was arrested, including 40 per cent of cases in which the police themselves observed the offence. In 29 per cent of cases there was more than one source of evidence available at arrest.

- In 60 per cent of cases officers felt that there was sufficient evidence to charge on arrest, rising to three-quarters in arrests for shoplifting, public order offences and prostitution. However, in 30 per cent of cases the evidence was not considered sufficient to charge at this point. (In the remaining cases, officers either were uncertain or provided no information.)

- In cases involving ethnic minority suspects, the evidence was less likely to be sufficient to charge at the time of arrest. This was not explained by differences in the kinds of offences for which ethnic minority and white suspects were arrested.

3 Arrival at the police station

This chapter deals with the initial stages of detention[1]. On the suspect's arrival at the police station under arrest, the custody officer must satisfy himself or herself that there are reasonable grounds for detention. If he/she is satisfied, he/she will formally authorise detention[2]. In common with other studies which have looked at this issue (see, for example, Morgan, Reiner and McKenzie (1991) and Brown, Ellis and Larcombe (1992)) the present study found that it was exceptional for detention not to be authorised. In only one case did the custody officer refuse to do so[3]. Morgan, Reiner and McKenzie (ibid) have suggested that detention is almost always authorised because of the lack of a clear procedure to do otherwise.

Figure 3.1 Time of arrival at police station

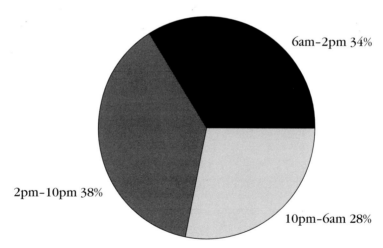

6am–2pm 34%

2pm–10pm 38%

10pm–6am 28%

Notes:
1. N=4,246 (all detainees). Data were missing in 4 cases.

---

1   In four per cent of cases suspects had previously been held in custody at other police stations immediately prior to their transfer to the stations in the study. Information was not available about their initial processing at these stations.

2   Under s.37 of PACE, the custody officer may authorise a person to be kept in police detention without charge where he/she has reasonable grounds for believing that this is necessary to secure or preserve evidence relating to an offence for which that person is under arrest or to obtain such evidence by questioning.

3   This case involved the arrest of a man who was suffering from senile dementia and was wandering lost. The custody officer instructed the arresting officers to find the family of the man and return him to his home.

Time of arrival

Figure 3.1 shows that the spread of times at which suspects arrived at the police station was fairly even. The quietest time, not suprisingly, was during the early hours of the morning.

Several factors contribute to the regularity of this pattern. Firstly, there is a ceiling to the number of arrests that can be made, even at busy times, given finite police resources. Once an arrest has occurred, the officers involved are occupied for some while with the processing and interviewing of their prisoner at the police station. Large numbers of arrests are sometimes made within a short time period where special operations are mounted and additional officers are drafted in. But these do not greatly affect the 'normal' pattern of arrests over a longer timescale.

Secondly, there is a certain amount of patterning to the incidents or other reasons which lead to arrests, meaning that there is a reasonably regular flow of people arriving at the police station. Where, for example, investigating officers have pinpointed a suspect for an offence, they often prefer to make an arrest early in the morning. This allows them the rest of their shift to interview and process the prisoner. During the day, there will in some areas be a steady flow of suspects arrested for shoplifting offences coming into custody. And, during the late evening and early part of the night, those arrested for public order and drink driving offences are a major element of the arrest population.

Nevertheless, all stations experienced periods which were very busy for no accountable reason. All observers witnessed such occasions, which could occur even at the quieter stations. This is a feature of custody office work, which others have previously noted (Brown, 1989; Morgan, Reiner and McKenzie, 1991; Brown, 1997).

There were some stations where the pattern shown in Figure 3.1 was distorted, but for reasons which custody officers could foresee. At Gateshead, for example, early on weekday mornings there would be a large influx of remand prisoners on their way from prison to court. At Croydon, the afternoon was a very busy time, attributable to the activities of shoplifters in the city centre. And at Birmingham Road a local prostitution problem led to a significant number of arrests in the evening.

Condition on arrival

Observers recorded any apparent abnormality in the suspect's condition on arrival at the police station. In three-quarters of cases nothing untoward was noted. The commonest abnormality was some degree of intoxication. Ten per cent showed clear signs of having been drinking, while a further four per cent were too drunk to be dealt with immediately and were consigned to a cell until they had sobered up. At the two London stations (Hackney and Croydon) the proportion of detainees who were suffering from the effects of alcohol was, at 16 per cent, slightly above average. The tendency for drunkenness to be more of a problem in the capital was also noted by Robertson, Pearson and Gibb (1995). Their study, which included a wider range of London stations, found that as many as 22 per cent of their sample were intoxicated on arrival at the station.

Two per cent of the sample in the present study appeared to be under the influence of drugs rather than drink. Three per cent were injured in some way or suffering from various kinds of sickness.

The bizarre behaviour of a small proportion of detainees – around one per cent – was clearly indicative of some kind of mental disorder[4]. A further one per cent were violent in the custody area; in some cases this appeared to be due to the influence of drugs or alcohol. Lastly, although not violent, another one per cent were very unco-operative, often refusing to give personal details to the custody officer.

Of those too drunk to be booked in immediately on arrival, two-thirds had been arrested for public order offences (particularly drunk and disorderly or drunk and incapable). Ten per cent had been arrested for theft and handling offences. Among those who had been drinking, but not as excessively, two-fifths had been arrested on suspicion of committing public order offences and nearly one-third for motoring offences. Suspects who were intoxicated were most commonly aged 30 to 59 years. Very few were black or Asian. Similar findings are reported by Robertson, Pearson and Gibb (1995).

Those under the influence of drugs had most frequently been arrested for theft and handling offences (in 40% of cases). However, it was rare for suspects who were arrested for drugs offences actually to be under the influence of drugs when they arrived at the station. Suspects who were suffering from an injury or some form of sickness on arrival were most likely to have been arrested for public order offences.

Those who were violent or unco-operative at the police station tended to have been arrested for violent or public order offences. Their response at the police station may simply have been an extension of their earlier offending behaviour. Detainees whom the police dealt with as mentally disordered were slightly more likely than average to be violent. However, the level of violence found in the present study is much lower than that reported by

---

4   In total, two per cent of those detained were treated by the police as mentally disordered (see Chapter 1). However, not all of this group displayed bizarre behaviour. Equally, not all those who behaved in a bizarre manner were treated as mentally disordered.

Robertson, Pearson and Gibb (1995). They found that 36 per cent of mentally disordered detainees used or threatened force or caused property damage while in custody.

Answering bail

Seven per cent (n=291) of the sample were suspects who, having previously been bailed to return to the police station pending further enquiries or the decision of a juvenile panel, returned to the station during the observation period. This proportion is the same as that reported in Robertson, Pearson and Gibb's (1995) study. The proportion of suspects answering bail varied from three per cent at Rochdale to 14 per cent at Luton. This gives an indication of the extent to which different forces tend to bail suspects to a later date, usually to allow them more time to complete enquiries.

Suspects most likely to be responding to bail were those arrested for drugs offences (19%), other theft and handling (15%), theft or taking of vehicles (13%t), robbery (13%) and violent offences (11%). In drugs cases bail would typically have been given while the police awaited the analysis of drugs samples. In theft cases suspects were often bailed while fingerprint evidence was investigated.

Arrests for additional offences

Eight per cent (n=294) of suspects were re-arrested while in custody for offences additional to those for which they had originally been detained. The majority were arrested for one further offence, but nearly a quarter were arrested for two offences, and eight per cent for three or more offences. Suspects arrested for property offences, particularly burglary, robbery, theft of vehicles, and other theft and handling, were most likely to be arrested for further offences.

Appropriate adults

Under PACE, the custody officer is obliged to secure the attendance of an appropriate adult to safeguard the interests of juveniles and suspects suffering from mental disorder or handicap. The role of the appropriate adult is to advise and assist the detainee, particularly during police interviews. The PACE Codes of Practice note that the appropriate adult should ensure that the conduct of the interview is proper and fair.

Juveniles

The vast majority of juveniles – 97 per cent (n=599) – had an appropriate adult in attendance for some or all of their time in police custody. In almost one-third of cases, the juvenile arrived at the police station with an appropriate adult. In many of these cases the police had arrested juveniles at their home address, or had gone with them to collect their parents before taking them to the police station. In 11 cases the police contacted an appropriate adult whilst the juvenile was at the police station, but they failed to attend. In a further nine cases the police made no observable attempt to contact an appropriate adult. In four of these cases the juvenile was arrested on warrant, and it is unlikely that they would have been interviewed. In the remaining five cases, the suspects were arrested for offences and there was no apparent explanation for the failure to secure an appropriate adult.

In 63 per cent of cases the appropriate adult was the juvenile's parent or guardian. In a further 10 per cent other family relatives attended. These figures are broadly similar to those obtained by Brown, Ellis and Larcombe (1992) in their study of the revised PACE Codes of Practice. Social workers attended in 20 per cent of cases. In over half of these cases the reason that a social worker was chosen was that the juvenile was in local authority care. In the remaining cases, parents were usually either unable or unwilling to attend.

Previous studies have suggested rather higher attendance rates by social workers. Brown, Ellis and Larcombe (1992), quoting a figure of 28 per cent, conclude that social workers are increasingly being asked to act as appropriate adults. Evans and Rawstorne (1994) draw similar conclusions on the basis of interviews with custody officers and social workers. The lower figure obtained in the present study may indicate that this trend has been reversed. This is certainly possible because the number of children in care has decreased (Department of Health, 1995) and, with it, the number of cases in which custody officers would automatically summon social workers. There are other possible explanations. One is that custody officers have become less willing to call upon social workers because, due to the number of demands placed upon them, they are not always able to attend quickly when required (Brown, Ellis and Larcombe, 1992). For their part, hard-pressed social workers may have become less prepared to act as appropriate adults where the child concerned is not already on the social services' caseload.

In two per cent of cases the adults who attended were from Panels of Appropriate Adults. These Panels exist in a few areas and consist of lay persons who are on call to represent the interests of vulnerable suspects at the police station. In another two per cent of cases, either a probation officer or children's home or care worker acted as appropriate adult. In the remaining four per cent some other person attended the police station.

The above pattern differed in the case of Asian juveniles. In particular, parents or guardians acted as appropriate adults in only 52 per cent of cases, compared with 65 per cent and 59 per cent respectively of cases involving white or black juveniles. There were two reasons for this. Asian parents were both more likely to refuse to come to the police station (in nearly 20% of non-attendances, compared with around 10% of cases involving white or black juveniles) and to say that they were unable to attend (in 36% compared with just over 20% for the other groups). The study was unable to go deeper and establish the factors which underlay refusals to attend. For example, it is not known whether they were prompted by parents' mistrust of the police or a desire to distance themselves from their children's alleged wrongdoing. The non-attendance of parents in cases involving Asians was compensated for by the attendance in their stead of another relative rather than social workers. Thus, 22 per cent of appropriate adults for Asian juveniles were relatives other than a parent, compared with nine per cent and 11 per cent respectively in cases where the suspects were white or black.

Time taken to obtain appropriate adults

Where an appropriate adult is needed, it is important that one is obtained quickly. Dixon (1990) has suggested that delaying the juvenile's stay in custody runs the risk that the suspect may say whatever he or she believes the police want to hear in order to secure release. However, previous research has drawn attention to lengthy delays in obtaining an appropriate adult in some cases (Brown, Ellis and Larcombe, 1992).

In the present study, appropriate adults were obtained reasonably quickly in most cases. In half, the adult attended the police station within one hour of being contacted by the police, and in a further 30 per cent within two hours. But, in a minority of cases the delay was much longer. In 14 per cent of cases the time taken was between two and four hours, and in seven per cent it was over four hours. On average, there was greater delay where a social worker was required.

Where there was a delay of more than an hour in securing the attendance of an appropriate adult, observers tried to find out the reasons. In nearly a third of cases there was no clear explanation. A common difficulty (in about a quarter of cases) was simply that of establishing contact because the adult was not at home. In a further quarter, appropriate adults were unable to attend immediately, usually because they were at work. In 13 per cent of cases an agreement was reached with the police that immediate attendance was not needed because officers were not yet ready to interview. The adult arranged to come shortly before the interview began. In nine per cent of cases the delay arose from the adult initially contacted refusing to attend the police station. It should be noted that the higher than average rate of refusal by Asian parents to come to the police station was not reflected in lengthier than average waiting times for appropriate adults in cases involving Asian juveniles.

Mentally disordered detainees

Sixty-seven detainees were treated by the police as mentally disordered or mentally handicapped[5]. Of these, 22 had been detained at the police station as a place of safety under s.136 Mental Health Act 1983, 44 had been arrested on suspicion of committing offences and one was held on warrant. As with juveniles, the custody officer is required under the PACE Codes of Practice to secure the attendance of an appropriate adult – usually a relative, carer or approved social worker. He/she must also arrange for a doctor to examine the detainee. Where the detainee is being held under s.136 of the Mental Health Act, the custody officer should arrange for a doctor and an approved social worker to interview and examine the detainee together.

In practice, the procedure followed by custody officers varied. The most common course of action was initially to call the police surgeon to examine the detainee. This occurred in nearly two-thirds of all cases where mental disorder was suspected. The proportion was higher (75%) in place of safety cases. The rate at which doctors were called is similar to that found by Brown, Ellis and Larcombe (1992) in their work on the revised PACE Codes of Practice. However, in over a quarter of cases there was no apparent attempt by the custody officer to call a doctor, notwithstanding the requirements of the PACE Codes of Practice and the Mental Health Act[6]. The reason for this failure would appear to be that custody officers decided on the basis of longer observation that their earlier fears about the detainee's mental condition were unfounded.

Appropriate adults were asked to attend less often than doctors. They were summoned in 33 out of 67 cases. In 20 of these cases an appropriate adult was called by the custody officer after an initial examination by a doctor. In only 13 cases was an appropriate adult asked to attend without the detainee having first seen a doctor. It should be noted, however, that the requirement in the PACE Codes of Practice to summon an appropriate adult is independent of that to seek medical advice. The tendency of custody

---

5   A further 13 detainees were perceived by observrs to be behaving in a way suggestive of mental disorder. However, none of these were treated by the police as mentally disordered and an appropriate adult was not contactred. See also footnote 4 above.

6   In a further nine per cent of cases the custody officer contacted a doctor but he or she did not attend the station. Advice was either given by telephone or the custody officer decided that it was unnecessary to hold the detainee until the doctor could reach the station.

officers to await the doctor's verdict has been noted by previous studies (Brown, Ellis and Larcombe,1992 and Bean and Nemitz, 1994). However, Savage et al. (1997) have pointed out that approved social workers in particular are not always readily available. In the present study, there were six cases in which the police sought in vain to secure the attendance of an approved social worker. Doctors, in contrast, are generally able to respond fairly quickly and so tended to be seen as the first port of call.

In the 33 cases in which someone other than a doctor was asked to attend the station, detainees saw one or more of the following: an approved social worker (20 cases); a psychiatrist (10 cases); or some other person acting as appropriate adult (usually a parent or relative) (14 cases)[7]. In the 22 cases in which detainees were originally detained at the police station as a place of safety, the full assessment procedure under the Mental Health Act, involving a doctor and an approved social worker, was carried out on just five occasions.

Of those initially identified by the police as possibly being mentally disordered or handicapped, 11 did not see a doctor, social worker or other professional or any other appropriate adult. Five had been detained at the police station as a place of safety; the others had been arrested for offences ranging from drunkenness to causing grievous bodily harm.

Delays in attendance

There were usually no major delays in the attendance of doctors, other professionals or appropriate adults. Doctors, on average, arrived within one hour of contact. Psychiatrists and other appropriate adults took about one and a quarter hours. These findings are similar to those reported by Brown, Ellis and Larcombe (1992).

The use of interpreters

The PACE Codes of Practice stipulate that, if suspects have difficulty in understanding English, they may not be interviewed by police officers in the absence of an interpreter. In the current research, an interpreter was required in two per cent of cases (n=61). In 15 the interpreter attended with the suspect; in the remainder the custody or investigating officer decided that one was needed. However, in three cases no action appeared to be taken by the police to secure an interpreter, despite the need for one having been established, while in one case efforts to obtain one failed. There was only one case in which a deaf detainee required an interpreter; one was successfully obtained.

---

7   Twenty-three detainees saw just one of the three (i.e. an approved social worker OR a psychiatrist OR some other person), nine saw two of them and one saw all three.

Key points

- Sixteen per cent of the sample were under the influence of alcohol or drugs on arrival, four per cent were injured, ill or acting in a bizarre manner, one per cent were violent and one per cent were very unco-operative. Typically, detainees in these groups had been arrested for public order offences.

- Appropriate adults, whose role is to advise and assist detainees who are believed to be at risk, were obtained in 97 per cent of cases involving juveniles. A parent or another family member usually attended in this capacity.

- In two-thirds of cases in which custody officers suspected that the detainee was mentally disordered or mentally handicapped a doctor was called.

- In 11 out of 67 cases in which custody officers were concerned about possible mental disorder or mental handicap, the detainee did not see a doctor, a social worker or other professional, or any other appropriate adult.

- A foreign language interpreter was required in only 61 cases. There was only one case in which a deaf detainee required an interpreter.

4 Legal advice

Legal advice is a key right for those held in police custody. There is strong evidence from previous studies that the demand for legal advice at the police station has been increasing in recent years (Brown, 1989; Brown, Ellis and Larcombe, 1992). This chapter provides an opportunity to examine recent trends in requests for legal advice.

Requests for legal advice

Previous research shows that the factors influencing the suspect's decision to seek legal advice include the nature and seriousness of the offence, time of arrival at the police station and previous criminal history (Brown, Ellis and Larcombe, 1992). The same research found that the basis for the decision to request legal advice is not always well thought through. Those who might benefit from legal advice often did not request it because they were anxious not to delay their time in custody or because they were told that they probably would not be charged. Others who did ask for a lawyer sometimes did so for inappropriate reasons: for example, to delay proceedings, to obtain items such as cigarettes and newspapers or to relay messages to family or friends. The researchers' observations of the interactions between custody officers and suspects in the present study confirm these findings.

Request rate

Thirty-seven per cent (n=1,564) of all detainees requested legal advice. The request rate was higher for suspects (38%) than for those detained for other reasons (for example, on warrant or as a place of safety) (31%). Three-quarters of suspects who requested legal advice did so on arrival at the police station. However, eight per cent arrived with a legal adviser and 16 per cent sought advice later.

The level of demand for legal advice was higher than that found by previous studies. For example, Brown (1989) found that in 1987 25 per cent of suspects requested legal advice. This rose to 32 per cent in a later study based on 1991 data (Brown, Ellis and Larcombe, 1992). The trend for increasing numbers of suspects to seek legal advice appears to be continuing. In research conducted since the present study, which drew upon 1995/96 data, Bucke and Brown (1997) found that 40 per cent of suspects asked for a lawyer.

Figure 4.1 shows considerable variation between stations in the request rate for legal advice. At Queens Road, Beaumont Leys, Fairwater and Hackney around half of suspects requested legal advice. At the other end of the scale, less than a quarter of suspects at Birmingham Road did so. This wide variation confirms the findings of previous studies (see, for example, Brown, 1989; Sanders et al., 1989; Brown, Ellis and Larcombe, 1992). Logistic regression analysis[1], carried out to determine which were the strongest predictors of demand for legal advice, showed that the station at which the suspect was held was a significant factor (see Appendix B, Table B.1).

Figure 4.1   Proportion of suspects requesting legal advice by station

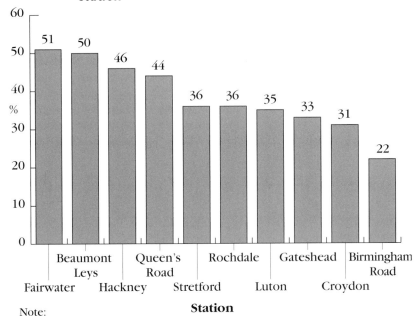

Note:
1. N=3,682 (all suspects).

Demand for legal advice also varied according to offence. Table 4.1 shows that the highest request rate was among those detained for robbery (68%) and sexual offences (66%). Over half of those arrested for burglary, violent offences and theft from vehicles also requested advice. The high figure for 'other offences' (53%) is explained by the fact that many of these were immigration offences where the suspect might be facing deportation. In less serious cases, suspects sought legal advice less often: the lowest figures were for shoplifting (25%), public order offences (23%) and motoring offences (21%). The logistic regression analysis referred to above showed that offence was the strongest single predictor of demand for legal advice.

---

1   This statistical technique examines which variables have a statistically significant association with a particular outcome variable - in this case requests for legal advice - once possible interactions with other variables have been taken into account.

Table 4.1 Proportion of suspects requesting legal advice by offence

Offence	%	(n)
Violence	52	(152)
Sexual	66	(35)
Burglary	52	(178)
Robbery	68	(54)
Theft and Handling:	36	(443)
Shoplifting	25	(79)
Theft of vehicle/TWOC	44	(164)
Theft from vehicle	54	(51)
Other theft and handling	35	(149)
Fraud and forgery	43	(59)
Criminal damage	37	(90)
Drugs	34	(43)
Public Order	23	(114)
Motoring offences	21	(70)
Prostitution	0	(-)
Other offences	53	(148)
Total	**38**	**(1,386)**

Notes:
1. N=3,682 (suspects only).
2. TWOC – unauthorised taking of a motor vehicle.
3. 'Other' offences include immigration offences and failure to appear at court.

Taken together, the variation in demand for legal advice according to offence and differences between stations in arrest patterns help to explain some of the variation in demand for legal advice from one place to another. Thus, the high request rate at Beaumont Leys was linked with the above average level of arrests for violent offences there, while the low rates at Birmingham Road and Croydon were linked, respectively, with high arrest figures for prostitution and shoplifting. Another factor accounting for some of the variation between stations concerns differences in the way in which custody officers present suspects with their rights. Both Sanders et al. (1989) and Brown, Ellis and Larcombe (1992) have observed that this can be influential in determining whether suspects request legal advice. Although such differences were observed during the present study, they were not systematically measured and it is not therefore possible to quantify their effect.

Predicting demand for legal advice

Besides station and offence, the regression analysis showed that the following were significant predictors of demand for legal advice: ethnic group; employment status; previous convictions; condition on arrival at the station; and whether answering police bail (see Appendix B, Table B.1).

Looking first at ethnic group, the request rates for legal advice among black people and Asians were, at 51 per cent and 44 per cent respectively, significantly higher than the rate for white suspects (35%). A number of surveys have pointed to mistrust of the police among ethnic minority groups, especially black people (Skogan, 1990, 1994; Southgate and Crisp, 1993). This may help to explain why, net of other factors, ethnic origin was a significant predictor of demand for legal advice upon arrest. The request rate was particularly high among black people arrested for burglary (nearly 80%) and violent offences (63%). For white suspects the equivalent figure for both offences was 49 per cent. Asian suspects arrested for violent offences were also particularly likely to seek legal advice (in 64% of cases).

Although ethnic group was independently a predictor of demand for legal advice, the high level of demand for advice among black people was also driven by their greater involvement in robbery and violent offences. These offences generate a high level of demand for legal advice, irrespective of the suspect's ethnic group. In contrast, white suspects were far more likely than black suspects to be arrested for public order offences and the demand for legal advice in such cases is relatively low.

Unemployed suspects were significantly more likely than those in employment, education or training to request legal advice: the figures were 43 per cent compared with 33 per cent. There was a similar difference between the request rate for those with previous convictions (42%) and for suspects with no previous record (31%). Undoubtedly, those who are familiar with the criminal justice system through previous contact will be more aware of their eligibility for free legal advice and prepared to take up this right.

Those whose condition on arrival at the station gave some cause for concern were significantly more likely to request legal advice. It is not clear why this should be so. Some may have felt that, because of their condition, they needed some form of outside help. In some cases appropriate adults may have summoned a lawyer on their behalf.

Suspects who were responding to police bail were also significantly more likely than other suspects to seek legal advice. The reason for this is almost certainly that those who are required to respond to their bail face the strong possibility of charges. Where charges are not to be laid, the suspect will usually be absolved from returning to the station. Those required to answer bail therefore often arrived accompanied by a lawyer.

Several other variables were found *not* to be significant in predicting demand for legal advice. Males were found to be much more likely than females to request a solicitor (in 40% of cases compared with 28%). However, this reflected differences in the types of offences for which they were arrested. For example, females were more likely to be arrested for shoplifting, for which the request rate for advice is low, while males were more likely to be arrested for burglary and robbery, offences for which the demand for advice is high.

Age was also not found to be significant. Juveniles were less likely than adults to request advice (in 33% of cases compared with 39%). But, again, this is related to offence, with juveniles being more likely than adults to be arrested for less serious offences for which suspects are less likely to seek legal advice, irrespective of their age. However, considerable variations were found between stations in demand for advice among juveniles. The range was from 11 per cent at Rochdale to 58 per cent at Hackney.

Type of solicitor requested

Suspects who require legal advice have two main choices: either to call their own solicitor or ask for the duty solicitor[2]. Of those who arrived at the station without a lawyer already in attendance and who requested advice, 65 per cent wanted their own solicitor and 35 per cent the duty solicitor[3]. This ratio varied considerably between stations. Only around 50 per cent of suspects asked for their own solicitor at Luton, Hackney and Croydon, but the figure was as high as 86 per cent at Fairwater.

There are several explanations for this level of variation. Very important are differences between areas in the way in which the legal profession is organised, as McConville et al. (1994) have emphasised. In some places, practices specialising in criminal work have a number of representatives on hand solely to provide advice at police stations. They may also be more proactive in advertising their services to those who might need them. Consequently, there is a high demand for 'own' solicitors in these areas.

Also relevant are differences between areas in the level of criminal experience of the arrest population and in the types of offences which predominate.

---

2   Section 59 of PACE required the Law Society to make arrangements for duty solicitor schemes covering police stations. Responsibility for administering the schemes has since passed to the Legal Aid Board. Under the schemes, local solicitors provide 24-hour cover to police stations within a particular area on either a panel or rota basis. For fuller details see Sanders et al. (1989) and McConville et al. (1994).

3   Two suspects sought the advice of a solicitor selected from a list provided by the police, and a further two requested advice both from the duty solicitor *and* their own solicitor.

Thus, suspects with previous convictions were significantly more likely to request legal advice from their own solicitor than the duty solicitor. Their prior experience of the criminal justice system had almost certainly put them in contact with lawyers. Also, higher proportions of those arrested for burglary, robbery, vehicle crime and violence against the person asked for their own solicitors. Again, this is linked with level of criminal experience since suspects in these categories were more likely to be repeat offenders.

Putting requests for advice into effect

Custody officers were successful in contacting a legal adviser on the suspect's behalf in 88 per cent of requests. Contact was usually with the solicitor requested by the suspect but in four per cent of cases the police contacted a solicitor other than the one originally requested. Comparison with previous studies is complicated by differences in the calculation of contact rates, but there is evidence to suggest that there has been an improvement since earlier studies by Sanders et al. (1989) and Brown, Ellis and Larcombe (1992). There are two reasons for this. One is that custody officers may well be going to greater lengths to obtain legal advice where it is requested (Brown, 1991). The other is that recent years have seen increasingly widespread use of solicitors' representatives who are more readily available than solicitors themselves (McConville et al., 1994)[4]. The contact rate varied considerably between stations, ranging from 98 per cent at Stretford to 77 per cent at Birmingham Road.

The main reason for failure to make contact was that suspects changed their minds about wanting legal advice (in 39% of non-contact cases). Inability on the part of the police to locate a solicitor was the reason in only nine per cent of cases. However, evidence from observers suggests that many suspects changed their mind because of difficulties in locating their chosen solicitor. One reason for widely different contact rates between areas was that the adequacy of arrangements for contacting solicitors or their representatives out of office hours varied. This is turn affected suspects''decisions whether to proceed with their requests for advice. Significantly, the majority of non-contact cases involved arrests made between 11pm and 2am. Suspects were probably unwilling to prolong their stay in custody any more than necessary at this time of night. They were most likely to change their mind in less serious cases, such as public order and motoring offences. Those arrested for drink driving often changed their minds when they realised that a request for legal advice would not delay the breath test procedure.

---

4 The most recent evidence suggests that the growth in use of representatives has now been reversed. This is the result of the introduction in 1995 of a Law Society accreditation scheme for police station representatives. Those who have not been accredited or have not registered to become accredited are not entitled to remuneration from the Legal Aid budget (Bridges and Choongh, 1996). Under the most recent revisions to the PACE Codes of Practice (Home Office, 1995a), accredited representatives also have fuller access to their clients than non-accredited or probationer representatives.

In 28 per cent of non-contact cases the suspect had been charged or released before contact could be made. Again, this is related to difficulties in establishing contact, particularly out of hours in some areas. In six per cent of cases suspects decided they would wait to see a solicitor at court. In a further six per cent appropriate adults decided that legal advice requested earlier by juvenile suspects was not needed after all. Solicitors were contacted in five per cent of cases but refused to give advice.

Under s.58 (6) PACE, a senior officer may authorise a delay in allowing the suspect access to legal advice in very restricted circumstances in serious cases. Previous research has shown that access to legal advice is now rarely delayed, following Court of Appeal decisions which have clarified the way in which the provision should be used (Brown, Ellis and Larcombe, 1992). In the present sample of 4250 cases, there was no example of the delay provision being used.

Consultations with legal advisers

Consultation rate

Thirty two-per cent (n=1,339) of the entire sample (i.e. whether suspects or detainees) had some form of consultation with a legal adviser while they were in police custody. This is substantially higher than the figure of 25 per cent obtained by Brown, Ellis and Larcombe (1992) in an earlier study, but similar to that found by Bucke and Brown (1997) in their recent research. The consultation rate was somewhat higher for suspects (33%) than for those detained for other reasons such as warrants (25%). A further one per cent of suspects secured the services of a lawyer but had no direct consultation. These were usually cases in which the adviser asked to be kept informed of developments and, when told that the suspect was not to be interviewed or charged, felt that no intervention was needed.

Reflecting differences in the request rate for advice, far more males (34%t) than females (24%) consulted a lawyer. Black (45%) and Asian (40%) suspects were also far more likely than white suspects (30% to have a legal consultation. There was also a small difference between juveniles (30%) and adults (33%).

Type of consultation

Figure 4.2 shows the kind of consultation suspects had with legal advisers. Nearly 80 per cent had a face to face consultation at the police station and less than one-fifth received legal advice purely by telephone. This contrasts with the situation found by earlier studies, in which advice was restricted to the telephone in up to a third of cases (Sanders et al., 1989; Brown, Ellis and Larcombe, 1992). Sanders et al. (ibid) have noted that duty solicitors are more likely than own solicitors only to give telephone advice. This held true in the current research. Duty solicitors gave telephone advice only in 29 per cent of cases compared with 16 per cent of cases in which own solicitors gave advice – a statistically significant difference.

Figure 4.2 Type of legal consultation

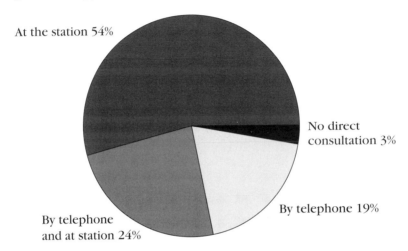

At the station 54%

No direct consultation 3%

By telephone 19%

By telephone and at station 24%

Note:
N=3,682 (all suspects).

There continue to be big variations between stations in the level of telephone advice provided. At Gateshead, only eight per cent of advice was provided purely by telephone, but at Croydon the proportion was 45 per cent. Generally, the facilities for private telephone conversations between lawyer and client were limited. At seven of the ten stations, suspects had to conduct telephone conversations with their lawyers in the custody office itself and could be overheard by anyone nearby.

Confirming previous research (Brown, 1989), it was found that legal advisers were more likely to attend the police station where the suspect had been arrested for a serious offence. Figure 4.3 shows that almost all those arrested for serious offences who obtained legal advice had a consultation at the police station. In contrast, a quarter of those arrested for moderately serious offences and 17 per cent of those arrested for less serious offences received advice solely by telephone.

Figure 4.3 Type of legal consultation by seriousness of offence

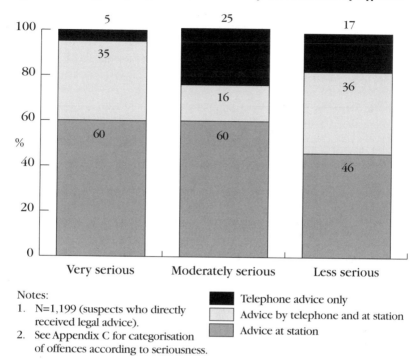

Notes:
1. N=1,199 (suspects who directly received legal advice).
2. See Appendix C for categorisation of offences according to seriousness.

■ Telephone advice only
▢ Advice by telephone and at station
▨ Advice at station

Type of lawyer consulted and their status

Suspects consulted their own solicitors or their representatives in 61 per cent of cases and duty solicitors or their representatives in 39 per cent of cases. The reason that more people consulted duty solicitors than initially requested them (see above) was that some who had asked for their own solicitor opted to switch to the duty solicitor where the police could not make contact.

Several studies have drawn attention to the practice of some solicitors' firms using legal representatives[5] to provide advice at police stations. The estimates they have provided vary widely (because of differences in methodology and geographical coverage) and range from nine per cent (Brown, Ellis and Larcombe, 1992) and 30 per cent (Sanders et al., 1989) to 76 per cent (McConville and Hodgson, 1993). There is agreement, however, that duty solicitors are far less likely than 'own' solicitors to use representatives because the Legal Aid Board's Duty Solicitor Arrangements limit the scope for duty solicitors to do so.

---

5 The term 'legal representative' is taken here to refer to a range of non-solicitor staff, ranging from articled clerks to former police officers and representatives with no formal legal qualifications

Previous research has suggested that the advice given by non-solicitor staff is sometimes of questionable quality (Bridges and Hodgson, 1995)[6]. The Law Society has recently tried to improve the quality of advice provided by legal representatives by introducing an accreditation scheme. Once accredited, representatives enjoy a similar status to solicitors under PACE Code of Practice C in terms of their rights of access to their clients. The present study was undertaken before the new scheme came into effect. In cases where the status of the adviser attending the police station was known[7], it was found that 74 per cent were qualified solicitors and 26 per cent legal representatives. Confirming the findings of earlier research, Figures 4.4 (a) and (b) show that representatives mainly provided advice in cases in which suspects had requested 'own' solicitors. Representatives provided advice in only 10 per cent of cases in which the duty solicitor had been requested.

Figure 4.4(a) Status of own legal adviser

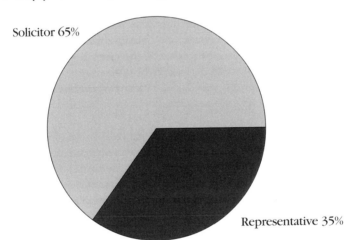

Solicitor 65%

Representative 35%

Note:
N=776 (suspects who received legal advice at the station). No information was available about the adviser's status in 194 cases.

---

6   However, other research has also questioned the quality of advice given by solicitors themselves: see Baldwin (1992).

7   Data were missing in 19 per cent of cases (n=189). The observers reported great difficulty in finding out whether a legal adviser was a qualified solicitor or a legal representative.

Figure 4.4(b) Status of adviser attending under the duty solicitor scheme

Solicitor 90%

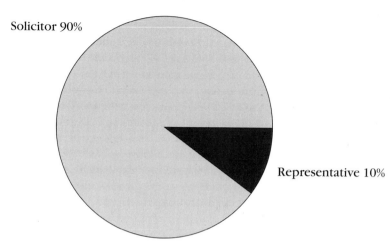

Representative 10%

Note:
N=776 (suspects who received legal advice at the station). No information was available about the adviser's status in 194 cases.

Number of consultations

In more than 90 per cent of cases in which legal advice was given by telephone, this was given in a single call. In eight per cent of cases there were two or more calls. Where advisers attended the station, they made just one visit in nearly 80 per cent of cases. There were two visits in 17 per cent of cases and three or more visits in a further 4 per cent of cases. The suspect was more likely to require more than one consultation where the offence was moderately or very serious. Those arrested for burglary, robbery, and theft and handling offences were particularly likely to have two or more consultations.

Interviews before a request for legal advice

Fifty-nine suspects had been interviewed by the police before deciding to request legal advice. Anecdotal evidence from observers suggests that some changed their mind because they had not initially realised the full extent or seriousness of the allegations against them.

Key points

*   Thirty eight per cent of suspects requested legal advice. The proportion ranged from 22 to 51 per cent at different stations.

*   Those arrested for serious offences were most likely to seek legal advice.

*   Males were more likely than females and black or Asian suspects more likely than whites to request legal advice.

*   Thirty three per cent of suspects had a consultation with a legal adviser. There were several reasons why some suspects who had requested a lawyer failed to talk to one, including changes of heart and difficulties in contacting lawyers out of office hours.

*   Of those advised, over three-quarters were seen by a legal adviser at the station, whilst slightly less than one-fifth obtained legal advice by telephone only.

*   Of those who consulted a legal adviser at the police station, 61 per cent saw their own solicitor and 39 per cent the duty solicitor.

5 Interviews with suspects

This chapter deals with police interviewing, focusing firstly on the extent to which suspects provided admissions and on the surrounding circumstances. Whether suspects admit the offences for which they have been arrested is crucial to the way in which the police deal with their case because, without an admission, a caution cannot be given. This means that custody officers may sometimes have no option but to charge or to take no further action where a caution would have been the preferable option.

The other focus of this chapter is the suspect's right of silence. Information is provided about the frequency with which suspects provide 'no comment' interviews and the circumstances in which they do so. This is useful baseline information against which to assess the effects of Criminal Justice and Public Order Act 1994 provisions, enacted since the research was undertaken. Under the Act it is now possible for courts in certain circumstances to draw inferences from the suspect's failure to mention when questioned by the police facts later relied on in his or her defence at court[1]. It should be noted that the Act provides no compulsion on suspects to answer questions and, to this extent, the situation is the same now as it was at the time of the research.

Admissions

Previous studies agree that rather more than 50 per cent of suspects provide admissions (Softley, 1980; Sanders et al., 1989; Moston, Stephenson and Williamson, 1992; Moston and Stephenson, 1993; Evans, 1993), although the precise figures vary. In the present study, 55 per cent of suspects provided some form of admission. In four-fifths of these cases suspects admitted the offence or all of the offences for which they had been arrested, while in the remaining one-fifth they admitted some offences only. This left 45 per cent of suspects who made no admission of guilt[2]. The 55 per cent admission rate is rather lower than the figure of 59 per cent obtained by Softley (1980) and Moston and Stephenson (1993) but very close to the rate of 54 per cent found by Sanders et al. (1989). It should be noted that the present study's figure relates to all suspects, not just those interviewed. A few suspects may have provided admissions prior to arrival at the police station and then not been interviewed. Others may have admitted the offence for the purposes of a caution, again without being interviewed.

---

1 A full evaluation of the effect of the new provisions is currently being undertaken by the Home Office Research and Statistics Directorate (Bucke, Street and Brown, in press).

2 These data are based on information supplied by arresting officers in 2,502 cases. In another 345 cases arresting officers returned questionnaires but failed to provide information about admissions and in 490 more failed to return questionnaires

Factors associated with admissions

The present study, in line with previous research (Sanders et al., 1989; Moston, Stephenson and Williamson, 1992), found that admissions were strongly linked with the provision of legal advice and the strength of the evidence. A logistic regression analysis, carried out to identify which variables predicted admission once other factors had been taken into account, showed that both these factors were highly significant (see Appendix B, Table B.2). Of those who saw a legal adviser at the police station, only 37 per cent provided admissions compared with 65 per cent of those not legally advised.

Nevertheless, the extent to which the advice given by lawyers is instrumental in persuading suspects not to provide admissions has been queried. Previous research has suggested that those who plan to contest the charges against them are most likely to seek legal advice and that the advice given often coincides with their own intentions (Sanders et a.l, 1989; Brown, Ellis and Larcombe, 1992; Baldwin, 1992; McConville et al., 1994). Furthermore, legal advisers seldom intervene during police interviews (Baldwin, ibid; McConville et al., ibid).

Those against whom there was strong evidence at the time of arrest[3] were far more likely to provide admissions than those against whom the evidence was weaker. The admission rate among the former was 67 per cent compared with 36 per cent for the latter.

Seriousness of offence was not in itself a significant predictor of admissions. It is true that suspects in less serious cases were far more likely to confess (in 72% of cases) than those in moderately serious (49%) and very serious cases (46%). However, this can be attributed to interactions with other variables. For example, in less serious cases suspects were less likely to seek legal advice and there was more likely to be sufficient evidence to charge upon arrest - both of which are factors strongly related to admission.

The regression analysis showed a number of other factors to be significant in predicting admission, once other variables had been taken into account (see Appendix B, Table B.2). These included: suspects' sex, ethnic origin and age; the station at which they were held; and their condition on arrival.

Taking each of these in turn, far more females (73%) than males (52%) provided an admission. To some extent this is related to differences in the kinds of offence for which men and women are arrested. In particular, women were far more likely than men to be arrested for shoplifting offences, for which the evidence is often cut and dried and there is little scope for

---

3   The strength of the evidence was measured by asking arresting officers whether there was sufficient evidence to charge at the time of arrest.

denial of involvement. However, when other variables (including offence) were controlled for, sex of suspect was still a significant predictor of admission.

White suspects were far more likely to provide admissions (in 58% of cases) than either Asians (48%t) or black people (44%). This finding is in line with the findings of previous research (CRE, 1992; FitzGerald, 1993). The relatively low admission rate among black people in particular increases the chances of them entering the formal criminal justice system because those who deny their guilt are ineligible for a caution.

Juveniles provided admissions in 62 per cent of cases compared with 54 per cent for adults. This confirms the findings of previous research by Evans (1993). Contrary to a suggestion made in a previous study by Dixon (1990), there was no evidence to suggest that delays in waiting for appropriate adults to attend the station increased the propensity of juveniles to confess.

The station at which the suspect was held was also a significant predictor of admissions. The highest admissions rates were at Croydon (65%) and Birmingham Road, Wolverhampton (62%) and the lowest at Queen's Road, Birmingham (46%) and Hackney (42%). The reason why station was a strong predictor of admissions is not obvious, bearing in mind that the regression analysis controlled for offence and a range of other variables. One possibility is that the prevailing culture among criminals in some areas may make them less inclined than in others to assist the police by providing admissions, even where the evidence against them is clear.

The suspect's condition on arrival was also a significant factor: those who were drunk, violent or unco-operative were less likely to provide an admission. This was almost certainly related to the nature of the offences involved in cases where suspects arrived in such a condition. They were likely to be cases in which suspects were not interviewed – typically minor public order offences and drink driving offences. It does not follow, therefore, that because there was no admission there was a denial. It was more the case that there was neither.

Admission of additional offences

Eleven per cent of suspects arrested admitted to offences additional to those for which they had been arrested. Some were further offences committed at the same time as the one which led to arrest, while others had been committed on different occasions. Those arrested for vehicle theft and motoring offences were most likely to admit to other offences (in 15% and 18% of cases respectively). These findings are not unexpected: those involved in car crime are often multiple offenders, while those held for motoring offences, such as disqualified driving, often turn out to be guilty of various other documentation offences.

Right of silence

Previous research

Several studies have looked at the frequency with which suspects exercise their right to silence during police interviews. However, as Brown (1994) has noted in a review of research on this topic for the Royal Commission on Criminal Justice (RCCJ), differences between studies in working definitions of 'silence' and in methodology have resulted in quite widely varying results. Studies have not usually discriminated between suspects' refusal to answer questions about their own criminal involvement and that of others. Under the new provisions of the Criminal Justice and Public Order Act 1994 (CJPOA) courts would only be able to draw inferences in the former situation. Some studies have used the interview and others the case as the basis for calculating how often suspects exercise silence. Some have used police officers and others independent observers to collect data. Sample size and representativeness also vary between studies. The most reliable studies are likely to be those which have used independent observers, drawn nationally representative samples of cases (separating out the Metropolitan Police area, where silence appears to be more common), and included a wide range of offences.

Providing a best estimate from these studies of the extent of silence at the time at which his review was undertaken (1992), Brown (ibid) suggests that around five per cent of suspects outside the Metropolitan Police and between seven and nine per cent in London refused to answer all police questions. A further five per cent of suspects in non-Metropolitan forces and around seven per cent in London were estimated to refuse some questions of substance about their involvement in the offence.

There is some evidence to suggest that recourse to silence increased further between the time that Brown's original review was carried out and the introduction of the CJPOA's provisions on inferences from silence. Firstly, a study, carried out by ACPO (1993), of 3,633 suspects processed for recordable offences in eight forces in the South East, showed that 10 per cent refused all questions and 12 per cent refused some. Brown (1997) comments, however, that no information is available on the methodology used in this study to confirm how dependable these figures are. Secondly, in their Crown Court study for the RCCJ, Zander and Henderson (1993) estimated that between 11 and 13 per cent of defendants had refused all police questions and that a further nine to 17 per cent had refused some. These figures can be compared with those obtained by studies dating back to the late 1970s and early 1980s, which also focused only on Crown Court cases. These showed that, at that time, a much lower proportion of defendants – between four and seven per cent – exercised their right of silence at the police station (see, for example: Zander, 1979; McConville and Baldwin, 1981; and Mitchell, 1983).

Frequency of silence in the present study

The present study collected data on the frequency of 'no comment' interviews by asking interviewing officers to record and return this information on questionnaires. They were asked to distinguish cases in which all questions were refused from ones in which refusal was selective. There are no grounds to doubt that officers completed questionnaires anything other than truthfully or that there are any systematic inaccuracies in the data. However, if there are any shortcomings, it might be argued that they are less likely to have occurred in relation to total 'no comment"interviews than selective refusals to answer questions. While, in the latter instance, officers were required to make judgements about the extent and nature of questions refused, where no questions were answered at all there was little scope for ambiguity in the way officers recorded this information.

Figure 5.1 shows that 10 per cent of suspects refused to answer all questions and that in a further 13 per cent of cases there was selective refusal. These figures are little different from those obtained in the ACPO (1993) study (see above). In line with previous studies, which have shown that suspects in London are more likely to remain silent, Figure 5.2 provides information separately about suspects' use of silence in the Metropolitan Police and other forces. On average, suspects at the two London stations were much more likely than their non-Metropolitan counterparts to refuse all questions (in 20% of cases compared with 8 per cent), although the figure for Hackney (27%) was far higher than that at Croydon (14%). The rate at which all questions were refused varied considerably outside London – from four per cent at Rochdale and Birmingham Road (Wolverhampton) up to 12 per cent at Fairwater (Cardiff). The rate at which suspects refused to answer questions selectively was, on average, little different between London and other forces.

Figure 5.1 Suspects' use of the right of silence

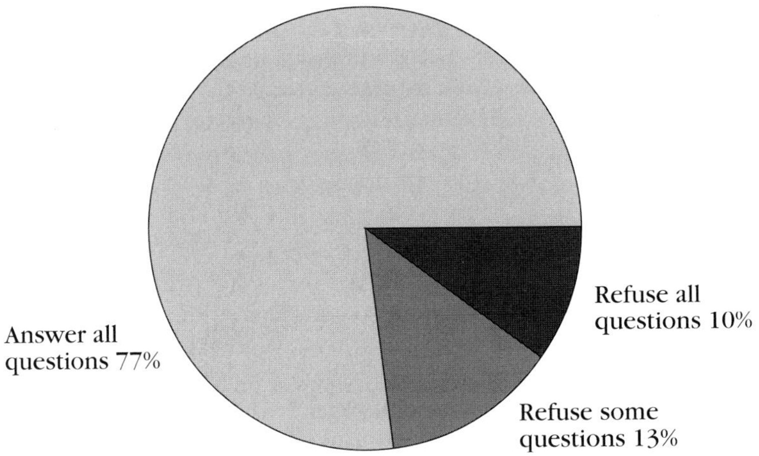

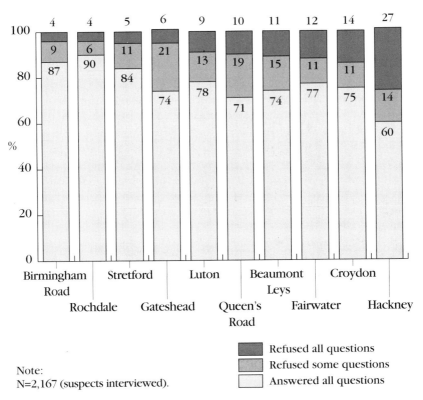

Answer all questions 77%
Refuse all questions 10%
Refuse some questions 13%

Note:
N=2,167 (suspects interviewed).

Figure 5.2 Suspects' use of the right of silence by station

4
4
5
6
9
10
11
12
14
27
100
80
60
40
20
0
%
9
87
6
90
11
84
21
74
13
78
19
71
15
74
11
77
11
75
14
60
Birmingham Road
Rochdale
Stretford
Gateshead
Luton
Queen's Road
Beaumont Leys
Fairwater
Croydon
Hackney
Refused all questions
Refused some questions
Answered all questions

Note:
N=2,167 (suspects interviewed).

Selective refusal to answer questions

Where the suspect's non-response was selective, interviewing officers were asked to indicate the nature of the questions refused. Table 5.1 shows that suspects were most likely to refuse to answer some or all questions about their own involvement in the offence. However, almost half of those who selectively answered questions refused to answer some or all questions about the criminal involvement of others. This is consistent with previous research which has suggested that there is strong resistance among criminals to 'grassing' on their co-accused (Hobbs, 1988; Foster, 1989). Only a very small number of suspects refused to answer questions unrelated to the offence. Such questions were generally ones designed to establish rapport.

Table 5.1   Selective responses to questioning: type of questions refused

Type of questions refused	%	(n)
All questions about suspect's involvement	31	(85)
Some questions about suspect's involvement	42	(115)
All questions about others' involvement	32	(88)
Some questions about others' involvement	15	(41)
Questions unrelated to the offence	5	(13)

Notes:
1.   N=273. Data were missing in 3 cases.
2.   Total percentage does not sum to 100, as multiple responses could be provided to this question.

Who remains silent?

There were significant variations in the rate at which suspects exercised their right of silence depending on: where they were held; whether they were legally advised; the offence for which they were arrested; their prior record; and their gender and ethnic origin[4].

Looking at these in turn, it has already been noted (see Figure 5.2) that the proportion of cases in which there were total 'no comment' interviews varied considerably from station to station. Suspects most often exercised their right of silence at the two London stations in the sample. Confirming the findings of previous studies (Moston, Stephenson and Williamson, 1990; ACPO, 1993), those who obtained legal advice were far more likely to refuse all questions (20%) than those who did not seek advice (3%). It is highly likely that those who plan to fight the case and who are not inclined to assist the police by answering questions are more likely to seek legal advice.

---

4   Age was also examined. There were no statistically significant differences between age groups in the likelihood of suspects exercising their right of silence. Juveniles were slightly less likely than older age groups to provide 'no comment' interviews

There was a tendency for the rate at which suspects exercised their right of silence to be higher at those stations where the demand for legal advice was also high. Thus, at Hackney, where nearly half of suspects requested a lawyer, over a quarter refused to answer all police questions. In contrast, at Birmingham Road less than a quarter of suspects asked for legal advice and only four per cent refused all questions. However, the link was not a straightforward one and there were examples of stations where demand for legal advice was relatively low but exercise of the right of silence above average (e.g. Croydon) and vice versa (e.g. Rochdale). Among the possible reasons for these discrepancies are that lawyers may vary from area to area in the readiness with which they advise suspects to offer 'no comment'. For their part, the extent to which suspects are prepared to co-operate with the police, irrespective of legal advice also varies between areas. Differences between stations in the kinds of offences for which suspects were arrested are also relevant.

Those arrested for very or moderately serious offences were significantly more likely to refuse all questions (13%) than those held for less serious offences (5 %). In less serious cases, the prospect of a caution if the offence was admitted may have been a factor encouraging suspects to respond in interviews. Suspects with a criminal record were much more likely to remain completely silent (13%) than those with no previous convictions (5%).

Males appeared to be significantly less willing than females to answer questions. Figure 5.3 shows that 11 per cent of male suspects refused all questions, compared with six per cent of females. They were also more likely to respond to questions selectively. Figure 5.4 shows that black suspects were significantly more likely than either whites or Asians to exercise their right of silence. Over 20 per cent refused to answer all questions, compared with 13 per cent and 8 per cent respectively of Asian and white suspects. Surveys have pointed to lower levels of confidence in the police among black people than among whites or Asians (Skogan, 1990, 1994; Southgate and Crisp, 1993). This may be one factor explaining why they are less inclined to assist them by answering questions.

Figure 5.3   Suspects' use of the right of silence by sex

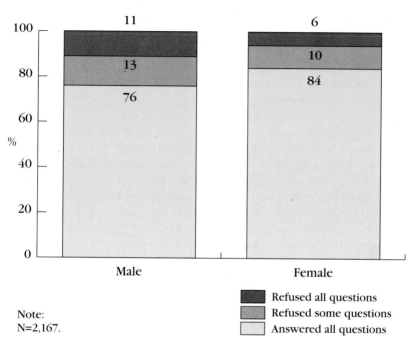

Note:
N=2,167.

Refused all questions
Refused some questions
Answered all questions

Figure 5.4   Suspects' use of the right of silence by ethnic origin

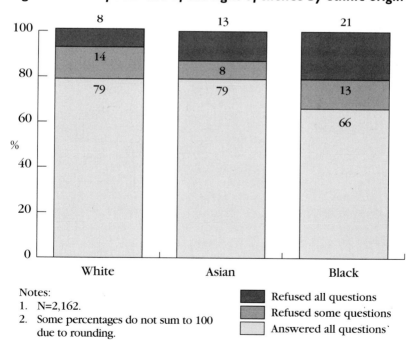

Notes:
1. N=2,162.
2. Some percentages do not sum to 100
    due to rounding.

Refused all questions
Refused some questions
Answered all questions

Key points

- Over half of suspects admitted the offence for which they had been arrested.

- Females were more likely than males and juveniles more likely than older suspects to provide admissions. White suspects also confessed more often than black or Asian suspects.

- The admission rate was also higher at some stations than others, as well as being higher where: the offence was less serious; the suspect was not legally advised; and the evidence was strong on arrest.

- Ten per cent of suspects refused to answer all questions during interviews and 13 per cent selectively refused to answer questions. Total 'no comment' interviews were more common in London (in 20% of cases) than elsewhere (8%).

- Among the suspects most likely to exercise their right of silence were: those who had received legal advice; those held for more serious offences; males; black people; and those with a criminal record.

- Where suspects selectively refused questions, they most frequently declined to account for own alleged involvement in the offence, but nearly half appeared to be trying to protect others by refusing to answer questions about the involvement of associates.

6 The outcome of custody: police decision-making

This chapter first provides a breakdown of the outcome of custody for members of the sample and some information about procedural aspects of decision-making. It then focuses on a range of factors which have a bearing on whether any official action is taken against the suspect. Finally, it considers how decisions are made about whether that action is to be in the form of charge or caution.

Case outcome

Previous studies have provided a range of figures on the proportion of arrests which result in charges. Differences in geographical coverage and in methodology largely account for the variation in their findings. In a study covering a range of stations (six in all), McConville, Sanders and Leng (1991) examined over 1,000 cases. They found that the police charged 50 per cent of suspects, took no further action against 25 per cent and cautioned 21 per cent[1]. A more limited study, set at just one Hampshire station (Portsmouth), found a rather higher prosecution rate. Of just over 1,000 suspects, the police charged or summonsed more than two-thirds, took no further action against 19 per cent and cautioned 13 per cent. In contrast, a study in the Metropolitan Police by Robertson, Pearson and Gibb (1995) found a considerably lower prosecution rate than either of these two studies. Set at seven stations and examining nearly 3,000 cases, they found that the police charged just 35 per cent of those arrested, cautioned 28 per cent, took no further action against 13 per cent and bailed 24 per cent pending further enquiries. The reason why the charge rate in this study is relatively low is partly that public order offences (which comprised a considerable proportion of arrests) were often dealt with by way of caution and partly that, where suspects were bailed for further enquiries, the final outcome was not known. Some of these cases would have resulted in charges.

The McConville study is the most representative of the three in that it included a range of stations in different forces. Coverage of a range of forces is important in order to average out the effect of differences between them

---

1   In the remaining four per cent of cases, either an informal warning was given or no information was available.

in cautioning practice. As other research has noted, cautioning rates vary markedly between areas, even for offenders in the same age group (Evans and Ellis, 1997). This was one reason why the present study was set in a number of forces, selected partly on the basis of differences in their cautioning rates.

Charge, caution and NFA

Table 6.1 provides details of the outcome of custody, taking suspects and other detainees separately. Fifty-two per cent of suspects were charged, a similar proportion to that found in the McConville, Sanders and Leng (1991) study.

The use of cautioning in the present study was lower than in the McConville research (17% compared with 21%). It is difficult for two reasons to relate this difference to national trends in the cautioning rate during the period between the two studies. One is that official statistics on cautioning are calculated on a different basis. Thus, the cautioning rate in Criminal Statistics England and Wales (Home Office, annually) relates to the proportion of offenders cautioned or found guilty who were cautioned[2]. The present study and that by McConville relate to the proportion of those arrested who were cautioned. The choice of stations in the two studies is also relevant. Unlike the present research, those in McConville's study were not necessarily chosen to be representative of the range of cautioning practice around the country and ones with high cautioning rates may have been over-represented.

In the present study, no further action (NFA) was taken against 20 per cent of suspects (a smaller proportion than the 25% found in McConville's study).

Bail for further enquiries

Just over 17 per cent of suspects were initially bailed for further enquiries before a final decision was made about what action to take. Juveniles were more likely than adults to be bailed: this occurred in 21 per cent of juvenile arrests[3] compared with 17 per cent of adult cases. The proportion of suspects bailed for enquiries varied quite considerably between stations, ranging from a fifth or more at Croydon, Gateshead and Luton to only 10 per cent at Fairwater.

---

2   Between the time of McConville's study (late 1980s) and the present research (1993/94), there was a rise of 10 percentage points in the cautioning rate as measured by official statistics (Home Office, 1997a).

3   This figure excludes juveniles who were bailed pending a decision by a juvenile panel.

Table 6.1   Outcome of detention

Disposal	Suspects		Other detainees		Total sample	
	%	(n)	%	(n)	%	(n)
Charge	52	(1,913)	7	(37)	46	(1,950)
NFA	20	(751)	4	(22)	18	(773)
Caution	17	(611)	1	(3)	14	(614)
Transfer	5	(180)	33	(185)	9	(365)
Held on warrant	2	(55)	45	(254)	7	(309)
Released	1	(23)	11	(60)	2	(83)
Other	2	(89)	1	(6)	2	(95)
Not Known	2	(60)	<1	(1)	1	(61)
Total n	3,682		568		4,250	

Notes:
1. N=4250.
2. Eighteen per cent (n=765) of suspects were bailed to return at the time fieldwork ended, either pending further enquiries (n=640) or the decision of an inter-agency juvenile panel (n=125). One per cent of suspects (n=59) were reported for summons. For all of these cases the final outcome is recorded. Where an information was laid in summons cases this is recorded as a charge.
3. 'NFA' refers to those cases which were taken no further by the police either because there was insufficient evidence to justify proceedings or a formal caution or because there were public interest considerations against taking the case further. The latter would count as detected but the former would not.
4. 'Released' covers cases in which suspects were released (without bail) pending further enquiries, ones where the offence was to be taken into consideration, and cases where the suspect was released under a warrant backed for bail. 'Other' disposals included informal warnings and fines paid.

There is evidence that the practice of using this kind of bail has risen in recent years. Research by Brown (1989), using 1987 data, found that only 12 per cent of adult suspects were then bailed. The rise since then may partly be related to the issuing of time limits within which the police should submit files to the Crown Prosecution Service after charge (Working Group on Pre-Trial Issues, 1992). There is evidence from recent Home Office research that officers sometimes use this form of bail to maximise the time available to them to prepare the case papers within the correct time limit[4].

Thirty per cent of those bailed for enquiries were charged, nine per cent were cautioned and 1 per cent reported for summons, while 17 per cent were dealt with in some other way. However, the highest proportion – 44 per cent – were NFAed. In contrast, among suspects who were not bailed, just 16 per cent were NFAed. Where those bailed were to be NFAed, they would usually be notified of this by letter and told that they need not answer their bail. These suspects represent what can be considered a 'dark figure' in the arrest population because the outcome of their cases is often not well documented. Because the pattern of outcomes for those bailed for enquiries is very different from the outcome of non-bail cases, it is likely that studies

4   Noted by Brown (unpublished) in a report to the Bail Issues Steering Group, July 1996.

such as that by Robertson, Pearson and Gibb (1995), which have not tracked the outcome of bail cases, have understated the proportion of detainees who are NFAed.

The fact that so many of those bailed for enquiries are finally NFAed highlights the gap in many cases between what is sufficient evidence to arrest and what is sufficient to charge. Whether a suspect is charged may often depend upon an admission being forthcoming during interviews after arrest. If it is not, officers may bail the suspect for enquiries in the hope that further evidence can subsequently be discovered. There must be some doubt, given pressures of work, whether officers are genuinely able in many cases to pursue further enquiries once bail has been given.

Figure 6.1 shows that the use of bail varied considerably according to offence. It was most frequently given where suspects had been arrested for fraud, sexual offences, robbery and drugs offences. However, the circumstances leading to the bailing of suspects varied. In some fraud cases, the complexity of enquiries could mean that officers needed to carry out further analysis of documents and talk to possible witnesses after their interview with the suspect. In drugs cases the most usual reason was to allow forensic analysis of suspected illicit drugs to be carried out. In some cases, particularly robbery, bail was given in order that an identification parade might be arranged. But, in all types of offence, the situation was often that the initial evidence against the suspect was insufficient to charge (particularly where it was circumstantial) and the suspect had made no admissions during interview. The suspect was bailed in the anticipation that further evidence would be uncovered.

Figure 6.1 Use of bail for enquiries by offence

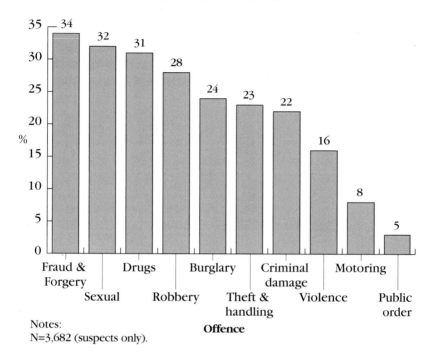

Notes:
N=3,682 (suspects only).

Suspects from ethnic minorities were significantly more likely to be bailed for further enquiries than white suspects. Whereas 16 per cent of the latter were bailed, this was true of 22 per cent of black suspects and 23 per cent of Asians. The reason was not that ethnic minority suspects were more likely to be arrested for the kinds of offences for which suspects are typically bailed. The discrepancy between bail rates was found for most of the main categories of offence. For example, while 14 per cent of whites were bailed for violent offences, this was the case for 21 per cent of black and 23 per cent of Asian suspects. And, in burglary offences, while 20 per cent of whites were bailed, this was true of 35 per cent and 38 per cent respectively of black and Asian suspects. Underlying these differences are the facts that black and Asian suspects were more likely than whites to be arrested where the evidence on arrest was insufficient to charge (see Chapter 2) and that they were less likely than white suspects to provide admissions during police interviews and more likely to exercise their right of silence. Where these factors coincided (i.e. there was insufficient evidence to charge and the suspect provided no admission/exercised the right of silence) the police may have had little alternative but to bail the suspect where no other evidence was forthcoming and where they were unwilling to choose to take no further action.

Summons cases

In only two per cent (n=67) of cases was the suspect reported for summons[5]. The summons procedure is most typically used instead of arrest in traffic offences where there is no need to protect the victim or suspect or secure evidence (Hallett, 1993). For this reason, reporting someone once they have already been arrested is quite rare. Moreover, it has become rarer. When PACE was first introduced Brown (1989) found that, at that time, 10 per cent of adult suspects were summonsed following arrest. The decline since then is largely due to the introduction of breath-test machines at police stations, which allow an instant decision to be made in most drink driving cases about whether to charge, without awaiting the analysis of samples of blood or urine. However, the summons procedure continues to be used in some borderline cases where such samples are still taken. It is used as an efficiency measure, in that the suspect is sent a summons to appear at court, without the officer in the case having to re-arrest the suspect.

Advice cases

The police may, in some circumstances, submit a file to the CPS prior to charge, typically in order to obtain a lawyer's view on the sufficiency of the evidence or the number and nature of the charges that are appropriate (Crisp and Moxon, 1995). In the present study, the police sought formal advice from the CPS in only seven cases. However, there was evidence of more frequent informal communication and advice between the two (although systematic data on this were not collected). In five of the cases where formal advice was requested, the purpose was to obtain a view on whether there was sufficient evidence to bring charges. In the other two cases, the police consulted about the number or type of charges. The cases in question ranged in seriousness from conspiracy to murder to section 5 of the Public Order Act 1986. The CPS advised the police to take no further action in two cases – advice which was followed. In the remaining cases they suggested that the police proceed, either on one or all offences. In only one case did the police not take the advice of the CPS.

Other detainees

The pattern of outcomes for other detainees was very different from that for suspects. The largest proportion (45%) were held in custody for court, having been arrested on warrant. One-third were transferred to court for the hearing of their case or returned to prison afterwards. The only other group of any size was the 11 per cent who were released, usually because they had been arrested on a warrant which authorised the police to bail the person to appear at court on a specified date.

---

5 Suspects are told that the allegations against them will be reported for a decision on whether or not they will be prosecuted. The 67 cases include 59 in which suspects were reported for summons when first released from custody and a further eight where they were later reported for summons, having first been bailed for police enquiries or, in the case of juveniles, referred for inter-agency consultation.

Factors related to case outcome

Offence type and seriousness

Case outcome varied according to the seriousness of the offence[6]. Figure 6.2 shows that serious offences were much more likely to result in charges than less serious ones (63% compared with 45%). Correspondingly, the less serious the offence the more likely were suspects to be cautioned. Those arrested for less serious offences were the least likely to be NFAed. This probably reflects the fact that it can sometimes be more straightforward to prove the essential elements of the offence in such cases. However, a logistic regression, carried out to identify factors which were significant predictors of whether suspects would be NFAed, showed that seriousness of offence was not in itself statistically significant (see Appendix B, Table B.3).

Figure 6.2 Outcome of custody according to seriousness of offence

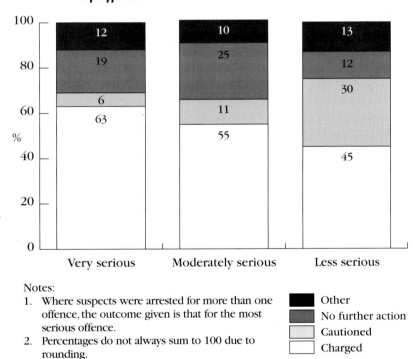

Notes:
1. Where suspects were arrested for more than one offence, the outcome given is that for the most serious offence.
2. Percentages do not always sum to 100 due to rounding.
3. 'Other' outcomes include transfer to another station and informal warnings.
4. See Appendix C for categorisation of offences according to seriousness.

■ Other
■ No further action
▨ Cautioned
□ Charged

Table 6.2 provides more detail about specific categories of offence. Among those most likely to be charged (in two-thirds of cases) were suspects

---

6   See Appendix C for details of the classification of offences according to level of seriousness

arrested for violence against the person. However, high charge rates were not confined to the more serious offences. A high proportion of those arrested for motoring offences were charged, for example. The majority had been arrested for driving after consuming excess alcohol and all forces had a mandatory charging policy for this offence. Almost all suspects arrested for prostitution offences were charged. Again, it was general police policy to charge those who had a previous record for this offence. In relation to property offences, the likelihood of the suspect being charged rather than cautioned increased with the value of the property stolen.

Table 6.2   Case outcome by offence

Offence	Charged	Cautioned	No further action	Other
	%	%	%	%
Violence against the person	67	11	13	9
Sexual	51	11	25	13
Burglary	52	9	29	11
Robbery	48	1	31	20
Theft/handling:	46	20	24	9
Shoplifting	44	40	10	6
Theft of vehicle/TWOC	52	7	30	12
Thefts from vehicle	51	16	26	7
Other theft & handling	42	17	30	11
Fraud and forgery	54	7	24	15
Criminal damage	50	19	22	9
Drugs	45	34	13	8
Public order	48	34	15	3
Prostitution	94	6	–	–
Motoring	72	3	18	7
%	52	17	20	11
Total n	1,913	611	751	407

Notes:
1.   Where suspects were bailed for enquiries or for the decision of a juvenile panel, the final disposal is recorded.
2.   Percentages do not always sum to 100 due to rounding.
3.   TWOC – unauthorised taking of a motor vehicle.

Generally, the cautioning rate was lower than the average (17%) for more serious offences, such as violence against the person, sexual offences, burglary, robbery and fraud. Those most likely to be cautioned had been arrested for shoplifting, drugs and public order offences. The research was carried out before the implementation of the most recent Home Office cautioning circular (18/1994). This advised that only in exceptional circumstances should offenders should be cautioned for indictable only offences. In the present study, out of just over 600 offenders cautioned, only one per cent (n=6) were cautioned for such offences[7]. One was a case of grievous bodily harm where the suspect was mentally disordered. The others were four cases of arson, involving juveniles with no previous convictions or cautions, and one case of rape and indecent assault on a female, where the complainant did not want to press charges and consented to the offender receiving a caution. While the offences were intrinsically serious, therefore, there were extenuating circumstances which led to the decision to caution.

The NFA rate also varied according to offence. In the logistic regression mentioned above, offence type was a significant predictor of whether suspects were NFAed (see Appendix B, Table B.3). Those most likely to be NFAed had been arrested for robbery, vehicle crime, theft & handling and burglary. There are probably two reasons why the NFA rate varies by offence. Firstly, it is less likely in some kinds of offence (such as burglary and robbery) that the suspect will have been caught in the act (as often occurs in shoplifting, public order, violence, prostitution and drugs cases). Short of an admission by the suspect, there may be difficulties in raising the evidence to the standard needed to charge. Secondly, the police may be reluctant to put forward serious cases for prosecution unless the evidence is watertight.

Strength of evidence

The study obtained a rough measure of the strength of the evidence on arrest by asking officers whether it was sufficient to charge at that point. Clearly, there is scope for the police to obtain further evidence after arrest, either by securing an admission from the suspect during interview or by pursuing other lines of enquiry. But, given that many suspects do not provide admissions and that the police have limited time after arrest to continue enquiries, it would be expected that those arrested where there was insufficient evidence to charge would be more likely to be NFAed. This was indeed the case. Figure 6.3 shows that NFA was the outcome in 40 per cent of cases where the evidence on arrest was insufficient to charge, compared with just 10 per cent where the evidence was sufficient. Multivariate analysis showed that, controlling for other factors, the strength of the evidence on arrest was one of the most important predictors of whether suspects would be NFAed (see Appendix B, Table B.3).

---

7   Official statistics also show that less than 1 per cent of those cautioned are cautioned for indictable only offences (Home Office, 1997a). However, it is not possible to verify whether the offences concerned were serious, objectively speaking, since there is no independent scrutiny of the appropriateness of the offences selected for caution in the way that the CPS examines the offences with which suspects are charged

Figure 6.3 Outcome of custody by strength of evidence on arrest

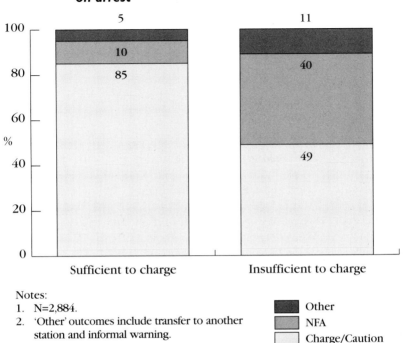

Notes:
1. N=2,884.
2. 'Other' outcomes include transfer to another station and informal warning.

Other
NFA
Charge/Caution

Station

There was considerable variation between stations in the way in which suspects were dealt with. For example, Table 6.3 shows that the proportion charged ranged from 40 per cent at Croydon to 71 per cent at Fairwater. There were corresponding variations in the proportion of suspects cautioned, ranging from just six per cent at Beaumont Leys to 22 per cent at Croydon. Previous studies have also drawn attention to the wide variation in the use of cautioning (see, for example, Brown, 1989; Evans and Wilkinson, 1988, 1990; Madison, 1994; Evans and Ellis, 1997), which is also evident from official statistics (Home Office, 1997a). The NFA rate also varied, from 10 per cent at Fairwater to 28 per cent at Luton. The station at which the suspect was held was a significant factor in predicting whether cases would be NFAed (see Appendix B, Table B.3).

There are a number of reasons for these variations. One is that stations vary considerably in the types of crime which are prevalent in their area. At Beaumont Leys, for example, the proportion of more serious offences was quite high, helping to explain the low cautioning figures here. In contrast, Croydon had more than its fair share of shoplifters, who contributed to a high cautioning rate.

A second important factor is that stations differed in the way in which they dealt with similar categories of offender. For example, at Beaumont Leys and Gateshead it was very unusual for burglary suspects ever to be cautioned; however, at Rochdale and Birmingham Road around one-fifth were given cautions. Again, whereas only five per cent of those arrested for ABH or GBH at Queen's Road and Fairwater were cautioned, the proportion was one-fifth or more at Rochdale and Stretford.

Table 6.3   Case outcome by station

Station	Charged	Cautioned	No further action	Other
	%	%	%	%
Stretford	63	14	18	6
Rochdale	56	18	19	8
Luton	44	19	28	9
Queen's Road	59	9	24	8
Beaumont Leys	53	6	19	22
Birmingham Road	54	18	22	6
Fairwater	71	12	10	7
Gateshead	51	19	22	9
Hackney	45	20	17	18
Croydon	40	22	22	16
%	52	17	20	11
Total n	1,913	611	751	407

Note: Percentages do not always sum to 100 due to rounding.

There are, in turn, several explanations for these differences in approach to the same kinds of offence. One concerns the extent to which forces have systematised the guidance given to decision-makers on how to deal with different kinds of offence. For example, two forces (Northumbria and Leicestershire) had introduced a system of gravity factors to help custody officers to decide when to caution and when to charge[8]. At station level commanding officers also influenced decision-making. Instances were found in which orders had been given to suspend cautioning for specific offences – typically of a public order nature – where these were of particular local concern. Lastly, while the provisions of the Police and Magistrates' Courts Act 1994 were not in force at the time of the research, it is possible that the

---

8   Since the research was conducted, guidance to supplement the 1994 Cautioning Circular has been issued by ACPO Crime Committee (ACPO, 1995). With the aim of promoting more objective and consistent decision-making on cautioning, the guidance incorporates a set of gravity factors. Essentially, these assign a weight to each kind of offence, and this is increased or decreased according to whether certain aggravating or mitigating factors are present. If the score arrived at falls at or below a certain level, the presumption is that the suspect will be cautioned. Recent research by Evans and Ellis (1997) suggests that these gravity factors are now widely used by forces throughout the country.

Act's requirement for chief officers to set key objectives for their forces may now affect cautioning practice. Where, for example, an offence such as burglary is targeted, this may predispose decision-makers within the force against cautioning for that offence.

Ultimately, whatever guidance or instructions are provided, decision-makers retain a residual discretion in deciding how best to deal with the suspect before them. It is likely that the individual practices of custody officers and inspectors played an important – albeit unquantifiable – role in accounting for differences between stations in patterns of cautioning and charging. This may help to explain why cautioning rates at individual stations were not always in line with those for the forces in which they were situated.

Age, sex, ethnicity and employment status

Figure 6.4a shows that males were significantly more likely to be charged than females and correspondingly less likely to be cautioned. Females were more likely to be cautioned because they were far more likely than males to admit their offences (see Chapter 5) and more likely to be arrested for less serious offences (typically shoplifting). They were also more likely than males to be NFAed. This was not a function of differences in the kinds of offences for which men and women are arrested. Regression analysis showed that, controlling for other factors (including offence), the sex of the suspect remained a significant predictor of NFA outcomes (see Appendix B, Table B.3). There are several reasons why this should be so. There may have been gender-related differences in the circumstances of the offences and suspects which the research could not measure. Or, as Hedderman and Gelsthorpe (1997) have suggested in relation to the sentencing of women, decision-makers (in this case custody officers) may treat men and women differently, even when their circumstances are to all intents and purposes similar.

The same proportion of white and black suspects were charged, but Asians were significantly less likely to be dealt with in this way (see Figure 6.4b). Both black and Asian suspects were significantly less likely than whites to be cautioned and significantly more likely to be NFAed. These findings are in line with the conclusions of previous research (Jefferson and Walker, 1992; FitzGerald, 1993)[9]. Regression analysis showed that, after controlling for other variables, the ethnic group of the suspect was not a significant predictor of NFA decisions. It is likely that the higher NFA rate for black and Asian suspects was associated with their lower admission rate and their involvement in certain kinds of offence which typically have above average NFA rates.

---

9   For a recent discussion of the relationship between ethnic origin and the disposal of cases involving male juveniles in the MPS see FitzGerald and Sibbitt (1997). They found that, once offence, admissions and previous convictions or cautions had been taken into account, differences in the use of cautioning between ethnic groups were generally slight.

Figure 6.4c shows that juveniles were considerably more likely to be cautioned than adults. However, those in the oldest age bracket, 60 years or more, were also significantly more likely than average to be cautioned (in 34% of cases). The different cautioning rates for these age groups were, to some extent, related to the offences for which they were arrested. However, the research also showed that, in relation to juveniles, the age of the suspect quite often weighed with custody officers as a factor in their decision to caution (see below).

Employed suspects were less likely than the unemployed to be charged, and more likely to be cautioned or NFAed (see Figure 6.4d). Those in full-time education or training were the most likely to be cautioned, reflecting the lower average age of those in this group.

Figure 6.4(a) Outcome of arrest by sex of suspect

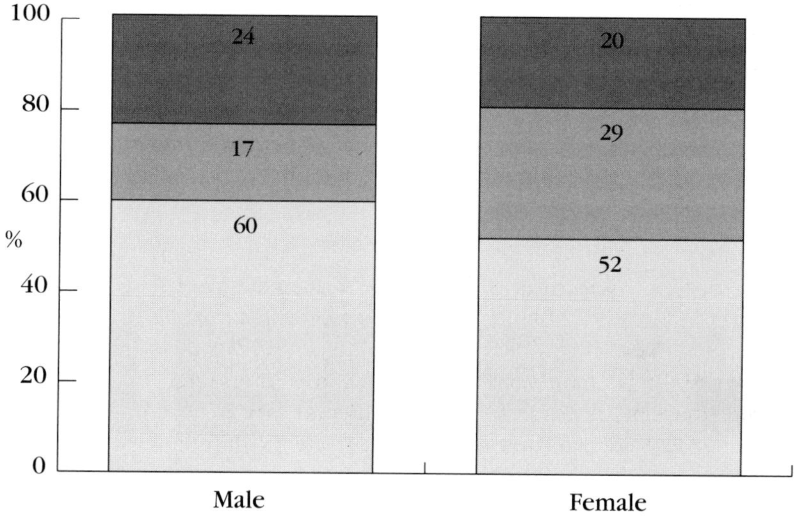

Notes:
1. N=3,682.
2. Percentages do not always add up to 100 due to rounding.
3. Where decisions were deferred, the final disposal is recorded.
4. 'Other' outcomes have not been included

NFAed
Cautioned
Charged

Figure 6.4(b) Outcome of arrest by ethnic origin of suspect

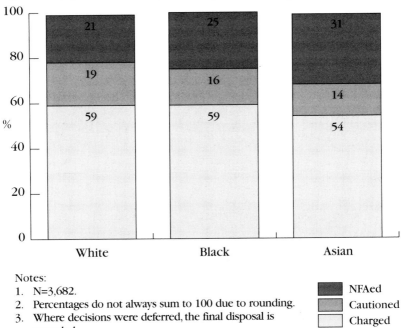

Notes:
1. N=3,682.
2. Percentages do not always sum to 100 due to rounding.
3. Where decisions were deferred, the final disposal is recorded.
4. 'Other' outcomes have not been included.

- NFAed
- Cautioned
- Charged

Figure 6.4(c) Outcome of arrest by age of suspect

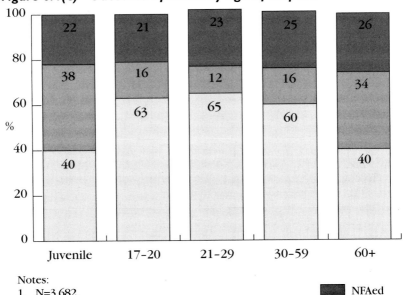

Notes:
1. N=3,682.
2. Percentages do not always sum to 100 due to rounding.
3. Where decisions were deferred, the final disposal is recorded.
4. 'Other' outcomes have not been included.

- NFAed
- Cautioned
- Charged

Figure 6.4(d)   Outcome of arrest by employment status of suspect

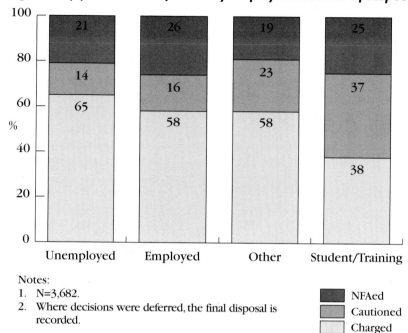

Notes:
1. N=3,682.
2. Where decisions were deferred, the final disposal is recorded.

■ NFAed
▨ Cautioned
□ Charged

Mental disorder

Those whom the police treated as mentally disordered were much less likely than average to be charged: this was the outcome in just 44 per cent of cases. The other outcomes were: caution – 12 per cent; NFA – 23 per cent; and transfer to hospital – 21 per cent. Robertson, Pearson and Gibb (1995) report a similar pattern in their research[10]. The below average charge rate for mentally disordered detainees partly reflects the fact that a third had been detained under the Mental Health Act and not for an offence. However, those arrested for offences were also less likely than average to be charged.

Domestic violence

Suspects arrested for domestic violence were no more likely than others to be subject to some form of action, whether by way of charge or caution. However, the difference between this group and other offenders was that the action taken was more likely to be in the form of charge rather than caution. Figure 6.5 shows that 57 per cent were charged and 13 per cent cautioned, compared with the study average of 52 per cent and 17 per cent. Not all the offences involved were ones of violence against the person: some were criminal damage or public order offences. However, where the offence was actually one of violence, the proportion charged was even higher (71%) and somewhat higher than the charge rate for offences of violence generally (67%).

---

10   However, they categorised case outcomes slightly differently and did not follow up cases where suspects were bailed for enquiries.

Figure 6.5 Outcome of arrests made in domestic violence cases

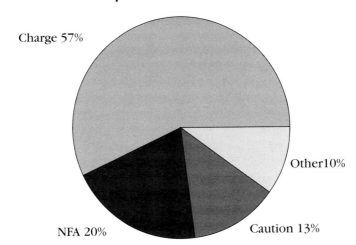

Charge 57%

Other 10%

Caution 13%

NFA 20%

Notes:
1. N=217.
2. Where decisions were deferred, the final disposal is recorded.

Previous research on domestic violence by Grace (1995) produced a roughly similar picture of police practice in dealing with domestic violence offenders, although also suggesting that there is variation between areas. She found that in the Thames Valley and South Yorkshire forces 60 per cent of those arrested for domestic violence offences were charged. But in a parallel exercise in three other forces she found a charge rate as high as 81 per cent, with only five per cent of suspects being cautioned[11].

Those charged with domestic violence offences were mainly male, although 10 per cent were female. Reflecting the age breakdown of those arrested (see Chapter 2), those charged were predominantly in their 20s (44%) or 30s (32%). Only 13 per cent were in their 40s and four per cent aged 50 or over; seven per cent were under 20. The ethnic breakdown for domestic violence offenders was similar to that for the sample as a whole.

Where suspects were charged, 60 per cent were held in custody prior to their first court appearance. In contrast, the figure for suspects generally was 29 per cent (see Chapter 7). The high rate of refusal of bail reflects custody officers' concerns about the risk of harm that suspects might pose to their (usually female) partners if released.

Stop/search

Given the controversy which police use of stop and search powers has generated, particularly in areas with high ethnic minority populations (see,

---

11 Grace used different methods of data collection in the two parts of her study and it is possible that this may account for some of the discrepancy in charge rates.

for example, Scarman, 1981), it is relevant to consider how frequently arrests following stop/searches led to some kind of action being taken against suspects. It was found that there was little difference in this respect between stop/search and other arrests. This was despite the fact that the proportion of stop/search cases in which the evidence on arrest was sufficient to charge was somewhat lower than for arrests generally (55% compared with 61%). It would seem that the police were generally able to remedy the shortfall in evidence after arrest.

However, the 'success rate' of stop/search arrests (the proportion leading to charge or caution) varied according to the reason for the search. Table 6.4 shows that, while nearly 80 per cent of arrests arising out of searches for offensive weapons and nearly three-quarters of those resulting from searches for drugs led to charge or caution, this was true of only 50 per cent of arrests arising from searches for stolen property[12]. These differences in 'success rates' raise the question of whether officers sometimes carry out searches and make arrests on less than reasonable suspicion. While this is a possibility, another explanation might be that officers' actions in searching and then arresting *are* generally based on reasonable suspicion, but that there are greater difficulties in some kinds of case than others in then raising the standard of suspicion to the level needed to charge. Thus, while the possession of drugs or a weapon may provide fairly incontrovertible proof of the commisison of an offence, it may be easier for suspects to provide plausible explanations for the possession of items which the police believe to be stolen. Short of other evidence, NFA may be the only option.

Table 6.4   Outcome of stop/search arrests by reason for search

Type of stop/search	Charge		Caution		NFA		Other	
	%	(n)	%	(n)	%	(n)	%	(n)
Stolen property	40	(31)	10	(8)	34	(26)	16	(12)
Drugs offences	27	(14)	46	(24)	19	(10)	8	(4)
Traffic offences	70	(32)	7	(3)	15	(7)	9	(4)
Excess alcohol	79	(27)	-	-	15	(5)	6	(2)
Going equipped	40	(10)	20	(5)	24	(6)	16	(4)
Offensive weapon	50	(7)	29	(4)	7	(1)	14	(2)
Other	63	(12)	5	(1)	32	(6)	-	-
All	**50**	**(133)**	**17**	**(45)**	**23**	**(61)**	**11**	**(28)**

Notes:
1.   N=267.
2.   Total percentages do not always sum to 100 due to rounding.

12   It is not known how often the items found in the course of a search differed from those initially sought. In common with the official Home Office statistics (see Wilkins and Addicott, 1997), the present research recorded the original reason for the stop/search

The likelihood of the suspect being charged or cautioned following a stop/search arrest was lower for black (63% than for white suspects (71%). Correspondingly, black suspects were more often NFAed: in 29 per cent of cases compared with 17 per cent for whites. The higher NFA rate for black people may be related to the kinds of offence for which they were arrested. In particular, compared to their overall presence in the arrest population, more black people than expected were arrested for robbery. For several reasons the NFA rate for robbery is considerably above average (see Table 6.2). Linking the offender to the offence may present difficulties, unless the victim makes a positive identification or the suspect provides an admission. However, black suspects are less likely than others to provide admissions and more likely to exercise their right of silence (see Chapter 5). The police may also be extra careful in serious offences like robbery to ensure that the evidence is 'cast-iron' and this may result in an above average level of rejection of cases for prosecution.

Right of silence and admissions

Moston, Stephenson and Williamson (1990) have suggested that whether suspects are charged is not strongly related to whether they have exercised their right of silence. More important is the availability of other evidence. Leng (1993) also examined the link between silence and case outcome. He found that in a sample of more than 250 NFA cases few suspects had exercised their right of silence and that, where they had, this generally had little bearing on the decision not to press charges.

The present study was also able to examine the relationship between suspects' use of silence and case outcome. An important preliminary point is that, of those who exercise their right of silence, more answer questions selectively than refuse to answer any questions at all (see Chapter 5) and that many of the former go on to provide admissions. Indeed, 43 per cent of those selectively refusing questions admitted culpability. Conversely, many suspects who answer all questions do *not* admit to any criminal involvement. The admission rate among those who co-operated with police questions was 59 per cent.

Any analysis of the relationship between case outcome and right of silence must therefore take admissions into account. One possible approach is to compare the outcome of all cases in which suspects provided admissions (whether or not in conjunction with selective refusal to answer) with the outcome of all cases in which there was no admission of guilt (whether due to silence in interview or the provision of an exculpatory explanation by a co-operative suspect). Figure 6.6 shows a clear difference in case outcome for these two groups. Nearly 90 per cent of those who provided admissions were charged or cautioned and seven per cent NFAed. But only 56 per cent of those who made no admissions were charged or cautioned, while 35 per cent were NFAed. Another difference between the two groups was that where there was an admission and some form of action was taken against the suspect, in one-third of cases it was in the form of a caution. In contrast, only two per cent of suspects who did not admit the offence (as far as is known) were cautioned[13].

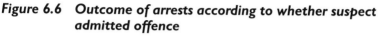

Figure 6.6   Outcome of arrests according to whether suspect admitted offence

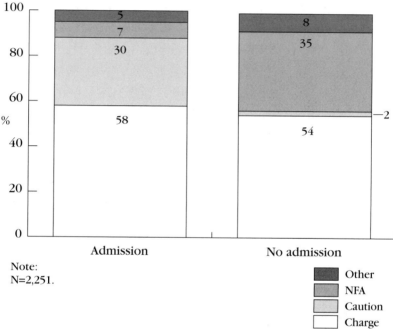

Note:
N=2,251.

A shortcoming of the above approach is that it treats those not providing admissions as an homogoneous group. However, it is reasonable to suggest that they consist of at least three factions: innocent suspects who, more often than not, seek to show this by answering questions; guilty suspects who seek to provide exculpatory accounts during interview; and guilty suspects who remain silent in the face of police questioning. If this is the case, it might be expected that the first two groups would be more likely to escape charges than the latter because they have taken the opportunity (sometimes successfully) to convince the police of their innocence. Those who refuse to answer questions have denied themselves of this chance. Figure 6.7 shows that there were indeed such differences. Only 43 per cent of those who answered all questions but admitted no criminal involvement

13   The National Standards for Cautioning (Revised), which accompany the most recent Home Office cautioning circular, stipulate that the offender must admit the offence before a caution may be issued (Home Office, 1994a). However, previous research has noted that in a small proportion of cases it is doubtful whether offenders do provide unequivocal admissions (Evans, 1993). This may explain why there were some caution cases in the present research in which there was no record of any admission. In all, 15 per cent of those cautioned had not apparently made any admission of guilt.

were charged or cautioned, while 48 per cent were NFAed. But, of those who refused to answer questions about their alleged involvement, 70 per cent were charged or cautioned and only 21 per cent were NFAed.

Figure 6.7 Outcome of arrests according to exercise of right of silence and admission

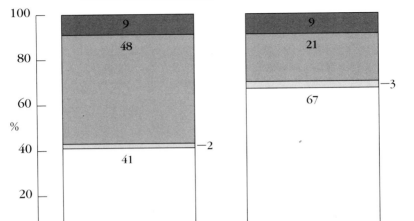

Note:
N=1,045.

However, a further important factor must be taken into account – the strength of the evidence against the suspect. It might be expected that, where the evidence is not strong, cases would be NFAed where suspects provide no admissions, regardless of whether they have answered or refused to answer questions. Equally, it might be expected that they would be charged where the evidence is strong, even without an admission. In the present study strength of evidence was gauged according to whether or not it was sufficient to charge on arrest (see above). Table 6.5 shows that, both where the evidence was strong *and* where it was less than adequate to charge, the chances of the suspect being charged (or cautioned) differed considerably according to whether he or she had answered police questions (but made no admissions) or had remained silent. Thus, 93 per cent of those who refused to answer questions were charged where the evidence was strong as against 67 per cent of those who answered during interview. Conversely, where the evidence was insufficient to charge on arrest, 49 per cent of those who remained silent were nonetheless charged, compared with just 27 per cent of those who answered police questions. Multivariate analysis confirmed that, taking account of other relevant factors, whether suspects exercised their right of silence was a highly significant predictor of whether they would be charged or NFAed (see Appendix B, Table B.3).

Table 6.5   Case outcome according to exercise of silence and strength of evidence

	Charge/caution		NFA		Other	
	%	(n)	%	(n)	%	(n)
Evidence sufficient to charge on arrest						
Questions about suspect's involvement refused	93	(114)	3	(4)	3	(4)
All questions answered	67	(159)	25	(60)	8	(18)
Evidence insufficient to charge on arrest						
Questions about suspect's involvement refused	49	(39)	33	(26)	19	(15)
All questions answered	27	(103)	62	(237)	11	(41)

Note: N = 820.

The most convincing explanation for these findings probably rests with factors which the research was unable to measure and, particularly, with what occurred during interviews. It is likely that those who answered police questions were often able to demonstrate their innocence, despite the evidence against them, or, at the least, provide a plausible story to explain the incriminating circumstances. Clearly, this task was easier where the evidence was not strong, thereby accounting for the particularly low charge rate among those who co-operated with questions in cases where the evidence at the time of arrest was insufficient to charge. In contrast, those who refused to answer questions in cases without strong evidence deprived themselves of the opportunity to offer any explanation. Their silence may have added to police suspicions and increased the chances of charges being pressed.

Looking at the sample as a whole, those who admitted guilt were far more likely to be charged or cautioned than those who made no admissions. In all,

87 per cent of the former were charged or cautioned and seven per cent NFAed, compared with 55 per cent and 36 per cent respectively of the latter. Multivariate analysis showed that whether suspects provided an admission was the single most important predictor of whether or not they would be NFAed (see Appendix B, Table B.3). In a high proportion (77%) of cases in which NFA was taken against those not admitting guilt, the evidence on arrest was insufficient to charge. The data point to the continued importance of admissions as a means of solving crime (Mawby, 1979; Morris, 1980; McConville and Baldwin, 1981; McConville, Sanders and Leng, 1991; Evans, 1993; Mortimer, 1994), despite moves in recent years to shift the emphasis of interviews away from interrogation to secure confessions towards a more neutral search for the truth (Brown, 1997).

Legal advice

Although the difference was not great, suspects who obtained legal advice were more likely to be charged or given a police caution than those not legally advised. Multivariate analysis showed that, after controlling for other factors, receipt of legal advice was a significant predictor of whether suspects would be charged/formally cautioned or NFAed (see Appendix B, Table B.3). Thus, of those legally advised, 63 per cent were charged and 17 per cent NFAed, compared with 59 per cent and 22 per cent respectively of those not advised. The most likely explanation for this difference is that those who are guilty are more likely to seek legal advice rather than that legal advice itself contributes to the probability of being charged.

Charge or caution?

Decision-making by custody officers

Assuming that there is sufficient evidence of the suspect's guilt to secure a realistic prospect of conviction, the question of whether the suspect is charged rather than cautioned depends on a range of public interest factors (although, if a caution is to be issued, the suspect must admit the offence[14] and consent to be cautioned). The charge/caution decision was made by custody officers in the great majority of cases – around 80 per cent[15] – often in consultation with inspectors or other officers. A key element of the research was to explore the factors which influenced custody officers' decisions. In each case in which a suspect was charged or cautioned custody

---

14   However, the present study found that there was no evidence of an admission in 15 per cent of cases in which cautions were issued (see above). Evans (1993) also found that a minority of juveniles who were cautioned had not apparently admitted their guilt.

15   In 17 per cent of cases a decision was deferred while the suspect was bailed for further enquiries (although, if the suspect was required to return to the station the decision whether to charge reverted to the custody officer), in three per cent juveniles were referred to juvenile justice teams for a decision, and in two per cent suspects were

officers were asked to indicate from a pre-prepared list which public interest factors were important in the particular case before them. These included items such as: seriousness of offence; recent previous convictions or cautions; likely court penalty; age of suspect; and continuing threat to the victim[16]. In this exercise custody officers were not asked to weigh evidential strength, since the only cases being considered were ones in which the evidence was already sufficient to justify proceedings.

Table 6.6 lists the reasons that custody officers gave for charging. Overall, the most frequently cited ones were: seriousness of offence (37%); need for a court sentence (36%); the offender's status as an adult (36%); recent or serious previous convictions (35%)[17]; and the degree of the offender's involvement (30%). The table also provides separate information for violent and property offences. In cases of violence, the seriousness of the offence and the views of the victim weighed most heavily (in 73% and 47% of cases respectively). The importance of the victim in such cases is further underlined by the fact that the continuing threat posed by the offender and the degree of harm or loss suffered were both significant considerations in more than a quarter of cases. Custody officers mentioned the need for a court sentence to deal with the suspect and the fact that the suspect was heavily implicated in the offence (i.e. they were the ringleader or prime instigator rather than being on the periphery) in one-third of cases.

For those charged with property offences, custody officers most frequently cited recent or serious previous convictions as influencing their decision to charge. Recent previous cautions were also mentioned in just under one-fifth of cases. The apparent determination by custody officers to deal strictly with repeat offending by property offenders is reflected in the latest Cautioning Circular (Home Office, 1994a), which emphasises that, unless there has been a considerable time-lag since the previous caution, second cautions should rarely be given. Custody officers also considered as important (each in about one-third of cases): seriousness of the offence; the offender being heavily implicated; the victim's wish to press charges; and the need for a court sentence. In 12 per cent of cases, the lack of an offer of reparation by the suspect was influential. Those arrested for property offences were also less likely than other suspects to have admitted their guilt. This meant that the custody officers did not have the option of a caution and effectively had to decide between charge and NFA.

---

16   The list was largely derived from the Code for Crown Prosecutors (CPS, 1994a) and the cautioning circular then in force, number 59/1990 (Home Office, 1990a). In addition to these factors, custody officers were asked to recall any other influences on their decision.

17   A logistic regression analysis, carried out to identify the strongest predictors of whether a suspect would be charged or cautioned, identified previous convictions as the most significant factor. Thus, the odds of suspects being charged rather than cautioned increased sevenfold where they had a criminal record (see Appendix B, Table B.4). However, the regression model is of limited value in the present context because it was not possible to measure systematically and build into it the range of qualitative considerations which custody officers take into account in deciding on the most appropriate disposal.

Table 6.6 Custody officers' reasons for charging suspects by offence type

Reason	Violence (n=236) %	Property (n=735) %	All offences (n=1,764) %
Seriousness of offence	73	36	37
Appreciable court penalty likely	19	18	16
Significant harm/loss to victim	26	15	12
Victim wishes to press charges	47	34	24
Offender heavily implicated	31	35	30
Continuing threat to victim	29	-	-
Offender shows no remorse	23	27	27
Lack of reparation	-	12	-
Recent/serious previous convictions	20	47	35
Recent previous cautions	-	17	13
No admission	28	30	22
Court sentence necessary	35	35	36
Offender is an adult	33	38	36
Offence not in cautioning guidelines	-	-	15

Notes:
1. No information was available in 101 cases in which suspects were charged.
2. Table includes reasons which were cited in 10 per cent or more of cases.
3. Offences against the person include violence against the person, sexual offences and robbery.
Property offences include burglary, theft and handling, and criminal damage.

Table 6.7 Custody officers' reasons for cautioning suspects by offence type

Reason	Violence % (n=27)	Property % (n=215)	All offences % (n=583
Triviality of the offence	11	36	34
Token court penalty likely	19	31	30
Little or no harm/loss to victim	30	34	26
Victim consents to caution	37	46	29
No offender threat to victim	22	21	14
Offender shows remorse	56	45	33
No recent previous convictions	67	67	55
No recent previous cautions	59	65	56
Offender admits the offence	85	83	72
Offender/parents consent to caution	15	25	25
Offender is a juvenile	33	25	19
Community support arrangements	11	-	2
Force policy	-	-	23

Notes:
1. N=583. Data were missing in 28 cases.
2. Table includes reasons which were cited in 10 per cent or more of cases.
3. Offences against the person include violence against the person, sexual offences and robbery. Property offences include burglary, theft and handling, and criminal damage.

Turning to those cautioned, Table 6.7 shows that (other than an admission of guilt) the most frequently mentioned reasons were: absence of recent previous cautions (56%) or convictions (55%); the triviality of the offence (34%); demonstration of remorse by the suspect (33%); and the likelihood of a token court penalty (30%)[18]. Relatively few suspects were cautioned for violent offences but, where they were, the factors weighing most heavily were the absence of previous convictions or cautions, a display of remorse by the suspect and the victim's agreement. In property offences, the lack of previous convictions or cautions also carried weight, as did the triviality of the offence, the likelihood of a token court sentence, and minimal loss to the victim.

It is apparent that the suspect's previous record played a significant role in custody officers' decision-making. Confirmation of this is provided by a comparison of case outcomes for those who did and did not have previous convictions. While 63 per cent of the former were charged and only nine per cent cautioned, the figures for those without previous convictions were 37 per cent and 29 per cent respectively.

---

18 As with charge, a logistic regression analysis was carried out to identify the strongest predictors of a suspect being cautioned. This showed that the fact that the suspect was a juvenile and had admitted the offence were the most significant factors (see Appendix B, Table B.5). However, for the reasons explained in footnote 14 (above), the regression analysis was unable to take account of many of the factors which are important to custody officers' decision-making.

The decision-making role of inter-agency juvenile panels

The decision whether to charge or caution does not always remain with the custody officer in cases involving juveniles. Custody officers first assess whether the case is one in which they are competent to make a decision. Typically, they will take responsibility where the offence is either so serious that charge is the only realistic choice, the offence is very minor or the suspect has no previous record. In other cases, they will refer the case to specialist juvenile justice teams[19], sometimes working alongside social services staff. A further filtering process then occurs as these officers consider whether to pass the case to their local inter-agency panel or bureau[20] for a recommendation about an appropriate disposal. This recommendation is not binding on the police, who, as Evans and Ferguson (1991) have noted, have the last say in the decision-making process. In the same research, the authors found that the proportion of cases referred for inter-agency consultation varied considerably between the areas of the West Midlands which they studied. Referral was routine in some places, but in others only took place in problematic cases, such as those where the juvenile already had previous cautions or convictions for like offences.

In the present study, custody officers referred 20 per cent (n=125) of all juvenile suspects to juvenile justice teams. The most significant factor predicting referral was the presence of an admission (see Appendix B, Table B.6). Without an admission there is (or should be) no scope to caution the suspect and custody officers may have felt that there was no point in passing on cases where decision-makers' discretion was fettered. However, in a fifth of cases referred there had been no admission. These cases may have been referred where custody officers felt that there were public interest factors to be considered in deciding whether the suspect should be NFAed rather than charged.

Black juveniles were significantly less likely than whites or Asians to be referred to juvenile justice teams. This confirms the findings of earlier research by Landau (1981) and Landau and Nathan (1983). While black suspects were less likely than others to provide admissions (see Chapter 5) this did not account for the low referral rate. Only five per cent of black juveniles who admitted their offences were referred, compared with nearly a quarter of whites.

A third predictor of referral was the station at which the suspect had been detained. Referral rates differed significantly between areas. Type and seriousness of offence and possession of previous convictions or cautions were not significant factors.

---

19   Officers are known as juvenile liaison officers in some forces.

20   These typically include members of the social services, education welfare service and the CPS. Some inter-agency panels form part of a wider diversionary scheme – 'caution-plus' – and panel participants may choose to refer juveniles to such schemes. These usually offer juveniles practical support and advice to encourage them to desist from offending.

Juvenile justice officers took unaided decisions about whether to charge juveniles in 46 per cent of the cases referred to them. But, in the remainder (67 cases) they referred the case for inter-agency consultation. Typically, these cases were moderately serious theft offences. The offenders were predominantly male (79%); 82 per cent were white, 10 per cent Asian and two per cent black.

The police did not usually recommend a specific course of action to the panel. However, in six cases they proposed cautioning and in six charging. In nine cases the panel accepted the reommendation. The police in turn generally accepted the recomendations made by panels. In only four out of the 67 cases did the police take a course of action other than that recommended. The bulk of recommendations (61%) were for a caution[21], 36 per cent were to charge and three per cent to take no further action. These findings confirm those reported by Evans and Ferguson (1991).

Key points

- Fifty-two per cent of suspects were charged, 20 per cent NFAed and 17 per cent cautioned. The remainder were released for various reasons or transferred elsewhere.

- Decisions were delayed in 17 per cent of cases while suspects were bailed for further enquiries and in four per cent for juvenile justice teams to consider what action was best. Forty-four per cent of those bailed for enquiries were later NFAed.

- Black and Asian suspects were much more likely to be bailed for enquiries than whites.

- Suspects were significantly more likely to be NFAed where they had not admitted guilt, where the evidence on arrest was insufficient to charge or where they had exercised their right of silence during interview. Suspects were also significantly more likely to be NFAed at specific stations and for particular categories of offence.

- Black and Asian suspects were more likely to be NFAed than white suspects, but this appeared to be related more to differences in the kinds of offences they committed and in admission rates than to ethnic origin.

---

21   Five recommendations were for cautions with intervention ('caution plus').

- Females were less likely than males to be NFAed; so too were suspects who had obtained legal advice compared with those who had not.

- Whether suspects were charged rather than cautioned varied with the seriousness of the offence, with charges being more likely in serious cases and cautions in less serious ones. Stations varied considerably in their use of cautioning.

- Charge rather than caution was also more likely where suspects were male, black or Asian, adult, had been arrested for a domestic violence offence, had previous convictions or had exercised their right of silence.

- Analysis of custody officers' decision-making showed that, in deciding to charge rather than caution, they were most influenced by the seriousness of the offence, the perceived need for a court sentence, the fact that the offender was an adult, the presence of recent and/or serious previous convictions and the degree of the offender's involvement in the offence.

- Where custody officers opted to caution the offender, they were most swayed by the absence of previous cautions or convictions, the triviality of the offence, a demonstration of remorse by the offender and the likelihood of a token court penalty.

- Custody officers referred 20 per cent of cases involving juveniles to juvenile justice teams, who in turn referred around half of these cases to inter-agency panels. Panels most often recommended a caution and the police generally complied.

- Black juveniles were significantly less likely than their white or Asian counterparts to have their cases referred for inter-agency consultation.

7 Leaving custody

This chapter gives details of the length of time that suspects were held in custody prior to charge or release and of the time spent by arresting officers on cases up to this point. It also provides information about the proportion of those charged who were already on bail at the time of charge and examines custody officers' decisions whether to grant bail after charge for the current offence.

Length of detention

A key aim of PACE was to keep detention without charge to a necessary minimum. Custody officers are required to charge a suspect where there is sufficient evidence to do so; if there is not such evidence, they may only authorise detention where it is necessary to secure or preserve evidence of an offence for which the suspect is under arrest, or to obtain evidence by questioning[1]. Except in limited circumstances in certain serious cases, an arrested person should not be held for more than 24 hours without being charged. Prior to this, an officer of at least inspector rank, who is not directly involved in the investigation, must review whether detention continues to be necessary. The first review takes place not more than six hours after detention was first authorised and the second not more than nine hours after the first[2]. Previous research suggests that the time which suspects spend in custody varies according to a range of factors, including the offence, the outcome of the case, and whether the police are required to secure the attendance of a lawyer or an appropriate adult (Irving and McKenzie, 1989; Brown, 1989).

In the present research, the average time that suspects were held without charge was six hours and 40 minutes. Confirming the findings of previous studies, the average time in custody before charge or release was much longer where the offence was very serious (e.g. murder or rape) and was just short of 22 hours. For moderately serious offences the figure was just over seven hours, while for less serious offences the average was just under four hours.

---

1   See PACE, s.37.

2   See PACE, ss.40 and 41

Figure 7.1 provides information about the time spent in custody according to case outcome. Suspects who were given an instant caution or NFAed were held for the shortest periods of time. Those charged and bailed were also dealt with relatively quickly. The longest periods in custody were spent by suspects who were charged and detained, reflecting the fact that the offences involved were often serious or complex and required lengthier interviewing and investigation.

Figure 7.1   Length of detention by outcome of custody

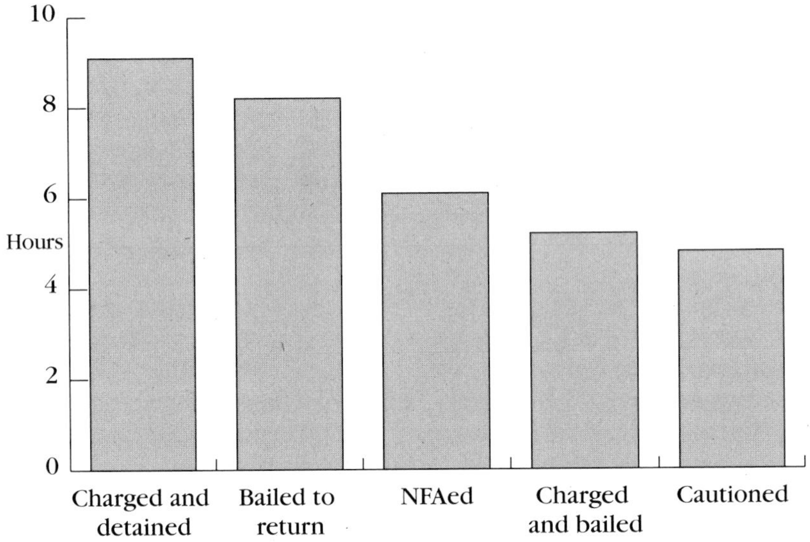

Note:
N=3,405 (suspects only). Data were missing in six cases.

The time which juveniles spent in custody varied considerably, depending on whether they arrived at the station with an appropriate adult or whether one had to be summoned. The former were held for an average of five hours, but the latter spent, on average, more than seven hours in custody. Mentally disordered suspects, for whom custody officers usually had to obtain a doctor and an appropriate adult, averaged just over five and a half hours in police custody.

In line with previous research, those who obtained legal advice spent longer in custody than those not legally advised: just over nine hours compared with five and a half hours. The longer time which legally advised suspects spent in custody was partly a function of the extra time spent waiting for advice to be provided; but it was also related to the generally higher level of seriousness of their offences.

One important factor in determining the time that suspects were held was the sufficiency of the evidence on arrest. Where arresting officers reported that it was sufficient evidence to charge at that point, the average length of detention was five and a quarter hours. This can be compared with a figure of more than eight and a half hours where there was insufficient evidence to charge the suspect at this point and the police needed more time to gather evidence. Again, these figures cannot be divorced from the seriousness of the case. It was more likely that sufficient evidence to charge would be available on arrest in certain less serious offences (for example, shoplifting), where offenders were often caught in the act, than in more serious ones requiring more complex proof of the act and intent.

Time spent by officers on the case

Data were collected on the amount of time which officers spent per case from the time that the suspect arrived at the police station up to the point when they were charged or released. This information is useful as a way of assessing the efficiency of investigations in different types of case. The time for which officers were asked to account includes that spent interviewing, conducting further enquiries and taking statements, completing necessary paperwork and awaiting the arrival of solicitors or appropriate adults where no other work could usefully be done on other cases during this time. Table 7.1 presents this information according to the outcome of the case. The time taken represents the collective time of all officers investigating each case. Cases in which suspects were cautioned were dealt with the quickest: around a quarter took less than one hour of an officer's time and two-thirds were dealt with inside three hours. The relatively quick turn-round reflects the fact these were usually less serious cases which did not involve complex investigation. Suspects had also admitted the offence, thereby avoiding the need to prove the essential elements of the offence by other means. Cautioned cases also involved far less paperwork than was required for charged cases, in which files had to be submitted to the CPS.

In contrast, charged cases and ones in which suspects were bailed for enquiries were much more time-consuming. Nearly 60 per cent took three hours or more of police time and a significant minority took far longer. Thus, nine per cent of charged cases and eight per cent of bail to return cases required over 20 hours of work collectively from investigating officers. The time taken to deal with NFA cases occupied an intermediate amount of time between cautioned and charged cases.

Some kinds of offence were particularly demanding of police resources. Those occupying most police time were violence against the person, sexual offences, burglary, robbery & fraud and forgery (see Appendix A, Table A.5). Public order, prostitution and motoring offences were dealt with the most speedily.

Table 7.1   Police time spent on cases by outcome

Outcome	Up to 1 hr	Over 1 hr up to 3hrs	Over 3hrs up to 7 hrs	Over 7 hrs
	%	%	%	%
Charge	14	27	29	29
Caution	28	42	21	8
Bail to return	10	34	33	24
NFA	25	29	26	20
Other	21	30	20	29
Total %	**17**	**31**	**28**	**24**
n	**544**	**992**	**895**	**768**

Notes:
1.   Some totals do not sum to 100 due to rounding.
2.   'Other' outcome includes transfers to prison, court and immigration authorities.

Offending on bail

In recent years there has been increasing concern about 'offending on bail' and several studies have been carried out to quantify its extent. However, Morgan (1992) notes that the definition of what amounts to 'offending on bail' has differed between studies and that the figures obtained vary accordingly. She identifies two basic measures:

- the proportion of persons given bail who commit offences while on bail;

- the proportion of persons charged who are on bail when charged.

Neither indicator is able to capture the true level of offending on bail, since a large proportion of offending does not result in the detection of an offender. The figures which the two indicators provide are therefore proxies for offending on bail. Bearing in mind this limitation, these indicators provide a rough guide to that proportion of offending which results in the detection of an offender and allow trends over time to be charted when comparisons are made with other studies using the same methods. The present study used the latter indicator because data about the bail status of those charged were readily available from arresting and custody officers[3].

3   In contrast, obtaining information on the first measure is a more time consuming operation, which involves tracking those given bail, using criminal record data, to see whether they are convicted of any offences committed during their bail period.

4   This is one reason why Morgan (1992) has advocated use of the first indicator. She points out that: this indicator counts the number of persons who offend rather than the number of times a person was charged; it relates to findings of guilt rather than to charges (some of which might later be dropped by the CPS or result in an acquittal); and it only counts offences actually committed on bail.

One shortcoming of this particular measure is that the offence with which the suspect was charged may not have been committed recently; so, although the suspect might be on bail when *charged*, he or she might not have been on bail when the offence was actually *committed*[4].

Previous studies have primarily been concerned with bail to appear at court, whether granted by the police after charge or by the court itself. However, the police also have the power to bail suspects before charge for further enquiries. The present study collected information about bail both before and after charge. Table 7.2 shows that 25 per cent of suspects who were charged were on bail to appear at court at the time of charge. This is slightly lower than the figures obtained by two other studies, reported by Morgan (1992), which have used a similar measure[5]. The first, carried out by Avon and Somerset police, used data from 1990/1991 cases and only counted charges for *notifiable* offences. The proportion of those charged who were on bail to appear at court when charged was 28 per cent. The other study, by Greater Manchester Police, was conducted in 1988 and produced a figure of 29 per cent. The Manchester study included notifiable and other offences, such as prostitution, as did the present research. The figure for the present study is, of course, the average for a range of stations in different forces and, given the wide variation between areas in rates of offending on bail to appear at court (as shown in Table 7.2), it would be unsafe to draw conclusions about trends in offending on bail from a comparison with figures from individual forces.

5   Morgan also draws attention to research conducted in Northumbria police force. This was based on a sample of persons *arrested* (but not necessarily charged) in 1989 (n=5,990). Of these, 23 per cent were on bail to appear at court or bail to return to the police station when arrested. In the present study, 24 per cent of those arrested were on bail to appear at court or the police station

Table 7.2 Proportion of suspects who were on bail at the time of charge

Station	Bail to appear at court		Police bail for enquiries		On any bail	
	%	(n)	%	(n)	%	(n)
Stretford	22	(36)	6	(10)	28	(46)
Rochdale	24	(52)	8	(18)	31	(68)
Luton	16	(37)	6	(15)	22	(51)
Queen's Road	29	(38)	9	(11)	36	(47)
Beaumont Leys	20	(31)	8	(12)	25	(38)
Birmingham Rd	42	(68)	6	(10)	46	(75)
Gateshead	29	(54)	3	(6)	31	(58)
Hackney	20	(29)	14	(20)	27	(39)
All	**25**	**(345)**	**8**	**(102)**	**30**	**(422)**

Notes:
1. N=1,399. Data were missing in 64 cases.
2. Some suspects were on both bail to appear at court and police bail for enquiries. The total in column 3 is not therefore the sum of the figures in columns 1 and 2.
3. Data on offending on bail were missing in more than 15 per cent of cases at Fairwater (16%) and Croydon (32%t) and these stations have been excluded from the table.

The station with the highest proportion of suspects who were on bail to appear at court when charged was Birmingham Road (42%). A high number of suspects here had been charged with prostitution. Many had a history of similar offending and were likely to be on bail for previous prostitution offences at any given time.

The proportion of suspects who were on police bail for enquiries at the time of charge was eight per cent. The figures for individual stations ranged from three per cent at Gateshead to 14 per cent at Hackney.

Whether suspects were on bail to appear at court when charged varied considerably according to the type of offence with which they were charged. The proportion ranged from just 11 per cent for those charged with drugs offences to 23 per cent for those charged with fraud and/or robbery, 27 per cent for theft and handling and 37 per cent for burglary. At the extreme (for reasons noted above) 82 per cent of those charged with prostitution offences were already on bail to appear at court when charged.

The likelihood of the suspect being on bail to appear at court when charged also varied according to age and sex (but not ethnic group). Suspects aged between 17 and 29 years were most likely to be on bail. They were more likely than members of other age groups to be arrested for property offences and the proportion of suspects who are on bail when charged with such offences is relatively high, irrespective of age. Females were more likely than males to be on bail when charged. This is explained by the high number of prostitutes on bail at Birmingham Road police station.

Since the present research was conducted a number of measures have been implemented in an attempt to curb offending by those on bail. The CJPOA 1994 contains six separate provisions which address the problem in different ways[6]. The 1990s have also seen the growth of schemes designed to improve the information available to bail decision-makers and to provide supervision and support for those on bail (Cavadino and Gibson, 1993; Morgan and Henderson, 1998). There is some evidence that these measures have helped keep offending on bail by older age groups in check, although there is some evidence of a rise in such offending by juveniles (Brown, 1998; Morgan and Henderson, 1998)[7].

Police bail after charge

The study collected information about the frequency with which suspects were given bail after charge and, where it was refused, the reasons. Since the research was completed the CJPOA 1994 has made important changes to police powers in this area (see footnote 6 above). The data presented here provide a useful baseline against which to assess the impact of these changes.

Of those charged, 28 per cent (n=444) were refused bail and kept in police custody until the next available court sitting. Brown (1989) has noted that there is considerable variation between stations in the extent to which bail is denied. The present study confirms this picture. Figure 7.2 shows that the proportion refused bail ranged from 15 per cent at Birmingham Road and Croydon (where the high proportions of prostitutes and shoplifters respectively help account for the low rate of custodial remands) up to 52 per cent at Stretford. Brown (ibid) has suggested that one factor affecting bail rates is the proportion of those charged who are juveniles. He notes that they are generally given bail and, therefore, the lower the number of juveniles the higher will be the rate at which bail is refused. The study provided little support for this suggestion. While, on average, 21 per cent of juveniles were refused bail (the figure for adults was 29%), there was considerable variation in bail practice between stations. Custody rates after

---

6   In particular, under s.28 of the Act the grounds on which bail after charge may be refused have been revised to allow the police to refuse bail to a person charged with an imprisonable offence where the custody officer has reasonable grounds for believing that this is necessary to prevent that person committing a further offence. Also, under s.27 the police now have the power to attach conditions to bail after a person has been charged.

7   Because of the shortcoming, noted above, that measures of offending on bail are unable to capture the true extent of offending, the possibility exists that apparent changes in levels of offending on bail may not necessarily reflect real changes in the amount of offending but changes in the amount of offending which comes to light. In view of the increased attention now being given to the supervision of those on bail and the monitoring of bail conditions, this is a real possibility.

charge ranged from six per cent (Rochdale) to 55 per cent (Hackney). However, the proportion of juveniles among those charged was low and never more than 10 per cent. The variations in the rate at which juveniles were refused bail therefore had little impact on the overall figures for refusal of bail.

Figure 7.2 Refused of bail by station

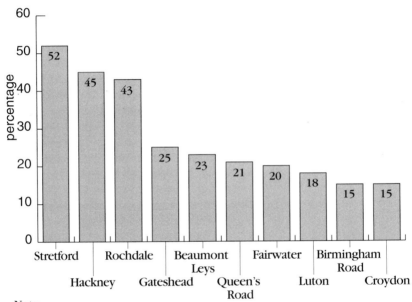

Note:
Table does not include those who were bailed for police enquiries and subsequently charged.

The rate at which bail was refused varied according to the seriousness of the offence. Over 60 per cent of those charged with very serious offences were refused bail, compared with 26 per cent of those charged with all other offences. Above average proportions of suspects were detained for robbery and violence against the person (both 40%) and burglary (38%).

Refusal of bail was related to the suspect's ethnic origin but not to sex. Whereas 26 per cent of white suspects were refused bail, the figures for black and Asian suspects were 35 per cent and 34 per cent respectively. Several factors associated with bail decisions were explored to see whether they accounted for these differences[8]. The discrepancy between bail rates for white and ethnic minority suspects persisted, largely irrespective of the offence with which the suspect had been charged and whether or not the suspect had previous convictions. The difference was less where the suspect was already on bail for another offence or where the suspect was a juvenile.

---

8 Numbers of ethnic minority suspects among those charged were too small to permit a full multivariate analysis.

But, conversely, where the suspect was not already on bail or where he or she was an adult, the difference between bail rates for ethnic minority and white suspects was even greater. Once again, these findings raise the issue of whether they provide evidence of discriminatory action against ethnic minorities. It would be unsafe to place this construction upon them. One difficulty is that bail decision-making is a complex process (Morgan and Henderson, 1998) and it was not possible to examine all the relevant risk factors which custody officers might take into account. Nor was it possible to examine whether, within particular categories of offence, those committed by ethnic minority suspects differed from ones committed by white suspects in terms of seriousness. But they do suggest that this is an area of police decision-making which supervisors might wish to examine in more detail.

Those who were of no fixed abode or whose name and address could not be verified were usually refused bail.

Table 7.3 shows the reasons custody officers gave for refusing bail. For offences generally, they most often cited the risk of the suspect failing to appear at court (in 32 % of cases). In offences against the person custody officers were more likely to quote the risk of the suspect causing physical injury to another (in 49% of cases). In property offences, a common reason for refusing bail was the risk that the suspect might cause further loss or damage to property while on bail (in 29% of cases). As Burrows, Henderson and Morgan (1994) have noted, custody officers appear often to have treated the risk of the suspect causing physical injury to another or causing loss or damage to property as tantamount to the risk that the suspect would reoffend if released on bail. Under section 28 of the Criminal Justice and Public Order Act 1994 the latter can now explicitly be given by custody officers as a reason for refusing bail in imprisonable offences.

Table 7.3 Reasons for refusing bail by type of offence

Reason	Offences against the person %	Property offences %	All offences %
Risk of failure to appear at court	19	35	32
Risk of physical injury to another	49	11	24
Risk of loss/damage to property	4	29	14
Risk of interference with the administration of justice/investigation of the offence	17	10	12
Name or address could not be ascertained	5	10	12
For detained person's protection	6	4	4
Detention of juvenile in their own interests	–	2	1

Notes:
1. N=314. Data were missing in 104 cases.
2. Offences against the person include violence against the person, sexual offences and robbery. Property offences include burglary, theft and handling, and criminal damage.
3. Where custody officers listed more than one reason for refusal of bail, they were asked to state which was the most important. The Table lists the most important reasons only.
4. Percentages do not always sum to 100 due to rounding.

Key points

- On average, suspects were held for six hours and 40 minutes prior to charge or release.

- Cases in which suspects were charged were more consuming of officers' time than those where the outcome was a caution. Less than a third of caution cases took up more than three hours of police time, compared with 60 per cent of charged cases.

- Twenty-five per cent of those charged were on bail to appear at court when charged and eight per cent were on bail for police enquiries. The proportion on bail to appear at court was much higher at certain stations. It also varied according to the offence with which suspects were charged and their age and sex.

- Overall, 28 per cent of those charged were refused bail but there was considerable variation in bail practice between stations.

- Suspects from ethnic minorities were more likely than white suspects to be refused bail, irrespective of offence charged and whether they had previous convictions. The difference was particularly great among adult suspects and those not already on bail at the time of charge.

- The risk of the suspect failing to appear at court was most often given as a reason for refusing bail. Those arrested for offences against the person were most often refused bail on account of fears of them causing further physical injury.

Part 2: The CPS follow-up study

The second phase of the study looked at the outcome of cases in which suspects had been charged by the police. The aim was to complete the picture of the criminal justice filtering process which determines whether suspects become defendants and whether defendants are convicted. In a significant minority of cases, charges do not result in convictions. The Crown Prosecution Service (CPS)[1] terminates some cases either becausPe the evidence is deemed insufficient or because there are public interest reasons for not proceeding. In some cases it is impossible to proceed because, for example, the defendant has died or cannot be traced. Other defendants are acquitted at trial. Then again, some cases result in conviction but not for the charges originally brought by the police. This occurs where the CPS increase or reduce the seriousness of the offences charged or prefer alternative charges.

This part of the report focuses particularly on the way in which the post-charge filtering process impacts upon sub-groups of suspects who were singled out for attention in the pre-charge phase of the project. These include: members of ethnic minorities; alleged perpetrators of domestic violence offences; suspects arrested following a stop and search; and those who exercised their right of silence during police interviews.

Chapter 8 presents information about the sample of cases put forward for prosecution, including details of the evidence on which CPS lawyers' initial review of cases was based. Chapter 9 documents the reasons why cases were terminated. Chapters 10 and 11 give details of the outcome of cases proceeding to the magistrates' courts and the Crown Court, while Chapter 12 presents an overall perspective on the attrition process between arrest and conviction, including consideration of the issue of charge reduction.

---

1   The Crown Prosecution Service was created by the Prosecution of Offences Act 1985 and became operational in 1986.

8 The CPS sample

Response rate

In part one of the study, 52 per cent of suspects (n=1,913) were charged with one or more offences by the police. To obtain information about the decision-making of the CPS in these cases arrangements were made for a questionnaire to accompany the file sent by the police to the CPS. Lawyers were asked to complete relevant sections of the questionnaire about their decision-making at key stages of the prosecution process. In the event, completed questionnaires were returned in 61 per cent of charged cases, resulting in a sample of 1,175 defendants for part two of the research.

The level of non-response means that it is relevant to consider whether there was any systematic form of bias. It was found that the response rate was far higher at some CPS branches than others and that, independently of this, it was more likely that forms would be returned for some categories of offence than others. At four branches the form completion rate was below average, although only at one was it significantly lower (just 17%). At the other six branches, completion rates ranged from 63 per cent to 93 per cent. The variations between branches were almost certainly related to differences in lawyers' workloads and in the efficiency of the local research liaison arrangements.

In terms of form completion rates according to offence, Figure 8.1 shows that above average proportions of those charged with theft and handling, criminal damage, public order, prostitution and motoring offences were successfully tracked through the CPS. But, below average numbers of those charged with sexual offences, burglary, robbery and drugs offences were successfully followed up. Generally, it was the case that the completion rate was lower for more serious offences. This is linked with the difficulties of tracking cases which proceeded to Crown Court, often up to a year or more after the original charges were brought. It was more likely that the requirement to complete monitoring forms would be overlooked the longer the case took and the more different personnel became involved with it.

Figure 8.1 Proportion of suspects charged whose cases were tracked through to CPS

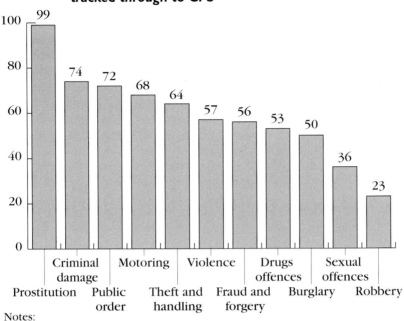

Notes:
1. N=1,705.
2. Figure does not include those charged with 'other' offences (n=208).

The offences

Table 8.1 give details of the offences comprising the CPS sample. By far the largest category (27%) were theft and handling offences, followed by motoring (15%) and public order offences (also 15%)[1]. The same table also compares the distribution of offences for those charged during the police station phase of the study. There is close conformity between the two samples. The small differences reflect the variations according to offence (described above) in the completion of monitoring forms by CPS lawyers. For example, compared with the police station sample, burglary and robbery offences are slightly under-represented in the CPS sample, while theft and handling, criminal damage, public order, prostitution and motoring offences are marginally over-represented. Offences which could be categorised as 'very serious' (see Appendix C for a list) comprised three per cent of cases in the CPS sample compared with 4.5 per cent of offences charged in the police station study.

---

[1] The proportion of motoring offences in the sample is, however, far lower than the proportion of such offences dealt with by the CPS since it only includes those in which the suspect had first been arrested. Most motoring offences - other than drink-driving offenders - are dealt with by way of a summons.

Table 8.1 Distribution of offences in part 1 (charged) and part 2 (CPS) samples

Offence	Phase 1 charged cases		Phase 2 CPS cases	
	%	(n)	%	(n)
Theft and handling	26	(498)	27	(317)
Motoring	14	(265)	15	(180)
Public order	13	(241)	15	(173)
Violence	10	(187)	9	(107)
Burglary	8	(147)	6	(74)
Criminal damage	6	(113)	8	(84)
Prostitution	3	(65)	5	(64)
Fraud and forgery	4	(71)	3	(40)
Drugs	3	(55)	2	(29)
Robbery	2	(31)	1	(7)
Sexual offences	1	(22)	1	(8)
Other	11	(208)	8	(92)
Total	100	(1,903)	100	(1,175)

Domestic violence cases

The proportion of cases in the CPS sample involving domestic violence related offences was, at six per cent, very close to the figure of seven per cent for those charged with such offences in part 1 of the study[2]. Half were cases of violence against the person (50%) but there were also some public order (26%), criminal damage (19%) and property offences such as burglary (5%).

Racially motivated offences

The most recent edition of the CPS Code for Crown Prosecutors (1994a) makes it clear that, if an offence is motivated by any form of discrimination against the victim's ethnic or national origin, this is a public interest factor in favour of prosecution. Earlier guidelines for the police, issued by the Association of Chief Police Officers' in 1985, state that an incident should be defined as racially motivated where the victim, investigating officer, or any person makes an allegation of racial motivation and this definition has

---

2   In part 1 arresting and investigating officers provided information on whether suspects had been arrested for domestic violence related offences. In the course of preparing cases for prosecution it is possible that interpretations of the circumstances of offences may change. Therefore, in part 2 the assessment of whether cases were domestic violence related is that of the CPS lawyers who dealt with them. This resulted in the exclusion of some cases in part 2 that were formerly categorised as domestic violence ones and the inclusion of others not previously so defined.

broadly been accepted by the CPS. A potentially wide range of cases is therefore included. CPS respondents were asked to say whether there was any evidence that the incident which led to charges was racially motivated or had a racial element to it. They reported that less than two per cent (20 cases out of the 1,175 reviewed) fell within this definition. These offences included public order, criminal damage and theft and handling charges. The suspect was only known to the victim in four of these cases (as an acquaintance or neighbour). In 14 cases suspects were white, in five they were Asians and one was black.

The defendants

Age and sex

Nine per cent of the CPS sample were juveniles. This compares with 11 per cent of those charged in the police station sample. The reason why there was less success in tracking cases involving juveniles was that the decision whether to charge was more often delayed than in adult cases, either pending further enquiries or reference to a juvenile bureau. It was more difficult in such cases to ensure that research monitoring forms were passed to the CPS along with the case file.

In the sample of cases reviewed by the CPS, 83 per cent of defendants were male and 17 per cent were female. In comparison, the ratio of males to females among those charged by the police was 86:14. One reason why a higher proportion of cases involving females was successfully tracked through to the CPS is that a significant minority of these cases were ones of prostitution and shoplifting. Such offences were usually disposed of quickly in the magistrates' courts and did not present the problems posed by more serious cases of keeping track of proceedings over a long period of time. Also, most of the prostitution cases came from one station where research liaison arrangements with police and CPS were particularly good.

Ethnic origin

A key issue is whether CPS lawyers are aware of the defendant's ethnic origin when they receive cases for review. If they are not then, clearly, there is no scope for conscious discrimination at this stage. The CPS have made a recent commitment to introduce ethnic monitoring by including an ethnic marker in a new computer system being developed for the service (CPS, 1997; Home Office, 1997b)[3]. However, at the time of the present research there was no systematic ethnic monitoring of files received from the police.

---

3   Procedures for ethnic monitoring have been in place in the prison service since 1985 and the probation service since 1992. More recently, prompted by the requirements of s.95 of the Criminal Justice Act 1991, the police have been required to monitor the ethnic origin of those stopped and searched, suspects arrested, offenders cautioned and homicide victims and suspects (Home Office, 1997b)

Crisp and Moxon (1995) have observed that it is often difficult for lawyers to deduce the ethnic origin of a suspect from the case file as this information is not always noted in a prominent place. The defendant's name may provide some indication, but is not an infallible guide. In the present study, CPS lawyers who carried out the initial review stated that they were aware of the ethnic origin of the defendant in only 40 per cent of cases . In over 80 per cent of these cases lawyers said that they knew this information from one or other of the documents on file – usually the custody record but sometimes the summary of evidence, criminal record printout, witness statements or other official forms. In the remaining cases, lawyers were aware of ethnic origin from prior knowledge of the defendant or from photographs on the file.

The fact that lawyers were often initially unaware of the ethnic origin of defendants was not problematic in terms of describing the CPS sample because data on ethnic origin were available from part one of the study. These showed that 83 per cent of defendants in the CPS sample were white, nine per cent black, five per cent Asian and three per cent of other ethnic origin. This is slightly different from the ethnic distribution of those charged which was: 80 per cent white; 12 per cent black; six per cent Asian; and two per cent other. The main reason for the differences between the part one and part two samples is that the rate at which CPS monitoring forms were completed was below average at the three stations which had the highest proportion of black suspects.

Previous convictions and cautions

Nearly two-thirds (62%) of suspects had previous convictions – marginally higher than the proportion of suspects in part one who were known to have a criminal record (61%). In most cases, the police had provided Crown Prosecutors with details of all previous convictions. However, in nine per cent of cases, lawyers were only provided with details of the most recent offences and in a further 11 per cent of cases they said that they were unaware of whether the defendant had previous convictions. This failure always to provide information about previous convictions contravenes guidance issued in October 1992 by the Working Group on Pre-Trial Issues[5], which aimed to standardise the content and format of prosecution files. This stated that, in both abbreviated and full files, the CPS should be provided with details of previous convictions.

Twenty-seven per cent of the sample had not been previously convicted, although a quarter of this group had previously been formally cautioned for an offence. Only 22 per cent of the sample were known never to have been convicted or cautioned before.

---

4   Of course, once cases came to court the lawyer presenting the prosecution case would usually be aware of the defendant's ethnic appearance from direct observation.

5   Now renamed the Trials Issues Group.

Key points

- Sixty-one per cent of cases from part one of the study were monitored in part two.

- The largest proportion (over a quarter) were theft and handling offences.

- Six per cent of cases were ones of domestic violence and two per cent were allegedly racially motivated.

- Nine per cent of defendants were juveniles; the male/female ratio was 83:17. Eighty three per cent were white, nine per cent black, five per cent Asian and three per cent of other ethnic origin.

- Sixty-two per cent of defendants had previous convictions. Twenty-two per cent had never previously been convicted or formally cautioned by the police.

9 Case review and bail decisions

Once the police have charged a person and forwarded the file to the CPS, one of the first tasks of the lawyer to whom the case is allocated is to carry out a review and to make an initial decision whether to continue with the prosecution or terminate proceedings. In order to make this decision, the lawyer needs to know details of the evidence in the case and of the existence of any relevant public interest considerations[1]. The basis for decisions to terminate cases is discussed in the next chapter. Here, attention is paid to the extent and nature of the information available to the lawyer at the review stage and to the frequency with which he or she has to seek further information from the police before being able to come to a decision.

The other focus of the chapter is bail decision-making. It is unusual for cases to be dealt with at first appearance in magistrates' courts[2]. Typically, cases will be adjourned twice (Home Office, 1998) for a range of reasons. The most common are: either the CPS or defence are not ready to proceed; the court requires further information; the case has to be adjourned to allow a trial date to be fixed; the case is awaiting committal to the Crown Court; or the defendant fails to appear (Whittaker and Mackie, 1997). On each occasion, the issue of whether the defendant should be given bail or remanded in custody arises. The role of the CPS in these proceedings is to put the prosecution point of view, taking into account any submissions from the police. This chapter considers how often the police made recommendations on bail and to what extent CPS lawyers followed them[3].

Evidence

The amount of information and level of detail which the police provide to the CPS depends on whether a file is classified as abbreviated or full. This in turn depends, broadly speaking, upon whether the defendant intends to plead guilty and upon the seriousness of the offence. In abbreviated files the

---

1   The criteria to be used in assessing evidential sufficiency and in deciding whether the public interest requires prosecution are set out in the Code for Crown Prosecutors, the most recent version of which was issued by the CPS in June 1994.

2   The exceptions tend to be minor public order and motoring offences, which are typically disposed of at first appearance.

3   The issue of bail decision-making is considered more fully by Morgan and Henderson (1998).

police will provide a summary of the evidence (including the victim's statement), a written record of any interview(s) with the defendant, any additional statements from key witnesses, details of previous convictions and cautions, and a list of witnesses. For full files, Crown Prosecutors should also receive details of witnesses' previous convictions and cautions, copies of interview tapes and original statements from all witnesses[4].

CPS respondents were asked to categorise the main grounds of evidence against each defendant. Figure 9.1 shows that the most commonly mentioned was eyewitness evidence from the police. Other eyewitness evidence, either from independent observers (25%) or victims themselves (22%) was also often important. Of equal value – both in just over a quarter of cases – were confession evidence and physical or forensic evidence.

Figure 9.1   Type of evidence available in cases reviewed by CPS

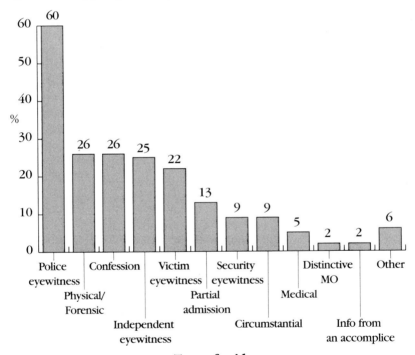

Notes:
1. N=1,108. Data were missing in 67 cases. In nine cases no evidence was cited.
2. Prosecutors could provide multiple responses to this question, hence percentages sum to more than 100.

---

4   Manual of Guidance for the Preparation, Processing and Submission of Files, 1992. Since the present research was undertaken, a pilot scheme has been implemented and evaluated in several areas, whereby the amount of information included on the file has been reduced in certain straightforward cases. Such files are now in use in almost all police forces (CPS, 1997).

The type of evidence available in cases reviewed by the CPS may be compared with the evidence available to the police on arrest (see Chapter 2, Figure 2.5). There are two main differences. Firstly, police eyewitness evidence is even more important in cases forwarded for prosecution than it was at the time of arrest. It was available in 60 per cent of the former compared with 40 per cent of the latter. This increase does not, of course, reflect a rise in the *number* of such cases at the prosecution stage; it simply reflects the fact that cases with police evidence were far more likely than those without such evidence to lead to charges and that they therefore constitute a larger percentage of a smaller base number of cases prosecuted. The second main difference is that confession evidence emerges as important at the prosecution stage. Clearly, such evidence is not usually available upon arrest but is obtained afterwards during police interviews. Although some studies have reported a decline in interviewing to secure confessions (Irving and McKenzie, 1989; Williamson, 1990), it is of note that in over a quarter of cases prosecuted such evidence features prominently in the case and adds significantly to the evidence available upon arrest. However, compared with the frequency with which those charged had provided confessions (around 49% admitted all offences for which they had been arrested), confession evidence was rated as significant in far fewer cases prosecuted. One possible explanation is that, in some cases in which the police had reported in part one of the study that the suspect had 'confessed', the confession was flawed in that it did not cover all the elements of the offence which needed to be proved. Or, it may be that where the other evidence in the case was overwhelming, confessions only provided the 'icing on the cake'.

The importance of different kinds of evidence varied considerably according to the offence (see Appendix A, Table A.6). Police eyewitness evidence was most important in a range of less serious – and usually victimless – offences which tend only to come to light where they are observed in progress by an officer. Thus, police evidence was significant in over 80 per cent of drugs cases and more than 90 per cent of public order, motoring and prostitution offences. It was also valuable in most cases of going equipped, many of which are detected as the result of stop/searches initiated by officers.

The other side of the coin to the overwhelming importance of police evidence in these offences is that in some crimes with a clear victim it was overshadowed by other sources of evidence. In offences against the person, evidence from the victim was most important, featuring in around 80 per cent of assaults, robberies and sexual offences. Uninvolved observers provided important evidence in cases of robbery (67%), burglary (47%) and criminal damage (47%).

Physical or forensic evidence came into its own in drugs cases (72%), where forensic analysis of substances in the suspect's possession could be crucial to the success of the prosecution, as well as in fraud and forgery (45%) and motoring (largely drink driving) cases (38%).

The likelihood that confession evidence would be important also varied according to the offence. It featured most often in fraud and forgery (58%) drugs (55%) and theft and handling (46%) cases. These are often cases in which there is other solid evidence against the suspect (for example, physical/forensic evidence in drugs and forgery cases and the first-hand observations of security staff in shoplifting cases) and suspects may have felt that it was futile to deny their involvement. Their confessions further bolstered the prosecution case against them.

In the average case there were usually two or three different kinds of evidence available to prosecutors: this was so in 56 per cent of cases. The evidence was particularly damning in a further seven per cent of cases in which there were four or more sources. In contrast, in a third of cases there was just one kind of evidence.

Sufficiency of the information on file

Crown Prosecutors were asked to indicate whether there was enough information on the police file to assess, for the first court appearance, whether the evidence was sufficient and whether the public interest required prosecution. In 94 per cent of cases, the CPS reported that there was sufficient evidential and public interest information to determine whether it was appropriate to proceed. In four per cent of cases the initial file sufficed to enable the Crown Prosecutor to decide whether the case required prosecution in the public interest, but there was insufficient information concerning the evidence. In a further one per cent of cases, lawyers reported that there was sufficient evidential information, but not enough public interest information. Therefore, in only a tiny minority of cases (1%) did the initial file contain insufficient information on both evidential and public interest grounds for prosecutors to proceed. Further, there was little difference in this pattern when offences were broken down into non-motoring and motoring[5].

The present findings may be compared with those obtained by Crisp and Moxon (1994). Their research, which was based on 1991 cases (before the Working Group on PRG – Trial Issues Group Manual of Guidance had been introduced – see Chapter 8 above), found that the initial file contained

---

5   There was sufficient evidential and public interest information in 93 per cent of non-motoring cases and 97 per cent of motoring cases.

sufficient information in only 74 per cent of non-motoring cases[6]. The proportion of files with sufficient evidential and public interest information has therefore increased dramatically[7]. In the current research there were a few types of offence in which Crown Prosecutors reported that they were less likely than average to find sufficient information on file to carry out their initial review. Thus, in fraud and forgery cases files came with sufficient evidential information in only 84 per cent of cases. And, in the category of 'other' notifiable offences (which included violent disorder and going equipped) the figure was 83 per cent. In fraud and forgery cases, which could involve a mass of complex documents, it is possible that forensic or other physical evidence was outstanding at the time case files were initially reviewed. However, it is less clear why police officers should not have provided sufficient information about the evidence in 'other' notifiable offences since they, as eyewitnesses, were often the main source of evidence in such cases.

Whilst, overall, 98 per cent of files contained sufficient information to determine whether the public interest required prosecution, the figure – at 88 per cent – was again below average for 'other' notifiable offences. For robbery too the figure was relatively low (89%) (although there is a need for caution here because the number of cases was small).

Particular problems can arise for the police in providing sufficient information to the CPS where the defendant is remanded in custody after charge to appear at court the next day, since there is relatively little time to assemble a file. Previous research on bail decisions by Burrows, Henderson and Morgan (1994) has shown that CPS lawyers often reported inadequacies in police files in such cases, particularly with records of police interviews and witness statements being missing. However, in the present study Crown Prosecutors did not generally complain that information was lacking in 'overnight' cases.

Requests for additional information

Although only a very small percentage of files lacked the information which lawyers required to make their assessment of evidential and public interest factors, they still needed to go back to the police for more information in 29 per cent of cases. In two per cent of cases lawyers also sought information from other bodies. These tended to be defence solicitors or probation officers, but they also included doctors, other CPS branches, complainants and public officials. The reason why CPS staff needed more information in such a large minority of cases is almost certainly that there is a difference

---

6   The figure for motoring cases was 91 per cent.

7   More recently, an initiative entitled Joint Performance Management, set up under the auspices of the Trials Issues Group, has pinpointed the quality of police files as a key area in which to identify and implement measures to improve performance. Evaluation of this initiative suggests that it has achieved some success (Hooke, Knox and Portas, 1996).

between files which, for the time being, are sufficient to proceed and those which are complete in every respect. For example, prosecutors may be able to proceed where they are still awaiting medical evidence, though they would require the information once the case reached court. Confirmation of this view is provided by the more recent work on Joint Performance Management (see also footnote 7 above). While less than half of police files were assessed as complete in all respects, in the great majority of cases lawyers stated that they were able to proceed on the basis of the information they were initially given (Hooke, Knox and Portas, 1996).

Specialist evidence

Forensic evidence was provided by the police in six per cent of cases. In a further two per cent Crown Prosecutors asked for additional forensic evidence or had to request forensic evidence because it had not been provided in the first instance. An expert witness was asked to provide evidence for Crown Prosecutors in six per cent of cases (including 2% of cases where the evidence had already been requested or arranged by the police), typically in violence against the person, theft and handling, and drugs offences.

Bail decisions

Previous research shows that an important factor in bail decisions is whether the suspect has been previously held in police detention before his or her first court appearance (Burrows, Henderson and Morgan, 1994). This is very likely to affect whether the CPS have had sufficient time to consider what recommendations to make regarding bail. In addition, denial of bail by the police is likely to influence the court's decision on bail. Conversely, the same study reports that, if the police had freed a defendant on bail after charge, Crown Prosecutors felt unable to request a remand in custody or the imposition of bail conditions unless, for example, the person could be shown to have interfered with witnesses while on bail.

In some cases – around a third in the present study – the police made specific recommendations to the CPS regarding bail. In 11 per cent of cases the recommendation was to oppose bail, in 12 per cent it was to support the granting of unconditional bail, while in the remaining 10 per cent it was to advise that the CPS request conditional bail (see Table 9.1)[8].

Police recommendations on bail tended to reflect the nature and seriousness of the offence with which the suspect was charged. Thus, the police never recommended unconditional bail in sexual offences. And bail was most often

---

8   At the time at which the research was carried out the police did not themselves have the power to place conditions on bail. This was given to them by s.27 of the Criminal Justice and Public Order Act 1994.

opposed by them in cases of violence against the person, burglary and robbery. The police were often likely to recommend that conditions be placed on bail in sexual offences and other indictable offences (which included the more serious public order offences such as violent disorder). Data on the type of conditions recommended were not collected, but Burrows, Henderson and Morgan (1994) and Brown (1998) note that the police often propose conditions such as residence, curfew and limitations on movement.

In 85 per cent of cases in which recommendations were made, the CPS followed them. They were least likely to do so (in only 71% of cases) where the recommendation was to oppose bail. The kinds of cases in which the CPS were most likely to take a contrary view to the police were ones of violence against the person, burglary, robbery and prostitution. In almost all of these cases the police had previously held the suspect in custody overnight. The most common explanations which the CPS gave for not going along with police wishes were: that conditional bail was more appropriate; that the offence was minor; and that an address provided by the accused had been verified. In comparison, police recommendations were followed by the CPS in 96 per cent of cases where unconditional bail was advised and 89 per cent of cases where the recommendation was for conditional bail. The most common reasons for the CPS dissenting from the need for conditions were: that they considered custody was necessary, usually because of past failures to appear; and that the defendant's good record of attendance at court meant that no conditions were needed.

Table 9.1   Police recommendations on bail and whether followed by the CPS

Offence	Police recommendation				Proportion of recommendations followed by the CPS	
	Oppose	Grant	Conditional	None		
	%	%	%	%	%	(n)
Violence	21	5	17	58	77	(33)
Sexual	14	-	57	29	100	(5)
Burglary	30	10	4	57	75	(24)
Robbery	44	22	-	33	67	(4)
Theft and handling	10	11	9	70	89	(77)
Fraud and forgery	13	20	7	60	92	(11)
Criminal damage	12	7	19	62	82	(22)
Drugs	-	29	-	71	100	(7)
Other indictable	13	9	47	31	86	(25)
Public order	5	11	4	81	92	(22)
Motoring	4	17	7	72	88	(36)
Prostitution	-	11	-	89	75	(3)
All offences	**11**	**12**	**10**	**67**	**85**	**(269)**
(n)	**(107)**	**(117)**	**(97)**	**(653)**		

Notes:
1. N=974: cases where defendant was not dealt with at first court appearance. In 125 cases the defendant was dealt with at first court appearance.
2. Percentages do not always sum to 100 due to rounding.

Key points

- The principal source of evidence available in cases reviewed by the CPS was police eyewitness evidence (in 60% of cases). Also important was evidence from independent eyewitnesses and victims, confession evidence and physical or forensic evidence.

- Police evidence was most important in victimless crimes such as drug and prostitution offences. Evidence from the victim was most important in offences against the person and confession evidence in fraud and forgery, drugs and theft & handling cases.

- In over 90 per cent of cases there was sufficient evidential and public interest information on the initial police file for the CPS to be able to decide whether to proceed with the case, although they later had to seek some further information (usually from the police) in nearly 30 per cent of cases.

- In around a third of cases the police made recommendations regarding bail and 85 per cent of them were followed by the CPS. The CPS were least likely to follow the police recommendation where it was to oppose bail.

10 Termination of proceedings

In carrying out its role of independently reviewing prosecutions initiated by the police, it is axiomatic that the CPS is able to terminate proceedings where appropriate. There has been some suggestion from earlier research that, despite their independence from the police, CPS lawyers are influenced in their decision-making by prior police action. McConville, Sanders and Leng (1991) argue that reviewing lawyers engage in routinised decision-making, with a strong tendency to prosecute cases on the basis that earlier police decisions to charge were correct and proper. However, their research was conducted very early in the life of the CPS when the agency was still coming to terms with its role and it is doubtful whether their conclusions remain valid. More recent research by Crisp and Moxon (1994) has pointed to a more detached relationship between the CPS and the police. Police officers interviewed emphasised their feelings of powerlessness over the final outcomes of cases because the decision whether the case would proceed was very much in the CPS's hands. Officers felt that the CPS sometimes discontinued cases which they thought worthy of prosecution.

In making their decision whether to proceed, Crown Prosecutors are required to employ a two stage test: is the evidence against the defendant sufficient to offer a realistic prospect of conviction; and (assuming the first test is satisfied) is prosecution in the public interest? In using these two tests, prosecutors are assisted by guidelines contained in the Code for Crown Prosecutors, which the DPP is required to issue under s.10 of the Prosecution of Offences Act 1985 (POA). The most recent edition was published in June 1994, but most of the cases in the present study would have been reviewed under the version issued in January 1992[1].

The evidential test is sometimes referred to as the '51 per cent' rule, on the basis that, if a court is more likely than not to convict, then the evidence should be deemed sufficient to proceed. However, the Explanatory Memorandum to the most recent version of the Code emphasises that the test is not so precise. Prosecutors must weigh both the quantity and quality of the evidence. They must have regard, for example, to the reliability of witnesses as well as to the content of their evidence (Ashworth and Fionda, 1994).

---

1   There were two main aims in issuing the revised Code in 1994: firstly, to simplify the language used; and, secondly, to clarify the evidential criteria and the requirement for a realistic prospect of conviction and to bring out the public interest *factors in favour* of prosecution. The 1992 Code only listed public interest factors that might work *against* prosecution.

If the evidential test is satisfied, the reviewing lawyer must then consider whether the public interest requires prosecution. It has long been accepted that there is no public interest in bringing to court every case in which there is sufficient evidence to do so (Ashworth and Fionda, ibid). The 1992 edition of the Code approaches this subject by listing factors which should normally weigh against prosecution. Among these are: the old age or infirmity of the defendant; the youth of the offender[2]; physical or mental ill health; and the likelihood of the court imposing a nominal penalty[3].

There are some cases which are dropped neither on evidential nor public interest grounds but, broadly speaking, on the basis that it is impossible to continue. The defendant may have died or be untraceable. In some cases the court may refuse a prosecution request for an adjournment and this may, effectively, make it impossible for the CPS to proceed if arrangements for all the necessary evidence and witnesses are not in place.

Where the CPS decide to terminate a case, this may be done in several ways, depending on the stage at which the proceedings are to be dropped. They may:

- discontinue proceedings under s.23(3) of the Prosecution of Offences Act during the early stages of the case before evidence has been presented at a summary trial or before committal to the Crown Court;

- offer no evidence in court;

- apply to withdraw proceedings.

The expression 'termination' is used in this report to refer to any of these procedures.

Termination rate

In the present study all charges against the defendant were dropped, either prior to first court appearance or later, in 14 per cent of cases (n=159). The remaining 86 per cent of cases (n=1,016) proceeded to court (although not necessarily on the charges originally preferred by the police – see Chapter 12). The termination rate of 14 per cent is very close to the figure of 13 per cent obtained by Crisp and Moxon (1994).

---

2   This is not included in the 1994 edition. The Explanatory Memorandum still advises that Crown Prosecutors should take account of the defendant's youth and the stigma that a conviction may carry. But, it also states that lawyers should not avoid prosecuting simply because of the defendant's age: the seriousness of the offence or past record may make prosecution necessary.

3   The 1994 edition lists factors which should tilt the balance towards prosecution, including: use of violence or a weapon; premeditation; the involvement of a group or a gang; and a discriminatory motive. In weighing up the factors for and against prosecution, the Explanatory Memorandum notes that the relative value of each may vary and that the calculation is not therefore a simple numerical one.

National statistics on termination for the period covered by the present study put the rate at 12 per cent (Home Office, 1997a). However, the national figures are not directly comparable with those obtained by either the present study or Crisp and Moxon. In particular, the official statistics include as terminated any cases in which charges are changed mid-term and ones in which one or more charges are dropped but where proceedings continue in relation to other offences. It has been estimated that in around a fifth to a quarter of cases officially categorised as terminated early, there is a conviction for a related offence in the same case (Home Office, ibid). It is likely, therefore, the proportion of cases nationally in which all charges are terminated is somewhat lower than the official figures suggest and is probably around nine to 10 per cent. The reason why the termination rate in the present study is rather higher than this is because the sample contained relatively few motoring offences. In these cases the termination rate is extremely low. Such cases do not generally come to court by way of arrest and charge but by way of summons without arrest. The study did not sample cases where suspects had not been arrested.

Reasons for termination

Reasons for termination were categorised as 'evidential', 'public interest' and 'other'[4]. The latter were used in cases where it was impractical for the CPS to continue with the case (see above). Evidential reasons were most often the grounds for termination, being cited in 57 per cent of terminated cases compared with 31 per cent in which public interest grounds underlay the decision. These findings confirm those of Crisp and Moxon (1994), who found that evidential and public interest factors accounted, respectively, for 58 and 29 per cent of terminations. They are also very similar to the results of discontinuance surveys carried out by the CPS itself in 1993 and 1994 (CPS, 1994b, 1995)[5]. Bearing in mind that the CPS areas taking part in the two studies were largely different, this suggests that there is a fair measure of consistency across the country and over time in the application of the guidelines for termination set out in the Code for Crown Prosecutors. The fact that public interest grounds were cited in a relatively large minority of cases in both studies casts doubt upon the conclusion reached by McConville, Sanders and Leng (1991), that prosecutors' decisions are dominated by the sufficiency of the evidence.

4　These categories should be mutually exclusive. Reviewing lawyers should first examine the sufficiency of the evidence. If it is insufficient to proceed, there should be no need for them to go on to consider public interest factors. In fact, both evidential and public interest grounds were cited as the reasons for termination in nine cases. Since Crown Prosecutors consider the evidence first, the evidential reasons are reported here.

5　This takes account of the fact that discontinuances were classified slightly differently in the CPS surveys than the present study. In particular, refusals of witnesses to give evidence or their failure to attend court were categorised by the CPS as 'Prosecution unable to proceed', while the present study classed these as evidential reasons for discontinuance. If these problems with witnesses are combined with reasons for discontinuance listed as evidential ones in the CPS surveys, the relative proportions of evidential and public interest discontinuances are very similar to those in the present research.

Twelve per cent of cases were terminated for 'other' reasons. In two thirds of them this was because the court refused a prosecution request for an adjournment[6]. The CPS most frequently sought adjournments where key witnesses had failed to appear or where vital evidence was missing. In the remainder, cases were usually terminated because the accused was not traceable or, in a few cases, because he or she had died.

Figure 10.1 provides a breakdown of the main evidential reasons for termination. The most frequently cited (in a third of cases) was the lack of supporting or corroborative evidence, followed by the shortage of evidence of a key element of the offence (in 24% of cases)[7]. These reasons were also the ones most often mentioned by lawyers in the Crisp and Moxon study. Various problems with witnesses also featured prominently. 'Witness failure' refers to those cases in which it was believed that a key witness would fail to attend court or fail to come up to proof if they did give evidence. Refusal of witnesses to give evidence was a problem in a significant proportion of cases. It is not known for sure why so many were reluctant but in recent years mounting concern has been expressed about the problem of witness intimidation (Maynard, 1994) and about the negative experiences of the court system reported by some witnesses. The 12 per cent of cases in which 'other problems' with witnesses were noted were ones in which Crown Prosecutors considered that witnesses were not credible or reliable or that their versions conflicted with those of other witnesses.

---

6   The technical means used to secure termination in these cases differed. In half of them the CPS offered no evidence and in the other half the case was dismissed for want of prosecution.

7   Either evidence of criminal intent or the commission of the criminal act were missing.

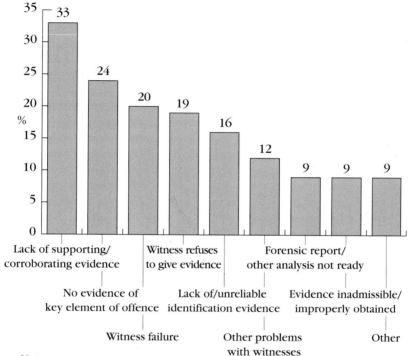

Figure 10.1 Reasons for case termination on evidential grounds

Notes:
1. N=90.
2. 'Other' problems with witnesses' include lack of credibility, unreliability and conflict between witnesses.

Whether cases were terminated on evidential grounds was strongly linked with the kind of evidence available. Figure 10.2 shows that cases in which the police themselves had observed an offence taking place were very rarely terminated. It was also less likely than average that a case would be dropped where the defendant had provided a confession or partial admission. Termination was most likely where the evidence was mainly circumstantial or related to the offender's *modus operandi*, with over a quarter of these cases being dropped. Cases where there were eyewitnesses other than police officers were also more likely than average to be terminated.

Figure 10.2 Termination of cases on evidential grounds by evidence available

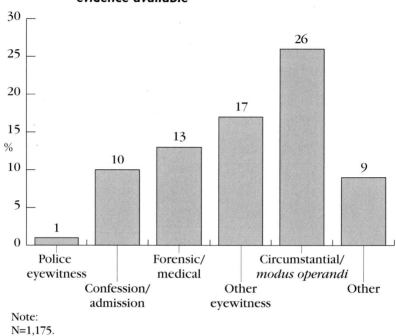

Note:
N=1,175.

Where cases passed the evidential test but were terminated on public interest grounds, the most common reason was the expectation that the court would impose only a nominal penalty (see Figure 10.3). In such cases prosecutors also sometimes pointed to the triviality of the offence or noted that a caution was a more appropriate disposal. In 17 per cent of cases the case was dropped because the defendant was due to appear on other charges, usually of a more serious nature. It was felt that no useful purpose would be served by proceeding with other offences which would probably add nothing to the sentence given. Also in 17 per cent of cases, the youth of the defendant was mentioned. It should be noted, however, that in the latest version of the Code for Crown Prosecutors this is not now listed as a specific factor tending against prosecution (see also footnote 2 above). The seriousness of the offence and the presence of previous cautions or convictions may now take precedence. This reflects changes in government cautioning policy, as set out in Home Office Circular 18/1994. Lastly, it was not unusual for considerations relating to the victim to arise. In 13 per cent of cases the victim's wish not to press charges was important while, also in 13 per cent of cases, the fact that the offender had compensated the victim swayed the prosecutor's decision.

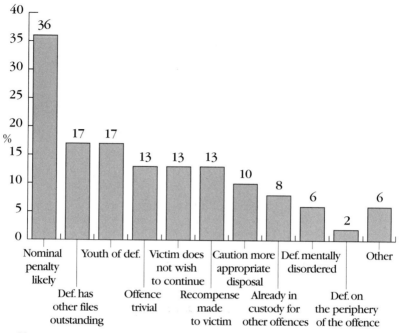

Figure 10.3 Reasons for termination on public interest grounds

Note:
N=47. Data were missing in one case.

The stage at which cases are dropped

The research by Crisp and Moxon (1994) highlighted that, where proceedings are terminated by the CPS, this does not generally occur before cases have reached magistrates' courts. A proportion of more serious cases reach Crown Court before weaknesses in the case result in judges ordering or directing an acquittal (Block, Corbett and Peay, 1993). As Crisp and Moxon (1994) note, it is in everyone's interest that cases that are going to be terminated are dropped as early as possible. Otherwise prosecution and defence will waste time on preparatory work, witnesses will attend court unnecessarily and court time will be wasted because other cases cannot always be scheduled in at short notice. Defendants will also experience unnecessary anxiety while court proceedings hang over them (Block, Corbett and Peay, 1993).

Despite the undoubted advantages of early termination, the present study found that very few cases were terminated prior to first court appearance. Figure 10.4 shows that only two per cent were dropped at this stage. Just nine per cent more were terminated at first court appearance. The great majority of cases were terminated after this point. Crisp and Moxon (1994) report very similar findings[9]. The main difference is that rather *more* cases in the present study were dropped at a late stage (at a subsequent court appearance). In fact, it might have been expected that *fewer* cases would have been dropped later. The Pre-Trial Issues Manual of Guidance (WGPTI, 1992) seeks to ensure that CPS lawyers have the prosecution file in their hands two weeks before first court appearance, thereby enabling them to reach a decision at an early stage about whether to proceed. Crisp and Moxon (1995) reported that this timescale was seldom adhered to and the same may have been the case at the time of the present study. Since then, however, efforts have been made – notably through the Joint Performance Management initiative – to boost the proportion of files which are delivered to the CPS on time. Evaluation of the initiative suggests that there has been some success in achieving target deadlines (Hooke, Knox and Portas, 1996). If so, it might be expected that a higher proportion of cases which are terminated would now be dropped at an earlier stage. The most recent CPS Annual Report provides some support for this view. While the present study showed that only 30 per cent of cases that were dropped were terminated after the first but before a subsequent court hearing, the figure for 1996-97 was 47 per cent (CPS, 1997).

Figure 10.4   Stage at which cases were terminated

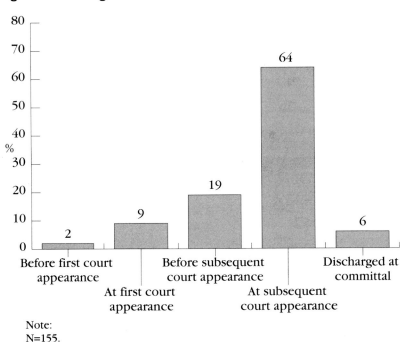

Note:
N=155.

---

8   In their study five per cent of non-motoring cases were dropped before first court appearance, seven per cent at first appearance and 37 per cent before, and 51 per cent at, a subsequent appearance

Consultation with the police

The Code for Crown Prosecutors advises that it should be normal practice for lawyers to consult the police when they propose to terminate a case. Generally such consultation did occur, either orally, in writing or both. There was no consultation in 21 per cent of cases, a very similar figure to the 22 per cent found by Crisp and Moxon (1994) in non-motoring cases. The most recent CPS discontinuance survey provides a somewhat higher figure of 26 per cent (CPS, 1995). However, this includes motoring cases. As Crisp and Moxon (ibid) point out, it is less common for there to be consultation in motoring cases, largely because many cases are dropped at court when the defendant produces relevant documents. The reason most frequently given by Crown Prosecutors for not consulting was lack of time. This might be because the file arrived late. Sometimes there was no possibility of consultation before termination because the decision to drop the case was forced upon the prosecuting lawyer at court when a key witness failed to turn up. With recent improvements in the timely delivery of police files (see above), there may now be more scope for consultation.

Bindovers and cautions

Termination of proceedings does not always mean that no action is taken against the accused. In certain circumstances the CPS may seek a bindover and this occurred in eight per cent (n=13) of terminated cases in the present study. These tended to be public order cases or ones involving domestic violence. Lawyers reported that the accused's willingness to accept a bindover influenced their decision to terminate proceedings. The effect of being bound over is that the accused agrees to keep the peace. Failure to do so means that he or she may be arrested, brought back before the court and required to forfeit a sum previously agreed as a surety.

Another option was for the CPS to recommend a caution (assuming that the accused had admitted guilt). Such recommendations were made in 8 per cent of cases (n=13) and the police acceded in all of them. A caution was sometimes considered appropriate where a nominal penalty was anticipated, should the case have gone to court.

Characteristics of terminated cases

Information has been given earlier about the evidential and public interest considerations which lead to termination. The issue addressed in this section is whether terminated cases have particular distinguishing features which mark them out from those proceeded with. Crisp and Moxon (1994) suggest that termination rates do not vary much according to offence, but that there is considerable variation between CPS branches in the rate at which cases are terminated. However, their study provides no information about the characteristics of defendants (for example, their age, ethnic origin and gender) in terminated cases. Nor is information available about the relationship between termination and other features of the case: for example, did the initial arrest arise from a stop search, had the defendant exercised his or her right of silence when interviewed by the police, and was the case one involving domestic violence? A wide range of such factors is considered below. Logistic regression analysis was carried out to determine which of these were, independently, predictors of termination (see Appendix B, Table B.7).

Age, sex, ethnic origin and employment status

Figures 10.5(a) to (d) show that the termination rate varied according to each of these variables. However, the only one which was a significant predictor of whether a case would be terminated, after controlling for other factors, was the defendant's ethnic origin. Thus, the odds of cases involving black or Asian defendants being terminated were, respectively, double and triple those for white defendants (see Appendix B, Table B.7). It is not easy to account for this finding. Since the logistic regression procedure controls for other key variables, including offence, the explanation is not that members of ethnic minority groups are disproportionately involved in offences for which the termination rate is above average. Nor is there any evidence that the higher termination rate for ethnic minority defendants reflects a pattern of intentional positive discrimination by Crown Prosecutors. There was a high initial level of unawareness among reviewing lawyers of the defendant's ethnic origin. The termination rate was almost identical where lawyers did and did not know the defendant's ethnic origin from the outset. And, although all lawyers might subsequently find this information out (often from direct observation at court) there are no good grounds for believing that the defendant's ethnic origin then influenced their decision-making. It is possible that the answer lies with the influence of factors not measured by the research. In particular, although details were known of the nature of the evidence against the defendant and other features of the case which may have had a relevance to the public interest, it was difficult to know what weight was attached to them in each case. The possibility must be considered that, where the defendant was from an ethnic minority group, the police were more likely to submit for prosecution cases in which the evidence was weaker than average or where the public interest was against prosecution.

Other characteristics of the defendant were not significant predictors of termination, despite variations in the termination rate, for example, according to whether the suspect was male or female (see Figure 10.5(a)). The reason that proceedings against females were less likely to be dropped was that prostitution cases (which made up a significant minority of cases against female defendants) were relatively straightforward to prosecute since they depended largely on direct eyewitness evidence from police officers.

Cases involving juvenile defendants were more likely to be terminated than those against members of other age groups (see Figure 10.5(c)). The 1992 Code for Crown Prosecutors (but not the 1994 version) specifically lists the youth of the defendant as a public interest consideration bearing on the decision whether to proceed. This almost certainly accounts for the higher termination rate in relation to juveniles.

Figure 10.5(a) Termination according to sex of defendant

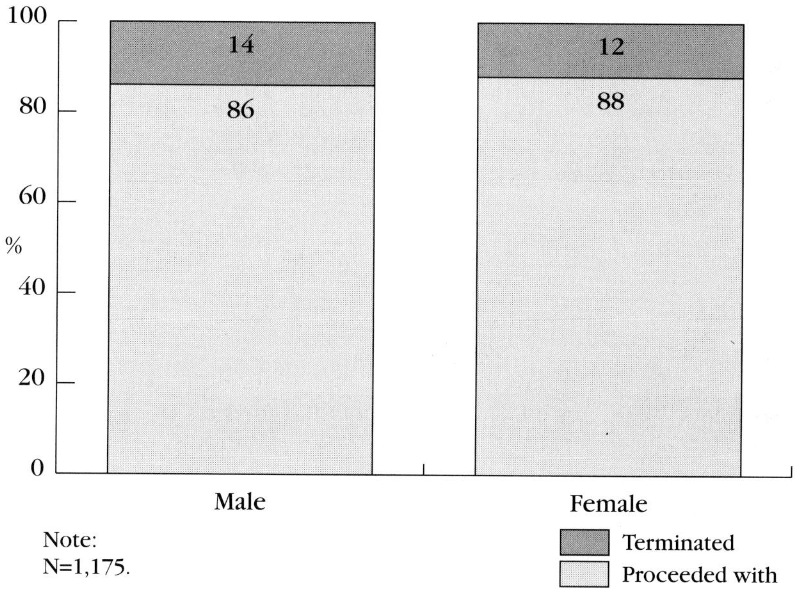

Note:
N=1,175.

Terminated
Proceeded with

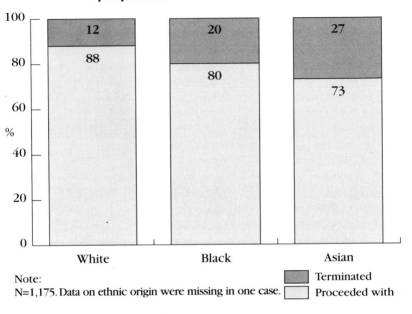

Figure 10.5(b) Termination according to ethnic origin of defendant

Note:
N=1,175. Data on ethnic origin were missing in one case.

Terminated
Proceeded with

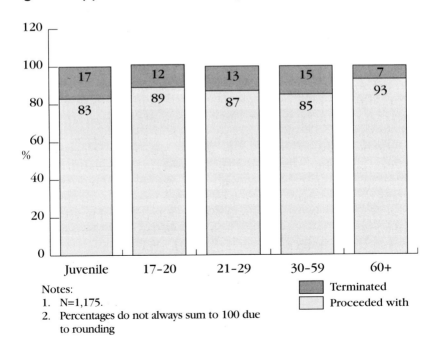

Figure 10.5(c) Termination according to age of defendant

Notes:
1. N=1,175.
2. Percentages do not always sum to 100 due to rounding

Terminated
Proceeded with

Figure 10.5(d) Termination according to employment status of defendant

Note:
N=1,175. Data on employment status were missing in 22 cases.

■ Terminated
□ Proceeded with

Offence type and seriousness

While Crisp and Moxon (1994) found that termination rates did not differ significantly between offences, the present study found considerable variation. Figure 10.6 shows that the highest termination rate (29%) was for offences of violence. This reflects the difficulties of proof in assault cases. Common problems in such cases included: conflict between witnesses; confusion over the relative culpability of defendant and victim; and the retraction of allegations in domestic violence cases (considered further below). The lowest termination rates were for prostitution (5%), drugs (3%) and motoring (1%) offences. These are cases which tend to be more evidentially straightforward[9]. When cases were grouped into categories according to their level of seriousness (see Appendix C), it was found that the termination rate for less serious cases (9%) was much lower than for moderately or very serious offences (both 16%). Offence type and seriousness were significant predictors of termination in the logistic regression model (see Appendix B, Table B.7)

---

9   In drugs cases this was true of simple possession but not necessarily of ones where the intent to supply must also be proven. The termination rate in drugs cases was also low because the police would often wait to charge the suspect until substances in his or her possession had been analysed and identified. If they turned out not to be controlled drugs, then no charges would follow. Therefore, only cases where there was incontrovertible forensic evidence tended to be put forward for prosecution.

Figure 10.6 Prosecution decision by offence type

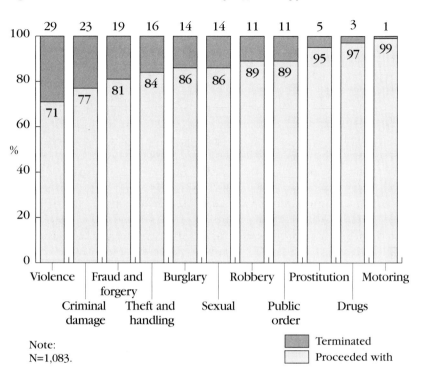

Note:
N=1,083.

■ Terminated
□ Proceeded with

Domestic violence cases

The termination rate in domestic violence cases was – at 37 per cent – rather higher than that for offences of violence generally. Domestic violence cases were considered separately in the regression analysis because they were not entirely a subset of violence against the person offences but included some criminal damage, public order and other offences. Whether a case was categorised as a domestic violence one was a significant predictor of termination. The main reasons for termination in these cases differed markedly from cases generally. In two-thirds of terminated cases refusal by a key witness to give evidence or other problems with witnesses were cited as a reason for termination[10]. Previous research on domestic violence has highlighted the difficulties in prosecuting such cases in the courts. Victims may be too fearful or too economically dependent on their partners or other family members to risk their wrath by co-operating with proceedings against them (Morley and Mullender, 1994). Some victims seek to achieve a reconciliation with the offender after charges have been laid. In nearly 40 per cent of terminated domestic violence cases this was noted as a reason why the victim either refused or was reluctant to testify. The difficulties in

---

10   These included the reluctance of witnesses to give evidence, the likelihood that the witness would not attend court or come up to proof, doubts about their credibility and conflict between witnesses.

securing a successful prosecution may not always reasonably be foreseeable when a suspect is charged. It was noted in part one of the study that the police press charges in a relatively high proportion of domestic violence cases.

Admissions and exercise of the right of silence

The provision of an admission during interviews with the police was a significant predictor of whether a case would be terminated. Where there was no admission, 16 per cent of cases were dropped, compared with only nine per cent where there was a full or partial admission. The absence of a confession is, of course, not necessarily fatal to the prosecution case if there is other strong evidence available. However, as Brown (1997) has noted, obtaining a confession continues to be an important part of police interviewing strategy, despite efforts in recent years to make the focus of interviews a more neutral search for the truth and to increase reliance on other evidence. It is possible, therefore, that in some cases where the file submitted to the CPS contained no confession, the evidence that was available may not have been as strong as in cases where there was confession evidence. The absence of any admission of guilt would also have put defendants in a stronger position to mount a defence in the face of the evidence that was available, and prosecutors would inevitably have taken this into account in deciding whether to proceed. While it might be thought surprising that as many as nine per cent of cases were dropped even though there was an admission, in some of these cases public interest factors may have pointed towards termination. And in some cases, either the admission was only partial or there may have been doubts about its admissibility.

Where suspects had exercised their right of silence, cases were more likely to be terminated (22% of cases compared with 15 % where they had answered police questions). However, right of silence was not in itself a significant predictor of case termination. This may have been because the number of suspects in the CPS sample who had exercised their right of silence was quite small. A more important consideration is that exercise of the right of silence did not necessarily mean that the suspect provided no admissions (some went on to do so in a later police interview). Equally, those who answered police questions did not necessarily admit guilt. This suggests that the more important relationship is between admission and case termination rather than right of silence and termination.

Previous convictions

Whether the defendant had previous convictions was a significant factor in predicting whether a case would be dropped. Where the defendant had no prior record, 17 per cent of cases were terminated, compared with 12 per cent where he or she had a criminal record. The lack of a criminal history could be relevant in less serious cases to deciding whether it was in the public interest to take an offender through the courts, with the resultant stigma that a conviction would bring.

Cases with co-defendants

The last factor in the logistic regression model which predicted whether a case would be terminated was the presence of co-defendants. Where the defendant had participated in a joint enterprise with others who were also charged, 26 per cent of cases were dropped compared with 11 per cent where the defendant was the only one accused. Cases involving more than one accused can present greater complexities of proof – for example, in terms of proving each person's separate part in the offence and of reconciling conflicting stories – and this may explain this finding.

Cases arising from stop/search arrests

Cases in which the defendant had originally been arrested following a stop/search were less likely than average to be dropped by the CPS (the termination rate was 7%t). This is significant because there has long been controversy surrounding the use of these powers (Young, 1994). In part one of the study it was noted that there was generally no significant difference in the frequency with which stop/search arrests led to charge or caution compared with other arrests. It would seem that the cases which are then forwarded to the CPS for prosecution are more evidentially sound than average. This is likely to be because police officers have either carried out the stop/search after witnessing the suspect commit an offence or because the search has revealed direct and tangible evidence of the person's involvement in an offence.

Legal advice

Twenty per cent of cases against those who had received legal advice at the police station were dropped, compared with 11 per cent where no advice had been obtained. However, securing legal advice was not in itself a significant predictor of termination. Rather, those suspects who consulted legal advisers tended to be ones who had been detained for more serious offences and who did not admit the offence. Both of these factors were significant pointers to case termination.

CPS branch

Although not a feature of the case itself, the CPS branch dealing with the case had a bearing on its outcome. Figure 10.7 shows that termination rates varied from eight per cent at Dudley (which dealt with the Birmingham Road police station cases) to 19 per cent at Leicester (dealing with the Beaumont Leys cases). Crisp and Moxon (1994) also report a similar level of variation in their study. However, CPS branch was not a significant factor predicting termination. Much of the discrepancy in termination rates probably stems from differences between branches in case mix. For example, Dudley (Birmingham Road) had a relatively large number of prostitution cases, which are rarely terminated, while Leicester (Beaumont Leys) had an above average proportion of more serious cases, for which termination rates tend to be high.

Figure 10.7 Prosecution decision by CPS area

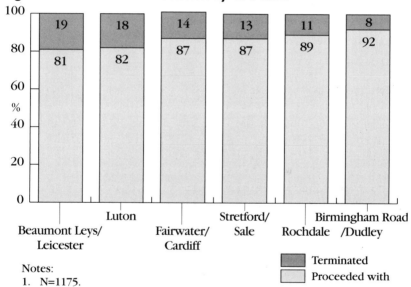

Notes:
1. N=1175.
2. Percentages do not awlasy sum to 100 due to rounding.

Witnesses' previous convictions

In cases involving witnesses with previous convictions, termination was far more likely than in cases where witnesses had no known criminal record. The respective termination rates were 24 per cent and 13 per cent. Issues of witness credibility and reliability tended to arise in such cases and have a bearing on lawyers' assessment of the evidential strength of the case.

Key points

- In 14 per cent of cases, all charges against the defendant were dropped, either prior to first court appearance or later.

- In 57 per cent of terminated cases the reasons for dropping the case were evidential. The most common evidential problems were lack of supporting or corroborative evidence, lack of evidence of a key element of the offence and various problems with witnesses.

- Public interest grounds were responsible for 31 per cent of terminations. The triviality of the offence and likelihood of a nominal court penalty were the most commonly cited reasons.

- Only just over 10 per cent of terminated cases were dropped prior to or at first court appearance; the remainder were terminated later. The police were usually consulted prior to termination; where they were not, this was due to lack of time or the unexpected failure of a key witness to attend court.

- Several factors were significant predictors of case termination. Termination rates were far higher where: the defendant was Asian or black; the offence was one of violence (and particularly domestic violence); the crime was classed as 'very serious'; the defendant had provided no admission of guilt; there were two or more co-defendants; and the defendant had no criminal record.

11 Court results

This chapter looks at the outcome at court of cases in which proceedings were continued by the CPS. These amounted to 86 per cent (n=1,016)[1] of cases forwarded to the CPS by the police for prosecution. In nine per cent (n=89) of these cases, the CPS dropped the principal charge against the defendant but proceeded with lesser offences. It should be noted that some cases in which all charges were terminated resulted in one or more hearings at magistrates' courts, since it was relatively rare for cases to be terminated prior to first court appearance. These cases are not dealt with in this chapter but in the earlier chapter on termination.

Plea and case outcome: magistrates' courts

The vast majority of cases (91% of those in which the CPS proceeded with the principal charges against the defendant) were dealt with at magistrates' courts. Figure 11.1 shows that 82 per cent of defendants pleaded guilty. A further eight per cent were convicted following magistrates' court trial and two per cent because the case was proven in their absence. Only two per cent of defendants had their cases dismissed following a not guilty pleas because the magistrates decided that the prosecution case had not been proven. A small proportion of defendants were bound over to keep the peace, most frequently in public order cases involving drunkenness offences and sections 4 and 5 of the Public Order Act 1986.

---

1   In 42 per cent of these cases, defendants had been charged with more than one offence. In all, the 1,016 defendants were charged with a total of 1,793 offences.

Figure 11.1 Outcomee of cases for defendants appearing at magistrates' courts

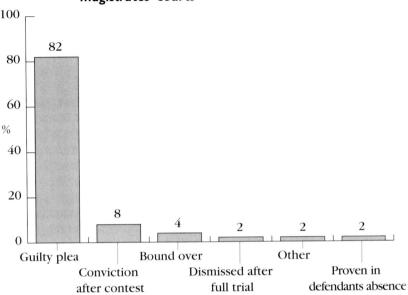

Notes:
1. N=780.
2. 'Other' includes warrant still live and transfer of case to another court.
3. Figure excludes cases committed to Crown Court.

In relation to plea, two points are worthy of note. Firstly, defendants appearing on domestic violence related charges were much less likely than average to provide a guilty plea, doing so in just 59 per cent of such cases. However, 31 per cent were bound over to keep the peace (compared with just 4% of defendants generally in magistrates' courts). Baldwin (1985) and McConville, Sanders and Leng (1991) have suggested that the prosecution may tend to seek bindovers in exchange for dropping the substantive charges where they foresee difficulties at trial or where they consider that the case is not serious enough to be worth fighting. Recent work on domestic violence prosecutions by Cretney and Davis (1996) also suggests that the CPS may sometimes seek a bindover where the incident is believed to be an isolated one and the parties are reconciled (a situation where the CPS's policy statement on domestic violence suggests that a bindover may be appropriate) but also where they have cause to think that the complainants are likely to withdraw their complaints. Whatever the truth of these contentions, it is undoubtedly true that domestic violence cases do present particular prosecution difficulties, as shown by the high proportion of cases discontinued due to problems with witnesses (see Chapter 10). The defendant's preparedness to accept a bindover may therefore have been seen as an acceptable outcome by the prosecution.

Secondly, plea was strongly related to whether the defendant had earlier admitted the offence during police interview. Of those who had provided an admission, 92 per cent pleaded guilty, compared with 76 per cent who had made no admission. A further 10 per cent of the latter group were convicted after a contest, resulting in an overall conviction rate of 86 per cent among those who had not admitted the offence during police questioning. The fact that defendants had provided no admission does not necessarily imply that they had exercised their right of silence during police interviews. Some may have sought to provide exculpatory accounts. In contrast, some of those who did exercise their right of silence later went on to provide admissions. Taken together, these factors help explain why right of silence was not in itself related to plea. Thus, broadly similar proportions of those who did and did not exercise this right (85% and 84% respectively) went on to plead guilty at court.

It should be noted that the present research was conducted before the inferences from silence provisions of the CJPOA 1994 were introduced. Research on the new provisions suggests that they have not altered the extent to which suspects provide admissions but they have led to reduced reliance on silence during police interviews (Bucke, Street and Brown, in press). It is not as yet clear whether this has altered the relationship between use of silence and plea. If it is the case, for example, that those who now exercise the right of silence are a hardcore of unco-operative offenders, it is reasonable to expect that members of this group may tend to plead not guilty more often than other suspects.

Sentencing at magistrates' courts

Figure 11.2 provides a breakdown of the sentences given to defendants dealt with at magistrates' courts. In line with national figures (Home Office, 1997a), the sentence most frequently given was a fine or compensation. In almost one-quarter of cases, the defendant received a conditional or absolute discharge. One in ten defendants were sentenced to immediate custody. Other studies have pointed to magistrates' general reluctance to resort to an immediate custodial sentence (Bond and Lemon, 1981; Rumgay, 1995). Together, community sentences (probation, community service and supervision orders) accounted for more than one-fifth of disposals. In recent years, however, there has been a steady growth in magistrates' use of immediate custody (Home Office, 1997a).

Figure 11.2 Sentencing at the magistrates' court

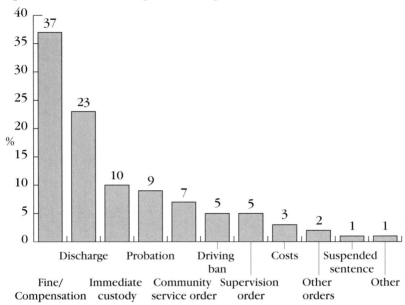

Notes:
1. N=679.
2. Figure provides details of the main sentence awarded in each case.
3. 'Other' includes bindovers after conviction and cases committed to Crown Court for sentence.

Seriousness of offence

While magistrates do not deal with the most serious offences, they hear a wide range of cases of intermediate seriousness, such as assaults, burglaries and thefts, as well as many less serious cases which typically involve breaches of public order. Thirteen per cent of those sentenced for offences categorised as moderately serious were given custodial sentences compared with just five per cent of those sentenced for less serious offences (see Appendix C for a categorisation of offences according to seriousness). A regression analysis, carried out to identify those variables which were, independently, predictors of a custodial sentence, found that seriousness of offence was one of four which reached statistical significance (see Appendix B, Table B.8).

Gender

Male defendants were far more likely than females to be given a custodial sentence (12% compared with 4% – see Appendix A, Table A.7). In line with the findings of a review of the research and statistical evidence on the sentencing of women (Hedderman and Hough, 1994), the present study found that this was only partly explained by males being likely to be charged with more serious offences and to have more previous convictions. Controlling for these factors, men were still more likely than women to be sentenced to custody and for longer periods. Hedderman and Hough (ibid) note that a factor accounting for some of the discrepancy is that fewer women than men are tried in the Crown Court, where the imposition of a custodial sentence is more probable and sentence length likely to be longer. The regression analysis found that gender did not reach significance as a predictor of receiving a custodial sentence (see Appendix B, Table B.8). However, this may be because the sample of sentenced defendants comprised only a small number of females.

Ethnic group

Type of sentence did not vary significantly according to ethnic group, although black defendants were slightly more likely to be sentenced to custody than whites or Asians (see Appendix A, Table A.7). Previous studies of sentencing in magistrates' courts have produced similar findings (Crow and Cove, 1984; Mair, 1986; Walker, 1989)[2].

Age

Almost one-half of sentenced juveniles received a community sentence – typically a supervision order (see Appendix A, Table A.7)[3]. Not surprisingly, given their low or non-existent income, few juveniles were ordered by magistrates to pay a fine or compensation. There was little difference in the proportion of juveniles and over-20s who received a custodial sentence (the figure was around 10%). In contrast, 14 per cent of 17- to 20-year-olds received custodial sentences. This was related to this group's greater involvement in theft and handling offences, which were more likely than average to attract a custodial disposal. Fines were most common among the 21 to 29 age group. One reason for this was that the bulk of those appearing on prostitution charges fell into this age group and a fine is the most usual disposal for such offences.

Employment status

Only three per cent of those in employment who were convicted were given custodial sentences compared with 14 per cent of the unemployed (see Appendix A, Table A.7). The former were far more likely than average to be fined or ordered to pay compensation. However, unemployed defendants were more likely than those in employment to receive a discharge. In part, this may have been because they were less likely to have the resources to pay fines (Flood-Page and Mackie, 1998).

---

2   However, attention has been drawn to methodological weaknesses of these studies, notably by Bowling and Phillips (forthcoming) and Smith (1994).

3   Supervision orders were made available for juveniles by the Criminal Justice Act 1991

Domestic violence

Relatively few domestic violence cases in the study led to a finding of guilt at magistrates' courts and it is therefore difficult to draw general conclusions about sentencing practice in such cases. However, of the 21 concerned, only one resulted in a custodial sentence. The most frequent outcome (in 9 cases) was a conditional discharge. Five defendants were fined (between £50 and £200), four were given probation orders, one was ordered to pay compensation and one was bound over after conviction.

Previous convictions

Table 11.1 shows that a custodial sentence was much more likely to be given where the defendant had previous convictions. The regression analysis showed that having previous convictions was a significant predictor of a custodial sentence and increased the odds of receiving such a sentence by a factor of four (see Appendix B, Table B.8). Of those sentenced to imprisonment, only one per cent had not previously been convicted. For those with no previous convictions, magistrates were most likely to order a conditional discharge of one year or more. Sentence was also related to the number of previous convictions. While 10 per cent of those with between one and five previous convictions were sentenced to custody, this rose to 19 per cent for those with six or more. The use of imprisonment was also related to previous experience of custody: 24 per cent of those who had served a custodial sentence before received custody on the present occasion compared with nine per cent of those with no previous custodial experience. The regression analysis showed that prior custody was a significant predictor of receiving a custodial sentence.

Table 11.1 Number of previous convictions and sentence imposed

	Custody		Other sentence	
	%	(n)	%	(n)
No previous convictions	1	(2)	99	(173)
Previous convictions:	14	(64)	86	(384)
Up to five previous convictions	10	(18)	90	(164)
Six or more previous convictions	19	(42)	82	(185)
No previous custody	9	(26)	91	(259)
Previous custodial sentence	24	(36)	76	(112)

Note: Percentages do not always sum to 100 due to rounding.

Court

In line with official statistics (Home Office, 1997a), the relative use of custody and other sentences was found to vary between courts. The proportion of those convicted who were given custodial sentences ranged from four per cent at Trafford to 21 per cent at Leicester. These variations were related to local differences in the proportion of more serious offences. However, they were not wholly explained by them and it seems likely, as other studies have observed, that magistrates differ greatly in their preparedness to resort to custodial sentences (see, for example, Rumgay, 1995).

Outstanding files

The existence of outstanding cases against defendants was a significant predictor of them receiving a custodial sentence, increasing the odds of receiving such a sentence by a factor of three (see Appendix B, Table B.8). These defendants were also likely to have multiple previous convictions. However, this factor did not explain the relationship with sentence because the regression analysis showed that having outstanding files was independently a predictor of custody. Possibly, the fact that the defendant had other outstanding cases to answer may have been one further factor which convinced magistrates that the person before them was a serious criminal and should be dealt with accordingly.

Cases committed to the Crown Court

Nine per cent (n=87) of cases proceeded with resulted in Crown Court trial[4]. Two per cent involved indictable only offences, so there was no choice as to venue. The remainder were triable either way. In three per cent the magistrates' declined jurisdiction and in two per cent the defendant elected Crown Court trial[5].

The factors which enter into magistrates' and defendants' decisions as to venue have been fully explored elsewhere, notably by Hedderman and Moxon (1992). The present study did not include interviews with magistrates or defendants about their decision-making, but it was possible to examine the characteristics of cases which went to Crown Court. A logistic

---

4   For the purposes of the present study, the committal rate was expressed as the proportion of *all* cases proceeded with (including summary offences) which were committed for Crown Court trial. This is somewhat different from the definitions used in official statistics. *Criminal Statistics England and Wales* (Home Office, annually) express the committal rate either as the proportion of those proceeded against for indictable only and triable either way offences who were committed for Crown Court trial, or as the proportion of those proceeded against for triable either way offences who were committed for trial. In 1996 committal rates were 20 per cent and 16 per cent respectively according to these definitions.

5   In the remaining two per cent of cases it was unclear whether the defendant had elected Crown Court trial or the magistrates had declined jurisdiction.

regression analysis was carried out to identify those which, after taking account of other relevant variables, were predictors of venue (see Appendix B, Table B.9). Five factors (discussed further below) reached statistical significance. It is certain, however, that there are other important predictor variables. The reason they were not picked out in the present model was because the sample of Crown Court cases was relatively small. For this reason, it was not viable to separate out cases in which magistrates declined jurisdiction from those in which defendants elected Crown Court trial.

Three of the significant predictor variables are included in Table 11.2: age of defendant; number of charges; and exercise of the right of silence during police interviews. The other significant factors were the seriousness of the offence and the magistrates' court where the defendant first appeared.

Looking first at age, it was rare for cases involving juveniles to be committed to the Crown Court. This occurred in only two cases: one of fraud and one of robbery. The fact that few juveniles were tried at the Crown Court is not surprising because there are statutory restrictions on the kinds of cases which may be sent there. Generally, those aged 17 or under are dealt with in the youth court unless they are charged with murder, manslaughter or certain other serious offences or are charged jointly with another person aged 18 or more (Home Office, 1997a).

Confirming Hedderman and Moxon's (1992) findings, the seriousness of the offence and the number of charges were also found to be significant predictors of committal to Crown Court. The link between seriousness and Crown Court trial is only partly explained by the fact that some serious offences are indictable only. Either way offences at the more serious end of the spectrum – such as violence against the person, burglary, and some sexual and drugs offences – were also highly likely to result in Crown Court trial. The number of offences was independently a predictor of Crown Court trial. While the individual charges may not necessarily have been serious, in combination they raised the prospect of a stiff sentence. In such cases, either magistrates may have preferred to decline jurisdiction or defendants may have wished to take their chances before a jury.

It is less clear why exercise of the right of silence during police interviews should be a significant predictor of Crown Court trial. A possible clue is provided by Hedderman and Moxon's (1992) study. Their interviews with defendants revealed that many who elected to go to Crown Court were convinced that they would be more likely to receive a fair trial there, believing that the jury, in contrast to magistrates, would be less likely to be on the side of the police. It may be the case that those who distrust the police may both have been more likely to exercise their right to silence at the police station and to have opted to be tried in the Crown Court.

Table 11.2 Factors associated with committal to Crown Court

	Mags Court		Crown Court	
	%	(n)	%	(n)
Ethnic origin:				
White	91	(677)	9	(69)
Black	79	(45)	21	(12)
Asian	88	(37)	12	(5)
Other	95	(20)	5	(1)
Age:				
Juvenile	97	(74)	3	(2)
Adult	89	(706)	11	(85)
Number of offences:				
One charge	94	(515)	6	(35)
Two or more	84	(265)	16	(52)
Legal advice	81	(200)	19	(46)
Right of silence	61	(43)	39	(27)
All cases	**91**	**(840)**	**9**	**(87)**

Note: N=927.

Again confirming Hedderman and Moxon's (1992) findings, the area from which the defendant came was found to be a significant predictor of venue. Committal rates ranged from four per cent at Rochdale up to 15 per cent at Luton and Stretford/Trafford.

The committal rate also varied in relation to a range of other factors, although none of these emerged as significant in the multivariate analysis. One was the defendant's ethnic origin. Table 11.2 shows that black and, to a lesser extent, Asian defendants were more likely than whites to be committed for Crown Court trial. This picture is confirmed in the national statistics, which have shown that more black than white defendants are tried in the Crown Court. In part this is because they are more likely to be charged with indictable only offences, particularly robbery (Home Office, 1989; FitzGerald and Sibbitt, 1997). Other research has also reported a higher committal rate for black defendants (Walker, 1988, 1989; see FitzGerald, 1993 and Smith, 1994 for reviews). The research evidence – and most recently Hood's (1992) study in the West Midlands – suggests that this may not be due to black defendants more frequently electing Crown Court trial. Hood found that there was little difference in the proportions of black and white defendants electing trial by jury. Similarly, research by Brown and

Hullin (1992) in Leeds magistrates' court also found no significant ethnic differences amongst those electing Crown Court trial. Since only 19 defendants elected to be tried in the Crown Court in the current research, the small numbers prevent consideration of the ethnic dimension in detail.

Trial venue was also associated with whether the defendant had received legal advice while in police custody: those who had been advised were much more likely to be committed to the Crown Court. Hedderman and Moxon (1992) also point to the relevance of legal advice where defendants elect Crown Court trial. However, receipt of legal advice at the police station was not, independently, a significant predictor of committal. The reason for this is probably that those who seek legal advice are more likely to have been arrested for more serious cases and to be inclined towards a not guilty plea.

Plea and case outcome: Crown Court

Figure 11.3 shows that just over half of those tried at the Crown Court pleaded guilty on some or all counts. In 16 per cent of cases the judge ordered an acquittal[6] after the prosecution had offered no evidence. Judge ordered acquittals represent another means by which the prosecution team (barrister on advice from the Crown Prosecutor) can withdraw from prosecuting a defendant because the case is weak. In a further seven per cent of cases, the judge directed[7] the defendant to be acquitted once the trial was underway. As in magistrates' courts, relatively few defendants – five per cent – were found not guilty. The four per cent of cases in which the outcome was classified as 'other' include ones in which defendants failed to appear and a Bench Warrant was issued, not guilty pleas to lie on file, and bindovers.

It is difficult to compare these figures with official statistics because the latter are calculated on a different basis. Moreover, the statistics published by the CPS are derived differently from those published by the Home Office. However, it is possible to draw upon the performance indicator information produced quarterly by the CPS to provide a comparable breakdown to that presented above. The results are as follows (the present study's figures are given in brackets)[8]:

- Guilty pleas: 68% (52%)
- Conviction after trial: 13% (16%)

---

6   A judge may order an acquittal at the beginning of a trial at the request of the prosecution. This is normally because there has been a significant change in the case, which means that it is no longer possible for the prosecution to proceed: for example a key witness has failed to appear.

7   Directed acquittals may occur at the conclusion of the prosecution case if the judge decides that the prosecution have not presented a case for the defence to answer.

8   The CPS data are taken from the CPS Performance Indicators bulletin for July–September 1997.

- Judge ordered acquittal: 7% (16%)
- Acquittal after trial: 7% (5%)
- Judge directed acquittal: 2% (7%)
- Other outcome (see above): 3% (4%).

The most significant differences between the CPS figures and those obtained by the present research are the higher number of guilty pleas and lower proportions of ordered and directed acquittals in the official figures. It is unlikely that the differences accurately reflect changes in the outcome of Crown Court cases over time. CPS statistics suggest that there are changes from year to year in the proportion of defendants pleading not guilty, for example, but not to the extent suggested by the comparison above. The differences probably arise because the study's sample of Crown Court cases was quite small (n=75) and not necessarily representative of Crown Court cases generally. However, it is probable that the reduction in ordered and directed acquittals is indicative of a trend which has been taking place. An important stimulus for change was research for the RCCJ, which suggested that many such acquittals could have been foreseen and a significant proportion avoided, either by the CPS discontinuing earlier or taking steps to remedy deficiencies in the evidence (Block, Corbett and Peay, 1993). Particularly in relation to judge ordered acquittals, which occur at the end of the prosecution case, the CPS has been concerned in recent years to reduce the proportion of cases which go this far before being aborted. Their most recent Annual Report points to a reduction since 1991/92 in the percentage of contested hearings which result in a directed acquittal.

Because the Crown Court sample was small, it was not sensible to analyse case outcomes there according to the ethnic origin of defendants. Previous research by Hood (1992) has shown that black defendants are much less likely to plead guilty than whites. There is some confirmation of this tendency by the present study, although the numbers involved are too low to be reliable when broken down by ethnic group.

Figure 11.3 Outcome at Crown Court

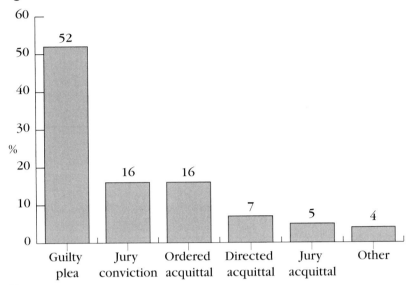

Notes:
1. N=679. Data on outcome were missing in 12 cases.
2. 'Other' includes not guilty plea to lie on file and bench warrant outstanding.

Sentencing in the Crown Court

Sentencing in the Crown Court has been fully considered elsewhere (see, for example, Hood, 1992; Hedderman and Moxon, 1992). Figure 11.4 provides details for the present study of the main sentence passed on those convicted in the Crown Court. Confirming previous studies, sentences were more severe for defendants found guilty in the higher court, with proportionately more receiving custodial sentences. Over 60 per cent of those convicted received an immediate custodial sentence. The main community disposal used was the probation order (in 22% of cases), with other sentences being relatively little used. The factors which most strongly predicted the passing of a custodial sentence have previously been described in relation to sentencing in the magistrates' courts. In brief, these were: having served a previous custodial sentence; possessing previous convictions; seriousness of offence; and having other files outstanding. The numbers of ethnic minority defendants who were convicted was too small to allow any meaningful analysis of Crown Court sentencing according to ethnic group. This issue has been fully examined by Hood (1992).

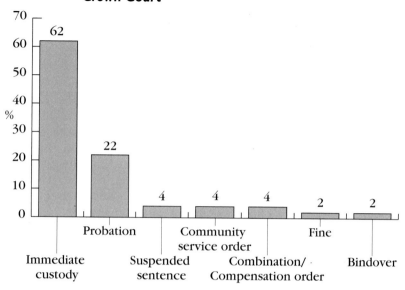

Figure 11.4 **Main sentence for those convicted at the Crown Court**

Note:
N=50. Data on sentencing were missing in one case.

Key points

- Over 90 per cent of defendants were dealt with at magistrates' courts: of these, 82 per cent pleaded guilty, 10 per cent were convicted following trial or in their absence, two per cent had their cases dismissed and four per cent were bound over.

- Defendants in domestic violence cases and those who had not admitted guilt when interviewed by the police were less likely than average to plead guilty.

- Fines were the most common sentence at magistrates' courts (in 37% of cases), followed by absolute or conditional discharges (23%). Ten per cent of those convicted were sentenced to immediate custody and nine per cent were placed on probation.

- Magistrates were most likely to use custodial sentences where the case was serious, and the defendant had previous convictions and other outstanding cases. Use of custody also varied considerably between courts.

- Nine per cent of cases were committed to the Crown Court, although committal rates varied between areas. Committal was more likely where the defendant was an adult, was appearing for serious offences, faced more than one charge, and had refused to answer questions during police interviews. Black and Asian defendants were also more likely than whites to be committed for Crown Court trial.

- The outcome of Crown Court cases was as follows: 52 per cent of defendants were convicted following a guilty plea; 23 per cent were acquitted at the order or direction of the judge; 16 per cent were found guilty; and five per cent were acquitted by a jury.

- Over 60 per cent of those convicted at Crown Court were sentenced to immediate custody, while 22 per cent were placed on probation. Other forms of sentence, including community sentences apart from probation, were relatively little used.

12 From arrest to conviction: an overview

This chapter pulls together information from the two phases of the study in order to provide an overall appreciation of the filtering process which occurs between arrest and conviction. It also touches on an aspect of this process which has not yet been dealt with in any detail, namely the alteration of charges by the CPS. While not having an impact on the number of cases coming before the courts, the alteration of charges has a number of other implications: it affects the number of charges heard, it determines the apparent level of seriousness of the case before the court, and it may be relevant to whether the case is heard in a higher or lower court.

The filtering of cases after arrest

The progress of individual offenders (rather than their offences) from arrest to trial is not well charted by official statistics. For example, while the Home Office's annually published *Criminal Statistics England and Wales* provide a figure for the total number of arrests made by the police each year, their outcome is not given. The number of offences cleared up is recorded, but it is not possible to tell how frequently clear-ups followed on from an arrest. There is a further problem in relating clearances by way of charge or summons either to any prior arrest or to the subsequent outcome of cases as they pass through the CPS and the courts. For, while clearances are expressed in terms of numbers of offences cleared up, proceedings are presented in terms of the number of persons proceeded against. Some suspects will have been arrested and subsequently dealt with for more than one offence. Indeed, the present study found that defendants faced an average of 1.75 charges each. Where a defendant faces multiple charges, it is possible for a case to proceed, even though one or more of the offences charged are dropped. The filtering process following arrest may therefore look rather different if it is examined from the point of view of suspects/defendants rather than offences[1]. Lastly, there are certain discrepancies between different sets of official statistics, depending on their derivation and the counting rules used. For example, the Home Office and CPS compile statistics on discontinuance on a different basis. The former include as discontinued any cases in which a charge is altered 'mid-term' or

---

1   See Barclay (1995) for an overview of the attrition process within the criminal justice system between the commission of an offence and conviction.

where one offence is dropped, even though proceedings continue on other charges (Home Office, 1997a).

It has been left to research studies to chart the progress of offenders through the criminal process. Prior to the present study, four are known to have been conducted. The most wide-ranging of these was that by McConville, Sanders and Leng (1991). They charted the progress of 1,080 cases from initial arrest or report for summons through to conviction, using file data and interviews with relevant decision-makers. Exactly 50 per cent of cases resulted in prosecution and 21 per cent in a caution, while no further action was taken in 25 per cent[2]. Of the entire sample, 37 per cent of cases resulted in conviction and two per cent in a not guilty verdict; six per cent (equating to 13% of cases where the police brought charges) were dropped by the CPS. While this study provides valuable information about the shape of the attrition process, it should be noted that it was conducted some while ago[3], in the very early months of the CPS's existence. Indeed, initial prosecution action on some cases was conducted before the introduction of the CPS. There have been various developments in prosecution policy and practice since then which are likely to have affected the attrition process. Nationally, for example, the proportion of cases discontinued increased considerably between 1987 and 1992 (Crisp and Moxon, 1994) (although, it should be noted that the discontinuance rate in the McConville study was, at 13 per cent, much higher than the national rate at the time of eight per cent).

A more recent study by Godson and Quade (1994) charted the progress of all those arrested and detained at one Hampshire police station during a three-month period in 1992. Unlike the McConville, Sanders and Leng research, this study did not examine police decision-making in any detail and CPS decisions not at all. They found that 68 per cent of their sample were charged or summonsed, 13 per cent cautioned and 19 per cent NFAed. In all, 50 per cent of arrests resulted in a conviction, two per cent in a not guilty verdict, and nine per cent in termination by the CPS. The value of the findings is limited by the restriction of the study to one station. This may help explain the higher charge and lower cautioning rates compared with the McConville work. The higher rate of termination by the CPS may reflect the upward trend nationally in the figures between 1987 and 1992.

A third study is that by Jefferson and Walker (1992). They examined the criminal justice outcomes for a sample of males aged 16 to 35 arrested in Leeds. While the study was able to compare cases involving white, black and Asian suspects, the range of information presented was limited and there was no assessment of CPS decision-making. Moreover, the study has been criticised on a number of methodological grounds, including its failure to take account of

---

2   In the remaining four per cent, the police either issued an informal warning, took some other non-prosecutorial action (e.g. TIC) or the outcome was not known.

3   The cases included in the research were drawn from six police stations in three forces, starting in March 1986

whether suspects were or were not eligible for a caution, depending upon whether they had provided an admission of guilt (FitzGerald, 1993).

The last study is that by Grace, Lloyd and Smith (1992), looking at the attrition process in rape cases. While providing useful insights into the reasons why many such cases fail, it is of limited relevance in the present context because of its restriction to the one category of offence and the fact that it was conducted prior to the introduction of the CPS.

Findings from the present study

Figure 12.1 provides an overall picture of the outcome of cases in the sample[4]. Forty per cent of suspects were convicted of an offence, either at magistrates' courts or in the Crown Court. This is close to the figure of 37 per cent found by McConville, Sanders and Leng (1991). One reason for the slightly higher figure for convictions in the present study is that the charge rate was higher (by two percentage points). The study's conviction rate is also likely to have been affected by the slight under-representation of serious cases in part two. Such cases are more likely to go to the Crown Court, where the acquittal rate is higher than in the magistrates' courts. The conviction rate, based only on those cases which it was possible to monitor (see footnote 4), may therefore be rather higher than would have been the case if it had been possible to track *all* cases.

Figure 12.1 From arrest to conviction: the final outcome of cases

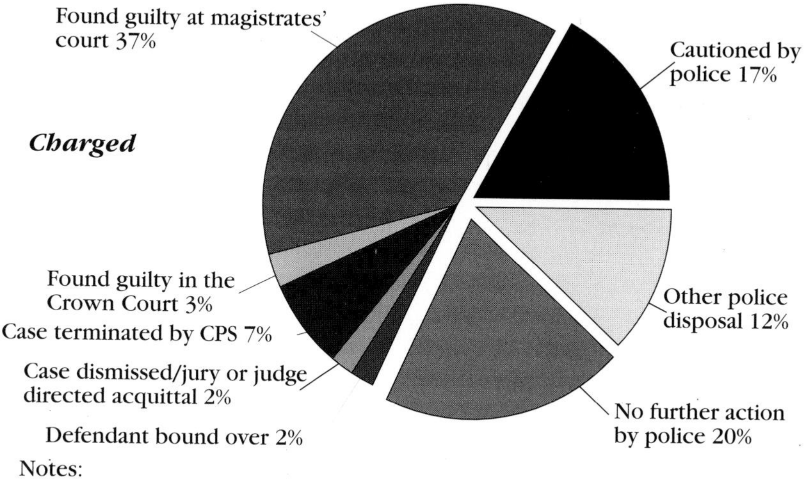

Found guilty at magistrates' court 37%

Cautioned by police 17%

Charged

Found guilty in the Crown Court 3%

Case terminated by CPS 7%

Case dismissed/jury or judge directed acquittal 2%

Defendant bound over 2%

Other police disposal 12%

No further action by police 20%

Notes:
1. 'Other police disposal' includes suspects transferred to other stations, informally warned and detained on warrant.
2. Those arrested for breach of the peace who were subsequently bound over were not technically charged. For convenience, they have been included with those charged with other offences, who were later bound over.

4   Not all cases in which the police brought charges were tracked through to the CPS. The discontinuance and conviction rates are based on those cases which were monitored and these rates were then applied to the sample as a whole.

The 40 per cent who were convicted were not, of course, the only suspects who were dealt with officially in some way. To these must be added the 17 per cent who were cautioned and the two per cent who were bound over by the court. Also, a small proportion of those classified under 'other police disposal' in Figure 12.1 were given informal warnings by the police, a few had offences taken into consideration at court, and a further small percentage were transferred to other police stations, where proceedings resulting in eventual conviction may have been instituted. Therefore, over 60 per cent of suspects – a best estimate is in the region of 63 or 64 per cent – were dealt with officially by the criminal justice system in some way. Correspondingly, around 36 or 37 per cent of suspects were not subject to any official action. For the most part, the decision that no action should be taken was made early on: the police themselves made the decision against taking any further action in well over 20 per cent of cases[5]. In a further seven per cent (equating to 14% of cases charged by the police), the decision was made by the CPS. In only two per cent was there a full court hearing resulting in dismissal or acquittal.

Stop/search arrests

The attrition rate in cases which originated from a stop/search was slightly lower than for cases generally. While, as has been noted earlier, those arrested following a stop/search were slightly less likely than other suspects to be charged and slightly more likely to be NFAed (the cautioning rate was the same as for suspects generally), in the later stages of the criminal process cases arising from stop/searches were slightly more likely than others to succeed. Thus, the termination rate for stop/search cases was only seven per cent, compared with the average of 14 per cent, and the conviction rate at court was slightly higher than average. The net effect was that 41 per cent of those arrested following a stop/search were convicted. This is very close to the figure of 39 per cent found by Young's (1994) study set in North London.

Domestic violence cases

Securing convictions in domestic violence cases presents particular difficulties. Attempts have been made by both the Home Office – notably through Circular 60/1990 – and the CPS in its guidelines on the prosecution of domestic violence cases to ensure that such cases are, where appropriate, pursued to conviction. As noted earlier, there appears to be some enthusiasm by the police to press charges in domestic violence cases. However, problems then appear to surface in taking cases to court. The termination rate is much higher than average, due to various problems associated with witnesses (the most common being refusal to give

---

5   A significant proportion of the 'other police disposal' category equated to 'no further action'. These were, for example, cases in which suspects were not charged with the offences for which they had been arrested but were found to be wanted on warrant for other offences and were detained for court. Also, in some cases suspects were released (rather than bailed) pending further enquiries, but no further action was subsequently taken.

evidence). These problems persist if cases reach court. The net effect of this attrition in the later stages of the process is that only around 21 per cent of those arrested for domestic violence offences are convicted. Even if those who are bound over by the court are included (a further 8 %), the attrition rate in domestic violence cases is considerably higher than average.

Right of silence

The proportion of arrests which led to a conviction differed considerably according to whether the suspect had exercised his or her right of silence during police interviews. Roughly half of all suspects who had refused to answer some or all police questions were convicted, compared with 37 per cent of those who had co-operated at interview.

These figures are the product of two competing influences. On the one hand, suspects who have not provided an admission are ineligible to be cautioned[6]. Clearly, those who have refused all police questions and some of those who have selectively refused to answer will not have provided admissions. If, therefore, the police decide to take some form of official action against the suspect, they are obliged to put the case forward for prosecution rather than administer a caution (see Chapter 6). It is also relevant that suspects who exercised their right of silence were more likely to have previous convictions and to have been arrested for more serious offences (see Chapter 5) - both factors which reduce the likelihood of a caution.

On the other hand, the CPS is much more likely to terminate cases in which the suspect has exercised the right of silence (this is related to the lack of an admission to assist the case - see Chapter 10) than those where there are admissions. Also, right of silence cases are slightly less likely when they reach court to result in a conviction. However, the effect of the first of these factors (i.e. the higher charge rate in right of silence cases) far outweighs that of the other two, resulting in the relatively high proportion of arrests resulting in convictions in right of silence cases. It should be noted that when convictions and cautions are added together, roughly similar proportions of right of silence and other cases result in some official action (55 % and 57% respectively).

It is likely that the dynamics of the process which result in different conviction rates for those who do and do not exercise their right of silence have changed since the introduction of the provisions of the CJPOA 1994. In some circumstances it is now possible for courts to draw proper inferences from the suspect's refusal to answer police questions. Research on the provisions suggests that far fewer suspects are now exercising their right of

---

6   However, the present study and previous research by Evans (1993) suggests that cautions are sometimes administered where the suspect has apparently not admitted guilt.

silence during police interviews (Bucke and Brown, 1997). And, it would appear that CPS lawyers and courts are prepared, where appropriate, to attach evidential significance to the suspect's silence (Bucke, Street and Brown, in press). This may have had some impact both on CPS and court decision-making as well as on that of defendants and their legal advisers.

Alteration of charges by the CPS

Besides the filtering out of cases at various points in the process between arrest and trial, a second, less visible form of filtering takes place in some cases. This is the alteration by the CPS of charges originally brought by the police. It would not be strictly accurate to refer to this process as case attrition, since a case against the suspect is proceeded with. Nor is it accurate to refer to it as charge attrition, for although the CPS tend most often to reduce charges, the research also found instances of charges being increased or ones of equivalent gravity being substituted.

McConville, Sanders and Leng (1991) argue that the criminal justice system in this country depends heavily on a high proportion of defendants pleading guilty and that bargains between prosecution and defence, whereby the defendant agrees to plead guilty to a lesser offence than that charged, are essential to avoid the courts being blocked with a plethora of contested cases. According to their argument, charges tend to be down-graded not as the result of any searching independent scrutiny of the case by CPS lawyers but in response to the defence signalling non-acceptance of the case as constructed by the police. The official view, as stated in the most recent CPS Annual Report (CPS, 1997) and in the Code for Crown Prosecutors (CPS, 1994a) is that a key task of CPS lawyers is to ensure that the right defendants are prosecuted on the right charges. Charges should: "reflect the seriousness of the offending; give the court adequate sentencing powers; and enable the case to be presented to the court in a clear and simple way" (CPS, 1997: 43). The Code goes on to emphasise that prosecutors should never press ahead with a serious charge just to encourage a defendant to plead guilty to a lesser one; nor should they accept a guilty plea to a lesser offence just because it is convenient, but should be satisfied that the court is able to pass a sentence that matches the seriousness of the offending. If the official view is accepted, the corollary is that much of the alteration of charges which occurs is a response to uneven charging practice by the police. It is for this reason that the CPS has recently begun to introduce a series of charging standards for different offences, in order to clarify what charge is appropriate for a given level of criminal behaviour or injury. The first to be issued related to assault offences (CPS, 1994c). Guidance has also been issued on public order charges and others are in preparation (CPS, 1997).

Whatever the reason for the alteration of charges (and both those mentioned above may have some validity), it is well established that in particular kinds of offence the CPS do quite frequently alter the charges brought by the police. Hedderman and Moxon (1992) found that this was particularly common practice in relation to section 18 charges of wounding with intent. More recent work by the Home Office Research and Statistics Directorate has confirmed that charge reduction in assault cases generally remains relatively common (Home Office, 1997c).

The present research presents a similar picture in relation to assault cases, as well as pointing to charge reduction in a significant minority of cases in other offence categories. For example, charges were altered in 22 per cent of fraud and forgery cases. The charge most often heard at court instead was one of theft. Figure 12.2 provides a more detailed breakdown of the way in which charges were altered for four groups of offences: assault; burglary; handling; and public order offences. Assault charges were the ones most often varied (in over one-third of cases) and nearly three-quarters of these changes amounted to charge reduction. The situation was less clear-cut in the other categories. In burglary cases it was more common to substitute an alternative rather than a lesser charge. Charge reduction occurred in public order cases, but it was nearly as common to prefer an alternative charge.

Figure 12.2 Alteration by the CPS of charges orginally brought by the police

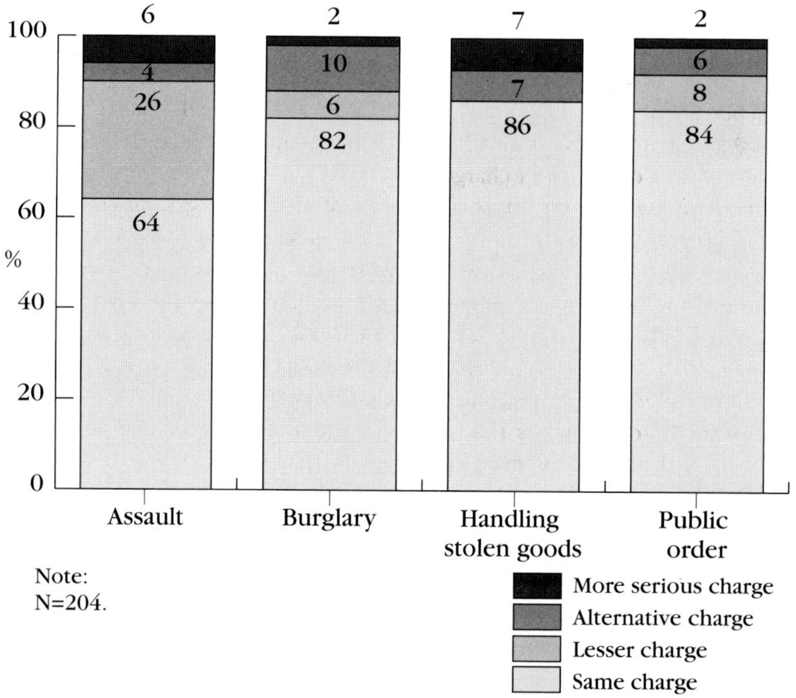

Note:
N=204.

Legend:
- More serious charge
- Alternative charge
- Lesser charge
- Same charge

Where charges were altered, CPS lawyers were asked their reasons for doing so. Those commonly cited were that the new charge more closely reflected the available evidence or that the defendant had indicated that he or she would plead guilty to a lesser or alternative charge. In the latter situation, some lawyers indicated that they were happy that the court possessed adequate sentencing powers to deal with the offender, no doubt prompted by the exhortation in the Code for Crown Prosecutors that they should not accept a guilty plea to a lesser offence simply for convenience's sake. However, Hedderman and Moxon's (1992) research suggests that a major factor in defendants changing plea prior to Crown Court trial was the expectation that a reduction in charges would lead to a lighter sentence. Without more detailed examination of the facts of individual cases it is not possible to say whether a reduction in charges did indeed help to ensure that defendants escaped lightly or whether the new charges simply reflected a more realistic appraisal of the salient features of the case.

Another important factor mentioned by lawyers as leading to the reduction of charges was the difficulty of proving intent. The downgrading of s.18 wounding with intent to s.20 wounding provides the best example of charge reduction for this reason. Where charges were upgraded, the gravity of the offence was most often cited as the reason for doing so.

As noted above, since the present research was conducted, the CPS has gradually been introducing charging standards for particular categories of offence. The first two to be implemented related to assault and public order offences. While it is too early to assess the impact of the latter, there are some indications of the effect of the former. In particular, the Home Office's annually published *Criminal Statistics England and Wales* show that the proportion of those proceeded against for indictable offences of violence who were committed for Crown Court trial has increased (Home Office, 1997a). Other work by the Home Office's Research and Statistics Directorate also suggests that there have been changes in police charging practice. In particular, many cases that would formerly have been charged as s.47 ABH are now being charged as common assault (Home Office, 1997c). However, the same work found strong evidence that assault charges continue to be reduced after committal and that, at court, more serious charges are still dropped in a significant minority of cases in return for a guilty plea to a less serious offence. It may be that what McConville, Sanders and Leng (1991) have referred to as the dependence of the criminal justice process on guilty pleas means that such practices will persist despite the development of charging standards.

Key points

- Of those arrested by the police, 40 per cent were eventually convicted of an offence, 17 per cent were cautioned and two per cent bound over. The police decided to take no further action against 20 per cent, while the case against a further seven per cent was dropped by the CPS. In only two per cent of cases was there a court hearing resulting in dismissal of the case or acquittal of the defendant.

- The proportion of arrests for domestic violence offences leading to conviction was, at 21 per cent, much lower than average. A further eight per cent of those arrested were bound over by the court.

- Suspects who had exercised their right of silence during police questioning were far more likely to be convicted than those who had answered police questions (around half compared with 37%). Many of the latter were dealt with early on by way of a caution. This option was ruled out for those who had exercised their right of silence, not only because of the lack of an admission, but also because they often had previous convictions and had been arrested for more serious offences.

- The CPS altered charges originally brought by the police in over a third of cases of violence against the person and nearly a quarter of fraud cases. Somewhat smaller proportions of burglary, handling and public order cases also proceeded on amended charges.

- Where charges were altered, this was most likely to amount to reduction in violence and public order cases and the substitution of alternative charges in burglary cases. In a small proportion of cases in all categories charges were increased in seriousness.

- The reasons most often cited for altering charges were: to reflect the available evidence; to respond to defendants' willingness to plead guilty to a different (usually less serious) charge; and to overcome problems in proving the requisite intent.

Part 3: Conclusions

The research described in this report constitutes perhaps the most thorough attempt so far undertaken to trace the progress of those arrested by the police from the time of arrival at the police station up to conviction. In doing so, it has provided a range of information of considerable value to policy makers and others. Four main themes can be emphasised. Firstly, at the most basic level, the study provides descriptive data about the arrest population in police stations. Secondly, the study charts the progress through the system of different sub-groups of suspects (for example, those from ethnic minorities and mentally disordered offenders) and shows how the path which they follow and the points at which cases drop out of the system vary. Thirdly, the research forms a useful baseline against which to assess the impact of a range of recent criminal justice initiatives. Lastly, it casts light on some of the dynamics affecting the processing of suspects, which have a bearing on the eventual outcome of cases (for example, the effect of exercise of the right of silence and custody officer and CPS decision-making). Each of these themes is considered in more detail below.

The arrest population

The original catalyst for the present research was increasing concern that, each year, around 1.75 million people are arrested by the police, but little information is known about who they are, what offences they are alleged to have committed, and what happens to them. Various studies have provided some information on these issues, but the present research is probably the most comprehensive and systematic attempt so far to establish such information. What, then, are the salient features of the arrest population at police stations?

- The bulk of suspects have been arrested for offences of intermediate severity: typically these are theft or handling offences, and of these, very many involve shoplifting or vehicle crime. Burglaries also feature prominently in crime at this level. Well over a third of suspects have been detained for relatively minor offences, typically against public order. Only around four per cent have been arrested for crime at the top end of seriousness: for example, serious violence against the person and rape.

- The sequence of events leading to arrest most frequently begins with the police being alerted by their control room or a member of the public that a crime is in progress or has recently occurred. Less than a quarter of arrests occur through proactive police tactics, such as conducting enquiries, surveillance or stop and search.

- At the time of arrest, the most important evidence against the suspect is usually eyewitness evidence, most often from the police themselves, but also from victims or observers. Physical evidence (e.g. goods believed to be stolen) or forensic evidence such as fingerprints also figure in around a fifth of cases.

- One feature of the arrest population, which is not often appreciated, is that a significant minority (13%) have been arrested not because they are suspected of having committed an offence but for a range of other reasons. Some have failed to turn up at court and there is a warrant for their arrest. Others are prisoners who are in transit between prison and court, either awaiting trial or escort to prison following the passing of a custodial sentence. Yet another group have been detained at a police station as a place of safety under the Mental Health Act 1983.

- Domestic violence features in an important minority of arrests: six per cent of all arrests and over a quarter of arrests for violence against the person relate to alleged incidents of domestic violence.

- The arrest population is far from representative of the general population. It is largely male. The ethnic composition also differs, with 13 per cent of those arrested being black and six per cent Asian (compared with 1.4% and 2.8% of the general population). Younger age groups feature predominantly, with 40 per cent being aged 20 or under and nearly three-quarters being less than 30. Well over half are unemployed at the time of arrest. Over 60 per cent already have previous convictions and over 40 per cent a previous police caution.

- A significant minority of those arrested are deemed to be vulnerable in some way. Thus, 15 per cent are aged 16 or under and two per cent are believed to suffer from mental disorder: both groups require special safeguards to be set in motion by the police. Other suspects also sometimes require particular care in the way they are handled: nearly 15 per cent are intoxicated to some degree on arrival and, of these, around a third are too drunk to deal with immediately; two per cent are clearly under the influence of drugs and three per cent are suffering from illness.

Groups of suspects raising particular concerns

The study made it possible to map the path through the criminal process of particular sub-groups of suspects who, for different reasons, have been the source of concern in recent years. Four groups were of particular interest: members of ethnic minorities; suspects arrested as a result of stop/searches; the mentally disordered; and those suspected of perpetrating incidents of domestic violence.

Ethnic minority suspects

There has long been a debate about whether the criminal justice system discriminates against members of ethnic minorities or whether ethnic minorities are disproportionately involved in crime. However, as FitzGerald and Sibbitt (1997) note, the debate was for long characterised by the lack of hard evidence. Gradually, ethnic monitoring has been introduced in different areas of the criminal justice system, beginning in the 1980s with prisons. This process was given impetus by the Criminal Justice Act 1991. Section 95 requires the Home Secretary to publish each year information to enable those engaged in the administration of criminal justice to avoid discrimination on grounds (inter alia) of race. Initially, in the early 1990s, it was apparent that relatively little such information was routinely collected in relation to the arrest process or subsequent police or CPS decision-making (Home Office, 1992a). Where data were available, they tended to be drawn from research which had examined specific aspects of the arrest or processing of suspects (for example, stop and search or police cautioning) (FitzGerald, 1993). A start has now been made on routine ethnic monitoring of certain police activity: thus, from April 1996, the police have been required to record the ethnic origin of those stopped and searched, arrested or formally cautioned (FitzGerald and Sibbitt, 1997). And, within the CPS, a start was made in 1996 on monitoring decision-making (CPS, 1997). However, at the time the present research was begun, these initiatives either did not exist or were embryonic. Moreover, some aspects covered by the present research – for example, exercise of the right of silence and police bail decisions – are not included within any ethnic monitoring programme.

The present study therefore provides a unique and integrated set of data about the processing of ethnic minority suspects compared with their white counterparts from the time of arrest up to disposal at court. It showed that there were ethnic differences – particularly between black and white suspects – at numerous points in this process. Some of the main ones were as follows:

- The proportion of black people among those arrested was much greater than their presence in local populations. They were more likely than whites or Asians to have been arrested following a stop/search.

- Black suspects were more likely to have been arrested for robbery than those from other ethnic groups, while Asians were more likely to have been arrested for fraud and forgery and theft from vehicle offences.

- Black and Asian suspects were significantly more likely than white people to request legal advice while in police custody.

- Black suspects were more likely to exercise their right of silence during police interviews and both they and Asians were less likely than whites to provide confessions.

- Black and Asian suspects were both less likely than white suspects to be given a police caution and more likely to have no further action taken against them by the police.

- Black suspects were significantly less likely than whites or Asians to be referred to juvenile justice teams for a decision about what action should be taken on their case.

- Black and Asian suspects were more likely than whites to be bailed for further enquiries.

- Both black and Asian suspects were less likely than whites to be given bail after charge.

- The CPS were significantly more likely to terminate proceedings in cases involving black or Asian defendants.

- Black defendants were slightly more likely than other groups to be sentenced to custody at magistrates' courts and both they and Asians were more likely than whites to be committed for Crown Court trial.

It is no easy matter to interpret the meaning and significance of these differences. The fact that they permeate each stage of the process from arrest to trial could perhaps be taken to suggest that they are systematic. In other words, they might suggest both that the criminal justice system treats ethnic minority suspects/defendants differently and that they react to it differently. In support of the view that there exists such an 'ethnic' effect it might be noted that some of the statistical analyses in this report show that the ethnic origin of the suspect was a factor which, independently of others, predicted particular outcomes (for example, demand for legal advice, admissions, referral to juvenile justice teams and case termination by the CPS).

However, for several reasons, interpretation is by no means this simple. Firstly and most importantly, it is certain in some instances and highly probable in others that the study was not in possession of information about all relevant variables to make a judgement that ethnic origin alone explained observed differences. For example, it would be necessary to know to what extent members of different ethnic groups were involved in different kinds of crime (particularly street crime) to know whether the disproportionate arrest of black people following stop/searches represented a discriminatory exercise of this power (Young, 1994). Both Reiner (1993) and FitzGerald and Sibbitt (1997) have pointed to the difficulties of pinpointing discriminatory practice in the criminal justice system through statistical analysis (see also Jefferson, 1993). In practice, it is possible to control for only a limited number of legally relevant variables when examining the relationship between ethnic origin and particular outcomes. Some cannot be controlled for, measured satisfactorily or even identified. There is a particular difficulty where information on decision-making is provided by the decision-makers (in this case, police custody officers and CPS lawyers) themselves. Ethnic origin of the suspect/defendant is not a legally relevant variable and might only very occasionally perhaps be relevant as a public interest consideration. However, given the sensitivity of 'race' issues, it is unlikely that decision-makers would refer to ethnic origin as a factor they took into account, even if it entered into their conscious decision-making at all.

Secondly, some differences between ethnic groups disappear or greatly reduce when account is taken of other factors. For example, the lower cautioning rate for black people and Asians is strongly linked with the lower admission rate among these two groups (although this in itself begs the question of why the admission rate is lower among ethnic minority suspects).

Thirdly, it is possible that differences in the treatment of ethnic minority groups at one stage in the process may be countered or compounded by differences at other stages. The higher than average termination rate of cases involving ethnic minorities may, for example, be a way in which one part of the system works to counteract a possible imbalance earlier on (i.e. preferral of charges by the police where the evidence is not sufficient for a successful prosecution). Equally, it is possible that an imbalance at one stage may be added to at a later stage.

These difficulties of interpretation suggest that the findings of the study on ethnic differences should not be taken as evidence that the criminal justice system does discriminate against ethnic minority suspects/defendants. Similarly, although the findings provide some prima facie evidence that members of ethnic minorities also react differently to the criminal justice system (for example, in terms of exercising their right of silence or admitting offences), there is a need for care in interpreting the meaning of this finding. The comments of FitzGerald and Sibbitt (1997) on police ethnic monitoring data on stop and search, arrests and cautions could be taken to apply equally appositely to the present study. They argue that ethnic monitoring data should be treated as 'indicators' which point to areas which require closer scrutiny in order to find out whether the patterns they show give cause for concern. They point to the need, for example, for operational police commanders to examine the way in which officers exercise their discretion when using their stop and search powers. The present study also implies the need to examine the qualitative nature of other decision-making within the criminal justice system to see whether decisions are correctly and fairly made: for example, police decisions whether suspects should be bailed or whether juveniles should be referred for inter-agency consultation, and CPS decisions whether to terminate proceedings. Equally, there is a need to explore decision-making by suspects. Little is known about the reasons why those from ethnic minorities disproportionately seek legal advice and exercise their right of silence. For example, are these decisions a reaction to the way members of ethnic minorities are actually treated as suspects or do they stem from generalised negative perceptions of the police, perhaps built up over a period of years? Or, are these two explanations mutually reinforcing?

Suspects arrested following stop/searches

The exercise by the police of their stop and search powers has often generated controversy. To a large extent this is because black people are significantly more likely to be stopped and searched and to be subject to multiple stop/searches (see FitzGerald, 1993 and Brown, 1997 for an overview of the main studies). As FitzGerald and Sibbitt (1997) point out, the rate at which black people are stopped, along with the quality and content of these encounters, has been seen as a major factor in shaping police–black community relations. In the light of perceptions, in the black community particularly, that stop/search tactics are sometimes unfairly targetted against them, it is important that the exercise of these powers should be shown to be fair and reasonable. Previous research has cast some doubt on the extent to which the police abide by the standard of reasonable suspicion when deciding whether to carry out stop/searches (Bottomley et al., 1989). Others have pointed to the difficulties in defining the concept of reasonable suspicion (Brown, 1997; FitzGerald and Sibbitt, 1997). Obviously, if the yardstick against which police actions are to be assessed is unclear, it is difficult to conclude whether stop and search powers are being exercised fairly and reasonably. These problems aside, it is clear that the great majority of recorded stop/searches[1] – currently around 89 per cent (Wilkins and Addicott, 1997) – produce no result in terms of arrest.

The present study was unable to examine police stop and search practice in the field, but it was able to consider the extent to which arrests following a stop/search were backed up by some kind of formal action against the suspect. This may be taken as another indicator of the fairness of the exercise of stop and search powers. Thus, if arrests following a stop/search are less likely than other arrests to result in such action, this might suggest an over-readiness of the police to make arrests in these circumstances on the basis of weak evidence.

Information from previous work on this issue is sparse. Young (1994) found that 40 per cent of cases arising from stop/searches in an area of North London resulted in a finding of guilt at court, but he provides no figures for cautions and makes no comparison with other arrests. The present study was able to fill in both these gaps. It found that, by and large, stop/search arrests resulted in action against suspects by way of charge or caution in roughly the same proportion of cases as arrests generally (although the charge rate was slightly lower and the NFA rate slightly higher than for other arrests). The proportion of cases in which the evidence on arrest was sufficient to charge was marginally lower than for other arrests. The differences found were not substantial enough to warrant drawing the conclusion that stop/search arrests generally are more weakly based evidentially than other arrests. Furthermore, where cases were forwarded for prosecution, the CPS terminated fewer than average and the conviction rate was also slightly above average. It would appear, therefore, that weak cases are generally being filtered out prior to arrest.

However, there are two caveats to this conclusion. Firstly, black suspects arrested following a stop/search were less likely than whites to be charged or cautioned and much more likely to be NFAed. The reasons for this difference require further exploration. It raises the possibility that arrests of this ethnic minority group are based on weaker evidence. However, there are other possible explanations which merit consideration. In particular, the higher NFA rate for black suspects may be linked with differences in the kinds of offences for which they and white people are arrested. For example, a relatively high number of robbery arrests are of black suspects and the NFA rate for this offence is significantly higher than average. Another factor may be that black suspects are less likely than others to provide admissions of guilt and more likely to exercise their right of silence. Where

---

1   However, an unknown proportion of stop/searches are not recorded by the police – see Chapter 2.

the evidence following arrest in stop/search cases falls short of the standard to charge and suspects themselves provide no further evidence, there may be no option but to take no further action.

The other caveat is that those arrested following stop/searches for stolen property were significantly more likely to be NFAed than those arrested as a result of stop/searches for other reasons. Again, this finding merits closer attention. It could indicate that the initial stop/search and subsequent arrest were not based on reasonable suspicion. But, again, there are other explanations to be explored. The standard of suspicion required to arrest does not have to be equivalent to that required to charge and it may well be the case that some kinds of stop/search create greater difficulty than others in raising the evidence to the level needed to charge. Thus, while the possession of drugs or weapons can provide clear proof of the commission of an offence which suspects are unable to explain away, it may be easier for suspects arrested in possession of items believed to be stolen to provide a plausible explanation when later interviewed.

The mentally disordered

Around two per cent of the sample in the present study were treated by the police as mentally disordered. This is consistent with the findings of other studies which have examined this issue (for example: Brown, 1989; Robertson, Pearson and Gibb, 1995; Bucke and Brown, 1997). The research was able to examine two key issues in relation to this group: their identification and their disposal. Previous research has suggested that by no means all of those suffering from mental disorder are picked up by custody officers (Robertson, 1992; Gudjunsson et al., 1993). However, studies which have reached this conclusion have included some form of assessment or observation by psychiatrists who are likely to pick up on cues missed by custody officers. The present study was not conducted by psychiatrists and cannot therefore pass comment on the proportion of cases which the police may have missed (other than noting that there were a few cases in which detainees behaved bizarrely but were not dealt with as mentally disordered). However, it is able to comment on the action taken by custody officers once they suspected that a person was suffering from mental disorder.

It was observed in Chapter 3 that the most common course of action was initially to call the police surgeon to examine the detainee and await his or her advice before summoning an appropriate adult. There are two points to note here. Firstly, as others have noted, police surgeons are often not well equipped to make judgements about mental disorder (Parker, 1992; Palmer and Hart, 1996; Laing, 1996). There is evidence that, generally, they may be no more likely than custody officers, and possibly less so, to raise concerns about the mental health of detainees and their fitness for detention or interview (Evans and Rawstorne, 1994). Secondly, where the detainee is suspected of an offence and appears to be suffering from mental disorder, under the PACE Codes of Practice the requirement to call an appropriate adult is independent of that to obtain medical attention. As others have again noted, it should be implemented as soon as practicable and not delayed until after the police surgeon's examination (Palmer and Hart, 1996; Brown, 1997; Bucke and Brown, 1997). The net effect of these two points is that there is a danger that some suspects who are suffering from some degree of mental disorder may be deprived of the advice and assistance which an appropriate adult may be able to provide.

The other issue examined was the way in which cases involving the mentally disordered were disposed of. Home Office, 1990c advised that, wherever possible, mentally disordered persons should receive care and treatment from the health and social services. Where there is sufficient evidence that such people have committed offences, consideration should be given to whether prosecution is in the public interest. Alternatives, such as a caution or admission to hospital, should be considered instead. The present research suggests that the police do indeed give serious attention to alternatives to prosecution in cases involving mentally disordered suspects. The proportion charged was below average, while no further action, sometimes in conjunction with admission to hospital, was much more common. It would seem that the main filter in cases involving the mentally disordered is at the police decision-making stage. Only three cases were noted in which the CPS terminated proceedings on the basis of the defendant's mental condition. And there was only one case in which the courts imposed a hospital order.

Suspects arrested for domestic violence

In recent years there have been important developments in the way in which domestic violence cases are dealt with by the police and the CPS. Home Office Circular 60/1990 recommended that the police take a more interventionist approach in such cases, with a presumption in favour of arrest (Grace, 1995). This echoes the introduction of pro-arrest policies in certain parts of North America (Cretney and Davis, 1996), which research has shown to have some success as a response to violent situations in the home (see, for example, Gamache, Edleson and Schock, 1988; and Sherman and Berk, 1984). For their part, the CPS have issued a statement of prosecution policy on domestic violence, the underlying message of which is that domestic violence cases will usually require prosecution if the evidence is available and that discontinuance should only take place when all other options have been considered and found to be inappropriate (CPS, 1993).

The present study was unable to examine police practice in responding to domestic violence incidents and whether the presumption in favour of arrest was being put into practice[2]. However, it was able to examine how domestic violence cases were handled after an arrest had been made. It showed that there appeared to be no want of firm action by the police against domestic violence suspects. They were more likely than other suspects to be charged rather than cautioned, and, where the offence was actually one of violence against the person[3], the charge rate was higher than for offences of violence generally. But once cases had been forwarded to the CPS for prosecution the picture was rather different. The termination rate for domestic violence cases was three times the rate for offences generally and the conviction rate was lower than average. The result was that only just over 20 per cent of those arrested in domestic violence cases were convicted. Other research has also pointed to the high termination rate in domestic violence cases and the difficulties of successful prosecution in the courts (Morley and Mullender, 1994; Cretney and Davis, 1996). In common with these other studies, the present research confirms that the reluctance of complainants to proceed with their complaint and give evidence in court was the most common reason for cases being dropped.

The issues raised by domestic violence cases are complex and, while it is tempting to conclude that the low conviction rate in domestic violence cases represents a high level of "failure", Cretney and Davis (1996) have pointed out that, from the victim's point of view, a discontinued case need not be a "failure" at all. Where the victim does not wish to end the relationship with the abusing partner, the experience of arrest and threat of conviction may be a sufficient deterrent from further violence (although it is arguable whether using the criminal justice system is the best way to achieve this end). Pursuing a prosecution would very probably have the unwanted result of ending the relationship. Cretney and Davis (ibid) also point to other issues: for example, the burden of undergoing the trial process, with all the associated anxiety and publicity, may be too high a price for the complainant to pay for an outcome about which he/she may be equivocal.

In contrast, some complainants opt to withdraw for the very different reason that they experience intimidation or pressure from the abusing partner to do so. The difficulty for the CPS is to get at the truth of the matter in deciding whether termination is the proper course where the complainant is unwilling to give evidence. The CPS's Statement of Prosecution Policy on domestic violence cases (CPS, 1993) makes it clear that the reasons for withdrawal should be gone into thoroughly and not accepted at face value. The statement details a range of measures that should be taken in this

---

2   Other research has examined this issue and has reported that officers are not always aware of the new guidance and, even where they are, considerations such as whether the complainant would be likely to support any police action frequently override the presumption in favour of arrest (Cromack, 1995; Grace, 1995).

3   Some domestic violence cases involved criminal damage or public order charges rather than ones of violence against the person – see Chapter 2

respect, as well as emphasising that options other than discontinuance (for example, compelling the victim to give evidence or proceeding without the victim's evidence) should be considered. While the present research was unable to enquire into the steps taken by the CPS prior to termination in domestic violence cases, Cretney and Davis (1996) reported that, in the area in which their research took place, the withdrawal procedure adopted tended to be much more ad hoc than that laid out in the CPS guidance and did not, for example, clearly address the issue of coercion to withdraw. The present study examined a broader range of areas than did Cretney and Davis. Given that it similarly found a high termination rate in domestic violence cases, it implies the need to examine whether termination in such cases is generally being managed in the careful manner proposed by the CPS's policy statement.

Recent criminal justice initiatives

The 1990s have, so far, been a period of considerable innovation in the criminal justice system. There is in government an assumption that all new initiatives should be evaluated to assess whether they are having the intended impact and to gauge their resource implications. In order to judge effects it is essential to have data about the pre-existing situation against which to measure the scale and nature of any changes. The present study has had a valuable role to play in relation to several recent criminal justice initiatives. One - ethnic monitoring in the police service – has already been discussed. Others include: the introduction of the inferences from silence provisions by the CJPOA 1994; the bail provisions of the same Act; and Home Office Cautioning Circular 18/1994.

Inferences from silence

At the time the present research was conducted, courts were not entitled to draw inferences from the refusal of suspects to answer police questions, nor could such silence be the subject of comment at court. The CJPOA changed this situation. Where those being questioned under caution by the police now fail to mention a fact which they later rely on at court in their defence (and it is something which, in the circumstances, they could reasonably have been expected to mention), then the court may draw such inferences as appear proper. This amounts to a major change in the law of evidence. It would be expected to have a range of effects on the way suspects respond to police questions, on the provision of legal advice to suspects and on the conduct and outcome of cases at court.

The present study was able to provide a range of relevant data about the situation as it was before the new provisions were introduced. In particular, it pointed to the prevalence of silence among suspects in police interviews, and was able to relate police and CPS decision-making, plea and the outcome of cases at court to the exercise of silence. This data has been used to make comparisons with the current situation in research on the CJPOA provisions being carried out by the Home Office's Research and Statistics Directorate. Findings so far published show that there has been a significant decline in the proportion of suspects now refusing to answer police questions during interview (Bucke and Brown, 1997). A further report which will examine the broader impact of the provisions on the prosecution and court process is in preparation (Bucke, Street and Brown, in press).

Bail

The CJPOA contains a range of provisions relating to bail. One underlying aim of them is to reduce the level of offences committed by those already on bail. One provision (s.28) now enables the police to detain for court those charged with imprisonable offences, where they have reasonable grounds for believing that this is necessary to prevent them from committing further offences. And, under s.27 the police are now able to attach conditions to bail once a person has been charged. Previously, the police had little choice where they wished to constrain the offending behaviour of those charged but to detain them for the next available court (Raine and Willson, 1994).

The present study provides one source of information about police bail practice prior to the implementation of these provisions[4]. It details, for example, what proportion of suspects were refused bail after charge and on what grounds. It also provides a measure of the extent of offending on bail (the proportion of those charged who were on bail at the time of charge). Since the introduction of the new provisions, several studies have provided information about their effect and certain comparisons are possible with the present study's data. For example, Raine and Willson (1996) and Bucke and Brown (1997) found that the power to attach conditions to police bail is being used in roughly one-fifth of cases in which suspects are bailed after charge, but that there has been little reduction in the proportion detained for court. Rather, conditions are tending to be used where the suspect would formerly have been given unconditional bail. In terms of the impact of the provisions on levels of offending on bail, recent work by the Home Office's Research and Statistics Directorate suggests that offending by adults is being held in check, but that there has been a continued rise in offending by juveniles (Brown, 1998).

---

4   Further information is provided in studies by Burrows, Henderson and Morgan (1994) and Morgan and Henderson (1998).

Police cautioning

There have been several Home Office circulars in recent years aimed at influencing police cautioning practice. While fieldwork for the present research was in progress, that in force was the 1990 circular. Like the previous 1985 circular, it sought to encourage consistency in caution decision-making and multi-agency consultation. It also emphasised the part that cautioning had to play in diverting juveniles and first-time offenders from formal proceedings. Up until the early 1990s, the cautioning rate for all age groups rose steadily. The 1994 circular again stressed the goal of consistency. But it also emphasised that cautions should not be used in inappropriate cases (particularly indictable only offences) and that those who had previously been cautioned should not generally receive a second caution. It was followed by more detailed guidance issued by ACPO (1995), which set out a system of 'gravity factors' to help the police decide on the most appropriate disposal for a given offence, taking into account any aggravating or mitigating circumstances that might be present.

The present research provided baseline information about police cautioning practice prior to the introduction of the 1994 circular and the ACPO guidance. In particular, it showed what proportion of those arrested are cautioned and identified the factors which decision-makers consider important in arriving at this disposal. Two studies carried out since point to some effects of the 1994 circular and the ACPO guidance. Evans and Ellis (1997) point to a decrease in the cautioning rate for juveniles and a levelling off for other age groups, while Bucke and Brown (1997) report a similar trend among a sample of suspects arrested by the police. As yet, no study has examined how the decision-making process may have changed. The present research suggests that the seriousness of the offence and whether the suspect had previous cautions were already factors which decision-makers considered important. If the circular is having the intended effect, it might be expected that yet further emphasis is now placed upon them. Another aspect of the decision-making process which awaits examination is the role of inter-agency consultation in cases involving juveniles. The cases considered by multi-agency panels often tend to be ones where the decision to caution is a borderline one, perhaps because the suspect has previous cautions. Evans and Ellis (1997) have suggested that one effect of the 1994 circular may have been to marginalise such panels. Firstly, the circular points out that the role of panels is purely *advisory*; secondly, that the final decision rests with the police in all cases; and, lastly, that repeat cautioning cannot usually be justified. However, there is no firm information as yet about the circular's effect on the working relationships between police and other agencies involved in caution decision-making.

The dynamics of the processing of suspects

An important theme to emerge from the research is the contingent nature of the processing of suspects after arrest. The study has shown that the path which they follow through the criminal justice system, the decisions made by and about suspects, and the eventual outcome of cases are dependent upon a range of eventualities. To expand on this point, the study examined several key events or stages during the course of the suspect's progression from arrest to trial. These included: the suspect's decision to seek legal advice; admission of guilt; police decisions whether to take any action against the suspect and, if so, whether this should be charge or caution; police decisions whether to refer juveniles for inter-agency consultation; CPS decisions whether to terminate proceedings; committal of cases to Crown Court; and the imposition of a custodial sentence. The study has shown how the outcome at each point is strongly associated with a range of key factors. It is not proposed to repeat these here because they have been fully documented earlier. But, as an example, the likelihood of suspects providing admissions is strongly related to the evidence against them, whether they have obtained legal advice, the type of offence for which they have been arrested, their ethnic origin, gender and age and the station at which they are being held.

Furthermore, there is what might be termed the theme of 'inter-relatedness'. There are two aspects to this. One is that decisions or events at one point in the system affect decisions or events at later points. An example is provided by the link between legal advice, admission and case outcome. Thus, having initially decided whether to obtain legal advice, whether the suspect then admits the offence is strongly linked with the outcome of that decision, while case outcome is in turn linked both with whether the suspect is legally advised and whether he or she has admitted the offence. The other aspect of the 'inter-relatedness' theme is that certain common factors appear to be significantly linked with decisions or events at a number of stages of the process. Two which stand out are the suspect's ethnic origin and previous convictions. Ethnic origin is strongly associated with requests for legal advice, admission, referral of juvenile cases for inter-agency consultation and case termination. And whether the suspect has previous convictions is closely related to demand for legal advice, whether the suspect is charged or cautioned, case termination and imposition of a custodial sentence.

These findings have more than academic interest. Their value is in enhancing understanding of the way in which the criminal justice system works. This, in turn, is essential for policy makers in helping them plan new initiatives and gauge their likely effect. Such information is particular crucial at a time of rapid innovation and change in the criminal justice system.

Appendix A
Supplementary tables

Table A.1 *Socio-demographic details of sample by ethnic origin*

	All		White		Black		Asian		Other	
	%	(n)	%	(n)	%	(n)	%	(n)	%	(n)
Male	85	(3,568)	84	(2,788)	85	(460)	96	(300)	69	(20)
Under 17	15	(635)	13	(462)	21	(116)	17	(54)	10	(3)
17–20	22	(936)	23	(766)	15	(82)	27	(84)	14	(4)
21–29	33	(1,393)	33	(1,102)	34	(185)	30	(94)	41	(12)
30 and over	30	(1,238)	30	(988)	29	(159)	26	(81)	35	(10)
Unemployed	55	(2,282)	57	(1,868)	50	(265)	46	(139)	39	(10)
Resident locally	76	(3,150)	76	(2,504)	69	(371)	84	(257)	64	(18)
Previous cautions	43	(1,426)	44	(1,155)	41	(177)	29	(85)	38	(9)
Previous convictions	63	(2,456)	65	(1,983)	60	(308)	49	(150)	56	(15)

Notes:
1. Table is based on all detainees: n=4,250.
2. Percentages do not always sum to 100 due to rounding.
3. 'Resident locally' refers to detainees who normally lived within the area covered by one of the police stations taking part in the research.

Table A.2　Reason for arrest by station

Offence/reason	Str %	Roc %	Lut %	QR %	BL %	BR %	Fai %	Gat %	Hac %	Cr %	All %
Offences											
Violence	8	7	5	9	11	6	7	4	9	7	**7**
Sexual	<1	1	2	2	3	1	1	1	1	1	**1**
Burglary	11	10	8	10	13	8	6	6	9	4	**8**
Robbery	3	1	2	3	1	2	2	1	3	2	**2**
Theft and handling:	28	30	34	28	34	21	30	27	16	36	**29**
Shoplifting	8	5	13	<1	5	3	6	4	2	21	**8**
Theft of vehicle/ TWOC	10	12	10	10	14	6	11	12	2	3	**9**
Theft from vehicle	1	4	4	5	2	1	2	1	2	1	**2**
Other theft & handling	9	9	7	13	13	11	11	10	10	11	**10**
Fraud and forgery	3	2	3	3	4	<1	4	2	5	5	**3**
Criminal damage	6	4	6	4	9	5	6	6	7	6	**6**
Drugs	3	4	4	2	2	1	3	1	6	3	**3**
Public order	11	10	10	13	5	10	11	13	18	16	**12**
Motoring	9	5	9	11	10	12	5	7	9	5	**8**
Prostitution	-	<1	1	<1	-	16	1	-	-	-	**2**
Other offences	4	3	2	4	3	4	8	3	2	2	**3**
Other detention Warrant, place of safety, transfers from prison to court, etc	11	18	12	7	6	9	12	27	10	8	**13**
Total n											**4,250**

Notes:
1. The table is based on all detainees.
2. Str=Stretford; Roc=Rochdale; Lut=Luton; QR=Queen's Road; BL=Beaumont Leys; BR=Birmingham Road; Fai=Fairwater; Gat=Gateshead; Hac=Hackney; Cr=Croydon.
3. TWOC – taking motor vehicle without lawful authority.
4. Other detention includes remands to police custody under s.48 PACE.
5. Percentages do not always sum to 100 due to rounding.

Table A.3   How incident came to police attention by offence

Offence	Command and control %	Info received %	Incident in progress %	Surveillance enquiries %	Stop search %	Call public %	Other %
Violence	36	22	11	11	1	10	9
Sexual	25	53	-	13	3	8	-
Burglary	24	23	10	17	3	10	12
Robbery	22	37	8	8	3	19	3
Shoplifting	61	18	4	3	2	11	1
Theft of vehicle	21	20	22	19	14	3	3
TWOC	15	18	25	12	22	5	3
Theft from vehicle	39	17	11	21	6	6	-
Other theft/handling	23	32	6	19	11	6	3
Fraud & forgery	17	31	4	22	4	14	8
Criminal damage	48	14	13	8	1	13	2
Drug	4	15	3	14	49	4	11
Other notifiable	24	15	11	28	17	4	1
Public order	34	6	37	3	5	12	5
Motoring	11	6	27	12	37	1	6
Prostitution	-	-	46	54	-	-	-
Miscellaneous	21	42	6	10	14	2	6

Notes:
1. N=3,161. Data were missing in 31 cases. Arresting officers failed to return questionnaires in a further 490 cases.
2. TWOC – taking a motor vehicle without lawful authority.
3. Percentages do not always sum to 100 due to rounding.

Table A.4 Main evidence available at time of arrest by offence

Offence	Material/ forensic	Medical	Indepen dent E/W	Police E/W	Security E/W	Victim E/W	MO	Circum.	Info O. sus Inform.	Info	Other
	%	%	%	%	%	%	%	%	%	%	%
Violence	9	19	28	23	3	69	1	7	2	2	2
Sexual	11	11	16	5	-	92	8	5	5	3	-
Burglary	30	2	37	31	3	14	2	21	6	7	4
Robbery	3	3	41	23	-	55	3	16	11	16	8
Shoplifting	10	<1	24	4	75	4	<1	5	1	1	3
Theft of veh.	27	1	25	47	1	8	2	20	4	5	4
TWOC	17	-	17	58	2	4	1	27	7	4	9
Theft fr. veh.	13	-	46	32	9	12	5	16	4	7	1
Other T & H	34	-	23	21	5	13	1	19	7	9	3
Fraud & forg.	46	1	23	17	12	11	5	17	9	6	7
Crim. damage	15	1	49	19	4	36	1	13	5	3	5
Drugs	47	-	5	48	1	-	-	6	2	23	4
Other not.	18	4	19	70	2	8	-	12	2	2	2
Public order	5	1	12	82	2	14	2	3	1	2	3
Motoring Prostitution	24	2	4	71	-	2	<1	4	<1	1	9
Miscell.	42	-	25	6	-	6	-	6	-	29	12

Note:
1. N=3,169. Data were missing in 23 cases. Arresting officers failed to return questionnaires in a further 490 cases.
2. TWOC – taking a motor vehicle without lawful authority.

Table A.5   Police time spent on cases by offence

Hours	Up to 1 hr	1-3 hrs	3-6 hrs	6-10 hrs	10-20 hrs	20-50 hrs	50+ hrs
	%	%	%	%	%	%	%
Notifiable							
Violence	9	32	28	13	10	2	6
Sexual	10	24	17	12	15	12	10
Burglary	6	26	27	20	12	7	3
Robbery	3	17	30	14	13	6	17
Theft & Hand.	8	32	37	10	7	3	4
Fraud & Forg.	11	22	31	15	11	6	4
Criminal dam.	12	39	27	12	4	2	4
Drugs	10	38	38	8	1	3	1
Other not.	10	30	29	19	5	2	5
Non-notifiable							
Public order	36	32	19	5	1	1	7
Motoring	37	38	14	5	1	1	4
Prostitution	96	3	-	-	-	-	1
Misc offs.	21	17	23	10	10	-	19
Detention	-	43	-	14	-	-	43
Total %	**17**	**31**	**28**	**10**	**6**	**3**	**5**
n	**544**	**992**	**895**	**332**	**190**	**87**	**159**

Notes:
1.   N=3,199. Arresting officers failed to return questionnaires in a further 490 cases.
2.   Percentages do not always sum to 100 due to rounding.

Table A.6 Evidence available to CPS at time of prosecution by offence

Offence	Physical/ Forensic	Medical	Indep EW	Police EW	Victim EW	Sec'y EW	Full Con	Part Admit	MO	Circ-st'l	Other	None
	%	%	%	%	%	%	%	%	%	%	%	%
Notifiable												
Violence	11	42	32	27	80	5	14	29	-	8	2	-
Sexual	14	-	29	-	86	-	14	29	14	14	-	-
Burglary	32	1	47	38	15	1	30	24	1	20	8	1
Robbery	33	-	67	11	79	-	22	33	-	-	11	-
Theft & hand.	32	1	31	43	13	26	46	14	<1	15	5	2
Fraud & forg.	45	-	23	29	29	13	58	23	3	26	7	-
Crim. damage	31	-	47	28	52	-	30	20	2	10	3	-
Drugs	72	-	3	83	-	3	55	7	7	-	-	-
Other not.	15	-	11	85	6	2	15	17	-	4	30	2
Non-notifiable												
Public order	6	-	11	91	15	2	5	4	-	3	-	-
Motoring	38	6	13	92	3	-	16	4	-	3	20	1
Prostitution	3	-	3	97	-	-	-	2	26	2	-	-
Miscellaneous	22	-	33	67	33	-	22	-	-	11	-	-
All offences	**13**	**3**	**12**	**29**	**11**	**4**	**13**	**6**	**1**	**5**	**3**	**<1**

Notes:
1. N=1,114. Data were missing in 61 cases.
2. Prosecutors could provide multiple responses to this question.

Table A.7 Main sentence for defendants found guilty in magistrates' courts, by age, sex, ethnic origin and employment status

	Custody	Community sentences	Fine/ compensation	Other
	%	%	%	%
Sex:				
Male	12	26	34	29
Female	4	13	46	38
Ethnic origin:				
White	10	23	36	31
Black	13	25	33	0
Asian	9	27	36	27
Other	18	18	47	18
Age:				
Juvenile	10	49	3	37
17–20	14	23	36	28
21–29	9	19	47	26
30–59	8	20	36	36
60+	14	14	43	29
Employment status:				
Employed	3	15	53	29
Unemployed	14	24	34	28
Other	8	37	10	45
Total (n)	**10 (68)**	**23(156)**	**37(248)**	**31(207)**

Notes:
1. N=679. Data were missing in 36 cases.
2. 'Other' includes discharge, driving ban, bindovers, costs, etc.
3. Percentages do not always sum to 100 due to rounding.

Appendix B
Multivariate analyses

Table B.1 Logistic regression model predicting requests for legal advice

Variable	ß	Significance	R	Odds Ratio
Offence		.0000	.1661	
Station		.0000	.1085	
Offence seriousness[2]:		.0000	.1044	
Moderate	-1.7531	.0000	-.0959	.1732
Less	-2.0182	.0000	-.1037	.1329
Ethnic origin[3]:		.0000	.0719	
Black	.5605	.0000	.0636	1.7515
Asian	.5490	.0004	.0476	1.7316
Other		n.s[4]		
Previous convictions	.3730	.0000	.0619	1.4521
Employed	.3458	.0000	.0589	1.4132
Answering bail	-.4878	.0011	-.0433	.6140
Condition on arrival	.3270	.0016	.0415	1.3868

Notes:
1. N=3,483 (suspects only). Data were missing in 199 cases.
2. Estimate of the increased odds of requesting legal advice for defendants arrested for offences of these levels of seriousness was compared with those arrested for 'Very Serious' offences (see Appendix C for a breakdown).
3. Estimate of the increased odds of requesting legal advice for defendants of these ethnic origins was compared with 'White' defendants.
4. Not significant.
5. Other variables tested were: age; mental health status; whether on s.48 remand; time of arrival at the police station; and place of residence.

Table B.2 Logistic regression model predicting admission by the suspect

Variable	ß	Significance	R	Odds Ratio
Sufficiency of evidence	1.2086	.0000	.1985	3.3488
Offence		.0000	.1506	
Legal advice	-1.0410	.0000	-.1746	.3531
Condition on arrival	-.4544	.0002	-.0577	.6348
Sex of suspect	.5266	.0001	.0585	1.6932
Ethnic origin[2]:	.	.0015	.0510	
Black	-.4530	.0029	-.0435	.6357
Asian		n.s.[3]		
Other	-.6851	.0067	-.0384	.5041
Juvenile	.3887	.0020	.0455	1.4751
Station		.0150	.0263	

Notes:
1. N=2,649 (suspects only). Data were missing in 1,033 cases.
2. Estimate of the increased odds of admitting the offence for defendants of these ethnic origins was compared with 'White' defendants.
3. Not significant.
4. Other variables tested were: seriousness of the offence; employment status; mental health status; place of residence; whether the suspect was answering police bail; whether on a s.48 remand; previous convictions and cautions; and time of arrival at the police station.

Table B.3 Logistic regression model predicting whether a suspect will be NFAed

Variable	ß	Significance	R	Odds Ratio
Exercise of silence	-1.0767	.0000	-.1263	.3407
Sufficiency of evidence	-1.3973	.0000	.2028	.2473
Admission-	2.9136	.0000	.3415	.0543
Condition on arrival	-.9011	.0005	.0730	.4061
Offence		.0002	.0798	
Station		.0003	.0813	
Legal advice	-.5129	.0018	-.0634	.5988
Sex of suspect	.5040	.0237	.0402	1.6553
Place of residence	.4295	.0267	.0389	1.5366
Circumstances of arrest[2]:		.0368	.0368	
Proactive		n.s.[3]		
Other	-1.0985	.0110	.0481	.3334

Notes:
1. N=1,819. Data were missing in 1,456 cases.
2. Estimate of the increased odds of being NFAed for defendants arrested in these circumstances was compared with those arrested as a result of 'Reactive Policing' methods.
3. Not significant.
4. Other variables tested were: ethnic origin; seriousness of the offence; previous convictions; age; employment status; mental health status; and whether on s.48 remand.

Table B.4 Logistic regression model predicting whether a suspect will be charged

Variable	ß	Significance	R	Odds Ratio
Previous convictions	1.9726	.0000	.2665	7.1893
Offence		.0000	.1743	
Offence seriousness[2]:		.0000	.1248	
Moderate		n.s.[3]		
Less		n.s.[3]		
Station		.0000	.1158	
Legal advice	.9487	.0000	.1019	2.5825
Juvenile	-1.0787	.0000	-.1065	.3400
Admission	-1.5319	.0000	-.1611	.2161
Place of residence	.4692	.0261	.0408	1.5987
Employed	.3470	.0450	.0337	1.4148

Notes:
1. N=1,689. Data were missing in 835 cases.
2. Estimate of the increased odds of being charged for defendants arrested for offences of these levels of seriousness was compared with those arrested for 'Very Serious' offences (see Appendix C for a breakdown).
3. Not significant.
4. Other variables tested were: exercise of silence; sufficiency of evidence; condition on arrival; sex of suspect; circumstances of arrest; ethnic origin; mental health status; and whether on s.48 remand.

Table B.5 Logistic regression model predicting whether a suspect will be cautioned

Variable	ß	Significance	R	Odds Ratio
Juvenile	1.5045	.0000	.1502	4.5020
Admission	1.3991	.0000	.1486	4.0516
Previous convictions	-1.6297	.0000	-.2184	.1960
Offence		.0000	.1667	
Offence seriousness[2]:		.0000	.1383	
Moderate		n.s.[3]		
Less		n.s.[3]		
Previous cautions	-.9737	.0000	-.1178	.3777
Legal advice	-.9576	.0000	-.1046	.3838
Station		.0000	.1032	
Place of residence	-.5090	.0180	-.0460	.6011

Notes:
1. N=1,546. Data were missing in 978 cases.
2. Estimate of the increased odds of being cautioned for defendants arrested for offences of these levels of seriousness was compared with those arrested for 'Very Serious' offences (see Appendix C for a breakdown).
3. Not significant.
4. Other variables tested were: exercise of silence; sufficiency of evidence; condition on arrival; sex of suspect; circumstances of arrest; ethnic origin; mental health status; employment status; and whether on s.48 remand.

Table B.6 Logistic regression model predicting whether juvenile suspects will be referred for an inter-agency decision

Variable	ß	Significance	R	Odds Ratio
Station		.0000	.2204	
Admission	.3584	.0294	.0755	1.9317
Ethnic origin[2]:		.0385	.0705	
Black	-1.2271	.0073	-.1039	.2931
Asian		n.s.[3]		
Other		n.s.[3]		

Notes:
1. N=502. Data were missing in 107 cases.
2. Estimate of the increased odds of being referred for defendants of these ethnic origins was compared with 'White' defendants.
3. Not significant.
4. Other variables tested were: sex; mental health status; place of residence; receipt of legal advice; sufficiency of the evidence; and exercise of the right of silence.

Table B.7 Logistic regression model predicting case termination decisions by the CPS

Variable	ß	Significance	R	Odds Ratio
Domestic violence	1.54	.0000	.1453	4.65
Co-defendants	1.13	.0000	.1635	3.10
Admission	-1.22	.0000	-.1772	.30
Offence type		.0017	.0947	
Ethnic origin[2]:		.0072		
Black	.68	.0312	.0568	1.98
Asian	1.11	.0033	.0901	3.02
Other		non-sig		
Previous convictions	-.47	.0357	-.0542	.63
Seriousness of offence		.0351	.0570	

Notes:
1. N=1,034. Data were missing in 141 cases.
2. Estimate of the increased odds of case termination for defendants of these ethnic origins was compared with white defendants.
3. Other variables tested were: area; legal advice; exercise of silence; outstanding files; and witnesses' previous convictions.

Table B.8 Logistic regression model predicting the imposition of a custodial sentence

Variable	ß	Significance	R	Odds Ratio
Previous custody	1.24	.0000	.1906	3.46
Files outstanding	1.23	.0000	.1914	3.44
Seriousness of offence[2]:		.0000	.2543	
Moderately serious	-4.07	.0000	-.1823	.0171
Less serious	-5.03	.0000	-.2338	.0050
Previous convictions	1.46	.0038	.1117	4.30

Notes:
1. N=648. Data were missing in 118 cases.
2. Estimate of the odds of a custodial sentence compared moderately serious and less serious offences with very serious offences (see Appendix C for a breakdown of offences according to seriousness).
3. Other variables tested were: sex of defendant; employment status; area; number of charges; type of offence; legal advice; exercise of silence; and plea.

Table B.9 Logistic regression model predicting committal to Crown Court

Variable	ß	Significance	R	Odds Ratio
Seriousness of offence[2]:		.0000	.2895	
Moderately serious	-4.64	.0000	-.2316	.0097
Less serious	-6.45	.0000	-.2934	.0016
Age	-2.27	.0048	-.1216	.10
Exercise of silence	.98	.0028	.1315	2.66
Number of charges	.74	.0222	.0897	2.09
Area		.0194	.0663	

Notes:
1. N=489. Data were missing in 438 cases. The same findings were produced when the model was re-run for only those cases where the suspect was interviewed at the police station (n=489; 34 missing cases).
2. Estimate of the increased odds of committal to Crown Court compared moderately serious and less serious offences with very serious offences.
3. Other variables tested were: ethnic origin; type of offence; co-defendants; and legal advice.

Appendix C
Model of seriousness of the offence

The classification of offences used by Brown, Ellis and Larcombe (1992) was expanded upon.

Very serious offences:

Murder
Attempted murder
Threat or conspiracy to murder
Manslaughter
Causing death by dangerous driving
Grievous bodily harm
Rape
Indecent assault on female
Gross indecency
Attempted abduction
Kidnapping
Blackmail
Riot

Moderately serious offences:

Actual bodily harm
Other violence
Indecent assault on male
Indecency between males
Other sexual offences
Burglary dwelling
Burglary other
Aggravated burglary
Robbery assault with intent to rob
Taking without the owner's consent
Aggravated vehicle taking

Theft from vehicle
Theft from person
Theft of pedal cycle
Theft of vehicle
Theft other
Theft from employer
Abstracting electricity
Going equipped
Found in enclosed premises
Interference with motor vehicle
Handling stolen goods
Fraud false accounting
Forgery
Obtain goods services by deception
Arson
Criminal damage – over £20
Criminal damage – value not known
Production / supply of controlled drug
Possession controlled drug
Violent disorder
Affray
Fear / provocation of violence
Other public order
Dangerous driving
Careless driving resulting in death
Careless driving
Driving after consuming drugs or alcohol
Driving whilst disqualified
Absconding from lawful custody
Pervert the course of justice

Less serious offences:

Common assault
Assault on constable
Prostitution
Shoplifting
Criminal damage – £20 or less
Harassment / alarm / distress
Breach of peace
Drunk and disorderly
Drunk and incapable
Vagrancy
Obstruction of police
Indecent exposure

Possession offensive weapon
Other licence insurance / documentation
Speeding
Other motoring
Failure to appear at court
Immigration offences
Miscellaneous offences
Warrant – non payment of fine
Warrant – failure to appear
Breach of injunction
S.48 PACE remand
Refusal to provide breath specimen
S.25 PACE

References

Ashworth, A. and Fionda, J. (1994). 'The new code for Crown Prosecutors: (1) Prosecution, Accountability and the Public Interest'. *Criminal Law Review,* pp. 894-903.

Association of Chief Police Officers. (1993). *ACPO Right of Silence Survey.* (Unpublished.)

Association of Chief Police Officers. (1995). *The Cautioning of Offenders.* ACPO Crime Committee. (Unpublished.)

Baldwin, J. (1985). PRG –Trial Criminal Justice. Oxford: Blackwell.

Baldwin, J. (1992). *The Role of Legal Representatives at Police Stations.* Royal Commission on Criminal Justice Research Study No.2. London: HMSO.

Barclay, G. (ed.) (1995). *Information on the Criminal Justice System in England and Wales.* London: Home Office Research and Statistics Department.

Bean, P. and Nemitz, T. (1994). *Out of Depth and Out of Sight.* Final report of research commissioned by Mencap on the implementation of the appropriate adult scheme. University of Loughborough: Midlands Centre for Criminology.

Block, B., Corbett, C. and Peay, J. (1993). *Ordered and directed acquittals in the Crown Court.* Royal Commission on Criminal Justice Research Study No.15. London: HMSO.

Bond, R.A. and Lemon, N.F. (1981). 'Training, experience and magistrates' sentencing philosophies'. *Law and Human Behaviour,* 5, pp.123-139.

Bottomley, A.K. and Coleman, C. (1976). 'Criminal statistics: the police role in the discovery and detection of crime'. *International journal of criminology and penology,* (4), 33-58.

Bottomley, K., Coleman C., Dixon. D., Gill, M. and Wall, D. (1989). *The Impact of Aspects of the Police and Criminal Evidence Act 1984 on Policing in a Force in the North of England.* Final report to ESRC. Unpublished.

Bowling, B. and Phillips, C. (forthcoming). 'Race', Crime and Criminal Justice. London: Longman.

Bridges, L. and Hodgson, J. (1995). 'Improving custodial legal advice'. *Criminal law review*, 101–113.

Bridges, L. and Choongh, S. (1996). *Evaluation of Training and Accreditation Scheme for Non-solicitor Police Station Advisers.* Report to Legal Aid Board and Law Society of pilot stage of research into the police station accreditation scheme. Unpublished.

Brown, D. (1989). *Detention at the Police Station under the Police and Criminal Evidence Act 1984.* Home Office Research Study No.104. London: HMSO.

Brown, D. (1991). *Investigating Burglary: the Effects of PACE.* Home Office Research Study No.123. London: HMSO.

Brown, D., Ellis, T. and Larcombe, K. (1992). *Changing the Code: Police Detention under the Revised Pace Codes of Practice.* Home Office Research Study No.129. London: HMSO.

Brown, D. (1994). 'The incidence of right of silence in police interviews: the research evidence reviewed'. *Research Bulletin,* (35), 57–75. London: Home Office Research and Statistics Department.

Brown, D. and Ellis, T. (1994). *Policing Low-level Disorder: Police Use of Section 5 of the Public Order Act 1986.* Home Office Research Study No.135. London: HMSO.

Brown, D. (1996). *Research Update on Offending on Bail.* Report to the Bail Issues Steering Group. Unpublished.

Brown, D. (1997). *Pace Ten Years On: a Review of the Research.* Home Office Research Study No.155. London: HMSO.

Brown, D. (1998). *Offending on Bail and Police Use of Conditional Bail.* Home Office Research and Statistics Directorate Research Findings No.72. London: Home Office

Brown, I. and Hullin, R. (1992). 'A study of sentencing in the Leeds magistrates' court: the treatment of ethnic minority and white offenders'. *British Journal of Criminology,* 32, 1, pp.41-53.

Bucke, T. (1995). *Policing and the Public: Findings from the 1994 British Crime Survey.* Home Office Research and Statistics Department Research Findings No.28. London: Home Office.

Bucke, T. (1997). *Ethnicity and Contacts with the Police: latest findings from the British Crime Survey.* Home Office Research and Statistics Directorate Research Findings No.59. London: Home Office.

Bucke, T. and Brown, D. (1997). *In Police Custody: police powers and suspects' rights under the revised PACE Codes of Practice.* Home Office Research Study 174. London: Home Office.

Bucke, T., Street, R. and Brown, D. (in press). *The Right of Silence: the impact of the Criminal Justice and Public Order Act 1994.* Home Office Research Study. London: HMSO.

Burrows, J., Henderson, P. and Morgan, P.M. (1994). *Improving Bail Decisions: the bail process project, phase 1.* Research and Planning Unit Paper 90. London: Home Office.

Cavadino, P. and Gibson, B. (1993). *Bail: the law, best practice and the debate.* Winchester: Waterside Press.

Cherrett, K. (1995). 'Policing the mentally ill: an attitudinal study of police contact with mentally disordered persons within the Gwent constabulary'. *The Police Journal,* January, 22-28.

Commission for Racial Equality. (1992). *Juvenile Cautioning - Ethnic Monitoring in Practice.* London: Commission for Racial Equality.

Crawford, A., Jones, T., Woodhouse, T. and Young, J. (1990). *The Second Islington Crime Survey.* London: Middlesex Polytechnic Centre for Criminology.

Cretney, A. and Davis, G. (1996). 'Prosecuting "domestic" assault'. *Criminal Law Review,* pp 162-174.

Crisp, D. and Moxon, D. (1994). *Case Screening by the Crown Prosecution Service: how and why Cases are Terminated.* Home Office Research Study No. 137. London: HMSO.

Cromack, V. (1995). 'The policing of domestic violence – an empirical study'. *Policing and Society*, vol.5, pp.185-199.

Crow, I. and Cove, J. (1984). 'Ethnic minorities and the courts'. *Criminal Law Review*, July, pp.413-417.

Crown Prosecution Service. (1993). *A Statement of Prosecution Policy: Domestic Violence.* CPS: London.

Crown Prosecution Service. (1994a). *The Code for Crown Prosecutors.* London: CPS.

Crown Prosecution Service. (1994b). *Discontinuance Survey November 1993: Report.* London: CPS.

Crown Prosecution Service. (1994c). *Charging Standard for Assaults.* CPS: London.

Crown Prosecution Service. (1995). *1994 Discontinuance Survey: Report.* London: CPS.

Crown Prosecution Service. (1997). *Annual Report for the Period April 1996 - March 1997.* London: CPS.

Department of Health and Home Office. (1992). *Review of Health and Social Services for Mentally Disordered Offenders and Others Requiring Similar Services.* Chairman: Dr John Reed. Cm.2088. London: HMSO.

Department of Health. (1995). *Child Protection: messages from research.* London: Department of Health.

Dixon, D., Bottomley, A.K., Coleman, C., Gill. M. and Wall, D. (1989). 'Reality and rules in the construction and regulation of police suspicion'. *International Journal of the Sociology of Law*, (17), pp 185-206.

Dixon, D. (1990). 'Juvenile suspects and the police and criminal evidence act'. In D. Freestone (ed.). *Children and the Law: essays in honour of Professor H.K.Bevan.* Hull: Hull University Press.

Dixon, D., Bottomley, K., Coleman, C., Gill. M. and Wall, D. (1990). 'Safeguarding the rights of suspects in police custody'. *Policing and Society*, (1), pp 115-140.

Evans, R. and Wilkinson, C. (1988). *The Impact of Home Office Circular 14/85 on Police Cautioning in England and Wales.* Report to the Home Office Research and Planning Unit. University of Birmingham. Unpublished.

Evans, R. and Wilkinson, C. (1990). 'Variations in police cautioning policy and practice in England and Wales'. *The Howard Journal of Criminal Justice*, (29), pp 155-176.

Evans, R. and Ferguson, T. (1991). *Comparing Different Juvenile Cautioning Systems in one Police Force Area.* A report to the Home Office Research and Planning Unit and Coventry Social Services Department. Unpublished.

Evans, R. (1992). *Evaluating and Comparing Young Adult Diversion Schemes in the Metropolitan Police Area.* Report to the Home Office Research and Planning Unit. Unpublished.

Evans, R. (1993). *The Conduct of Police Interviews with Juveniles.* Royal Commission on Criminal Justice Research Study No. 8. London: HMSO.

Evans, R. and Ellis, R. (1997). *Police Cautioning in the 1990s.* Home Office Research and Statistics Directorate Research Findings No.52. London: Home Office.

Evans, R. and Rawstorne, S. (1994). *The Protection of Vulnerable Suspects.* A report to the Home Office Research and Planning Unit. Unpublished.

FitzGerald, M. (1993). *Ethnic Minorities and the Criminal Justice System.* Royal Commission on Criminal Justice Research Study No.20. London: HMSO.

FitzGerald, M. (1995). 'Ethnic differences'. In Walker, M. (ed.). *Interpreting Crime Statistics.* Oxford: Oxford University Press.

FitzGerald, M. and Sibbitt, R. (1997). *Ethnic Monitoring in Police Forces: a beginning.* Home Office Research Study No. 173. London: Home Office.

Flood-Page, C. and Mackie, A. (1998). *Sentencing in the 1990s: an examination of sentencing practice in magistrates' courts and the Crown Court following recent legislation.* Home Office Research Study. London: Home Office.

Foster, J. (1990). *Villains: Crime and Community in the inner-city.* London: Routledge.

Gamache, D.J., Edleson, J.L. and Schock, M.D. (1988). 'Co-ordinated police, judicial and social service response to women battering: a multiple-baseline evaluation across three communities'. In **G.T.Hotaling, D.Finkelhor, J.K.Kirkpatrick and M.A.Strauss** (eds.) *Coping with Family Violence: research and policy perspectives.* Newbury Park, California: Sage.

Godson, D. and Quade, D. (1994). *Monitoring Arrest to Trial.* Report of a joint research project undertaken by Hampshire Police and probation services. Unpublished.

Grace, S., Lloyd, C. and Smith, L.J.F. (1992). *Rape: from Recording to Conviction.* Research and Planning Unit Paper 71. London: Home Office.

Grace, S. (1995). *Policing Domestic Violence in the 1990s.* Home Office Research Study No.139. London: HMSO.

Gudjunsson, G., Clare, I., Rutter, S. and Pearse, J. (1993). *Persons at Risk during Interviews in Police Custody: the identification of vulnerabilities.* Royal Commission on Criminal Justice Research Study No.12. London: HMSO.

Hallett, G. (1993). 'Better to summons than to arrest'. *Policing,* (9), pp 267–279.

Hedderman, C. and Moxon, D. (1992). *Magistrates' court or Crown Court? Mode of trial decisions and sentencing.* Home Office Research Study No. 125. London: Home Office.

Hedderman, C. and Hough, M. (1994). *Does the Criminal Justice System Treat Men and Women Differently?* Home Office Research and Statistics Department Research Findings No.10. London: Home Office.

Hedderman, C. and Gelsthorpe, L. (1997). *Understanding the Sentencing of Women. Home* Office Research Study 170. London: Home Office.

Hobbs, R. (1988). *Doing the business.* Oxford: Clarendon Press.

Home Affairs Committee. (1994). *Racial attacks and harassment. Volume 1: Report and Proceedings.* House of Commons Session 1993/4, Paper 71-1. London: HMSO.

Home Office. (Annually). *Criminal Statistics England and Wales.* London: HMSO.

Home Office. (1985). *The Cautioning of Offenders.* Circular 14/1985. London: Home Office.

Home Office. (1989). *Crime Statistics for the Metropolitan Police District by Ethnic Group, 1987: victims, suspects and those arrested.* Home Office Statistical Bulletin 6/89. London: Home Office.

Home Office. (1990a). *The Cautioning of Offenders.* Circular 59/1990. London: Home Office.

Home Office. (1990b). *Domestic Violence.* Circular 60/90. London: Home Office.

Home Office. (1990c). *Provision for mentally disordered offenders.* Circular 66/90. London: Home Office.

Home Office. (1992a). *Race and the Criminal Justice System.* London: Home Office.

Home Office. (1992b). *Gender and the Criminal Justice System.* London: Home Office.

Home Office. (1993). *Criminal Statistics England and Wales.* London: HMSO.

Home Office. (1994a). *The Cautioning of Offenders.* Circular 18/1994. London: Home Office.

Home Office. (1994b). *The Ethnic Origin of Prisoners.* Home Office Statistical Bulletin 21/94. London: Home Office Research and Statistics Department.

Home Office. (1995a). *Police and Criminal Evidence Act 1984 (s.60(1)(a) and s.66): Code of Practice Revised Edition (effective 10 April 1995).* London: HMSO.

Home Office. (1995b). *Criminal Statistics England and Wales.* London: HMSO.

Home Office. (1997a). *Criminal Statistics England and Wales.* London: HMSO.

Home Office. (1997b). *Race and the Criminal Justice System.* A Home Office publication under section 95 of the Criminal Justice Act 1991. London: Home Office.

Home Office. (1997c). *Wounding/Assault Offences: from prosecution to conviction.* (Unpublished.)

Home Office. (1998). *Criminal Justice Business Quarterly Report: fourth quarter (October – December) 1997.* London: Home Office Research and Statistics Directorate.

Hood, R. (1992). *Race and Sentencing: a study in the Crown Court.* Oxford: Clarendon Press.

Hooke, A., Knox, J. and Portas, D. (1996). *Evaluating Joint Performance Management between the Police and the Crown Prosecution Service.* Home Office Research and Statistics Directorate Research Findings No.40. London: Home Office.

Hughes, G. (1995). 'Beating the bandits'. *Police Review,* (103), pp 16–18.

Irving, B.L. and McKenzie, I. (1989). *Police Interrogation: the effects of the Police and Criminal Evidence Act 1984.* London: Police Foundation.

Jefferson, T. and Walker, M.A. (1992). 'Ethnic minorities in the criminal justice system'. *Criminal Law Review,* pp 83–95.

Jefferson, T. (1993). 'The racism of criminalization: police and the production of the criminal other'. In L. Gelsthorpe (ed.) *Minority Ethnic Groups in the Criminal Justice System.* Papers presented to the 21st Cropwood Roundtable Conference 1992. Institute of Criminology, University of Cambridge.

Jones, T., Maclean, B. and Young, J. (1986). *The Islington Crime Survey.* Aldershot: Gower.

Laing, J.M. (1996). 'The police surgeon and mentally disordered suspects: an adequate safeguard?' *Web Journal of Current Legal Issues,* (1), pp.29–36.

Landau, S.F. (1981). 'Juveniles and the police: who is charged immediately and who is referred to the juvenile bureau'. *British Journal of Criminology,* (21), pp 27–46.

Landau, S.F. and Nathan, G. (1983). 'Selecting delinquents for cautioning in the london metropolitan area'. *British Journal of Criminology,* (23), pp 128–149.

Leng, R. (1993). *The Right to Silence in Police Interrogation: a study of some of the issues underlying the debate.* Royal Commission on Criminal Justice Research Study No.10. London: HMSO.

Madison, D. (1994). *Instant Cautions for Summary Offences.* Report of work undertaken under the Police Research Group Police Research Award Scheme. London: Home Office Police Department.

Mair, G. (1986). 'Ethnic minorities, probation and the magistrates' court: a pilot study'. *British Journal of Criminology,* 26, 2, pp.147–156.

Mawby, R.I. (1979). *Policing the City.* Farnborough: Saxon House.

Mawby, R.I. (1980). 'Sex and crime: the results of a self-report study'. *British Journal of Sociology,* (31), pp 525-543.

Mayhew, P., Aye Maung, N. and Mirrlees-Black, C. (1993). *The 1992 British Crime Survey.* Home Office Research Study No.132. London: HMSO.

Maynard, W. (1994). *Witness Intimidation: strategies for prevention.* Police Research Group Crime Detection and Prevention Series paper 55. London: Home Office Police Department.

McConville, M. and Baldwin, J. (1981). *Crime, Courts and Conviction.* Oxford: Oxford University Press.

McConville, M., Sanders, A. and Leng, R. (1991). *The Case for the Prosecution.* London: Routledge.

McConville, M. and Hodgson, J., with the assistance of **Jackson, M. and Macrae, E.** (1993). *Custodial Legal Advice and the Right to Silence.* Royal Commission on Criminal Justice Research Study No.16. London: HMSO.

McConville, M., Hodgson, J, Bridges, L and Pavlovic, A.(1994). *Standing Accused: the organisation and practices of criminal defence lawyers in Britain.* Oxford: Clarendon Press.

Mirrlees-Black, C., Mayhew, P. and Percy, A. (1996). *The British Crime Survey.* Home Office Statistical Bulletin, Issue 19/96. London: Home Office Research and Statistics Directorate.

Mitchell, B. (1983). 'Confessions and police interrogation of suspects'. *Criminal Law Review,* 596-604.

Morgan, P.M. (1992). *Offending while on Bail: a survey of recent studies.* Research and Planning Unit Paper No. 65. London: Home Office.

Morgan, R., Reiner, R. and McKenzie, I.K. (1991). *Police Powers and Police: a study of the work of custody officers.* Full final report to the ESRC. Unpublished.

Morgan, P. and Henderson, P. (1998). *Remand Decisions and Offending on Bail: evaluation of the Bail Process Project.* Home Office Research Study No.184. London: Home Office.

Morley, R. and Mullender, A. (1994). *Preventing Domestic Violence to Women.* Police Research Group Crime Prevention Series Paper No.48. London: Home Office Police Department.

Morris, P. (1980). *Police Interrogation: review of literature.* Royal Commission on Criminal Procedure Research Study No.3. London: HMSO.

Mortimer, A. (1994). 'Asking the right questions'. *Policing,* vol.10, No.2, Summer.

Moston, S., Stephenson, G. and Williamson, T. (1990). *Police Interrogation Styles and Suspect Behaviour.* Final report to the Home Office Police Requirements Support Unit. University of Kent Institute of Social and Applied Psychology. Unpublished.

Moston, S., Stephenson, G. and Williamson, T. (1992). 'The incidence, antecedents and consequences of suspects' use of the right to silenc''. *Criminal Behaviour and Mental Health.*

Moston, S. and Stephenson, G. (1993). *The Questioning and Interviewing of Suspects outside the Police Station.* Royal Commission on Criminal Justice Research Study No.22. London: HMSO.

Painter, K., Lea, J., Woodhouse, T. and Young, J. (1989). *Hammersmith and Fulham Crime and Police Survey,* 1988. Centre for Criminology: Middlesex Polytechnic.

Palmer, C. and Hart, M. (1996). *A PACE in the Right Direction?* Institute for the Study of the Legal Profession, Faculty of Law, University of Sheffield.

Parker, C. (1992). *Confessions and the Mentally Vulnerable Suspect.* Thesis submitted for L.L.M. in Human Rights and Civil Liberties. Unpublished.

Raine, J. and Willson, M. (1994). *Conditional Bail or Bail with Conditions? The use and effectiveness of bail conditions.* A report for the Home Office: School of Public Policy, University of Birmingham. Unpublished.

Ratcliffe, P. (ed.) (1996). *Ethnicity in the 1991 Census. Volume Three: social geography and ethnicity in Britain: geographical spread, spatial concentration and internal migration.* London: HMSO.

Reiner, R. (1993). 'Race, crime and justice: models of interpretation'. In **L. Gelsthorpe** (ed.) *Minority Ethnic Groups in the Criminal Justice System.* Papers presented to the 21st Cropwood Roundtable Conference 1992. Institute of Criminology, University of Cambridge.

Robertson, G. (1992). *The Role of Police Surgeons.* Royal Commission on Criminal Justice Research Study No.6. London: HMSO.

Robertson, G., Pearson, R. and Gibb, R. (1995). *Entry of Mentally Ill People to the Criminal Justice System.* Final report to the Home Office Research and Planning Unit. London: Department of Forensic Psychiatry, Institute of Psychiatry.

Royal Commission on Criminal Justice. (1993). Chairman: Viscount Runciman of Doxford CBE, FBA. Cm. 2263. *Report.* London: HMSO.

Rumgay, J. (1995). 'Custodial decision making in a magistrates' court: court culture and immediate situational factors'. *British Journal of Criminology,* 35, 2, pp.201-217.

Sampson, A. and Phillips, C. (1992). *Multiple Victimisation: racial attacks on an East London estate.* Police Research Group Crime Prevention Unit Series: Paper No.36. London: Home Office Police Department.

Sanders, A., Bridges, L., Mulvaney, A. and Crozier, G. (1989). *Advice and Assistance at Police Stations and the 24-hour Duty Solicitor Scheme.* London: Lord Chancellor's Department.

Savage, S.P, Moon, G., Kelly, K. and Bradshaw, Y. (1997). 'Divided loyalties? - The police surgeon and criminal justice'. *Policing and Society,* vol.7, 79-98.

Scarman. (1981). *The Brixton Disorders 10-12 April 1981.* Report of an inquiry by the Rt. Hon. Lord Scarman, OBE. Cmnd.8427. London: HMSO.

Sherman, L.W. and Berk, R.A. (1984). 'The specific deterrent effects of arrest for domestic assault'. *American Sociological Review,* 49, 2, pp.261-272.

Skogan, W. (1990). *The Police and Public in England and Wales.* Home Office Research Study No.117. London: HMSO.

Skogan, W. (1994). *Contacts between Police and Public: findings from the 1992 British Crime Survey.* Home Office Research Study No.134. London: HMSO.

Smith, D.J. (1994). 'Race, crime and criminal justice'. In M. Maguire, R. Morgan and R. Reiner (eds), *The Oxford Handbook of Criminology.* Oxford: Clarendon Press.

Smith, D.J. and Gray, J. (1985). *Police and People in London.* Aldershot: Gower.

Smith, L.J.F. (1990). *Domestic Violence.* Home Office Research Study No.107. London: HMSO.

Softley, P. with the assistance of **Brown, D., Forde, B., Mair, G. and Moxon, D.** (1980). *Police Interrogation: an observational study in four police stations.* Home Office Research Study No.61. London: HMSO.

Southgate, P. and Crisp, D. (1993). *Public Satisfaction with Police Services.* Research and Planning Unit Paper 73. London: Home Office.

Steer, D. (1980). *Uncovering Crime: the police role.* Royal Commission on Criminal Procedure Research Study No.7. London: HMSO.

Stevens, P. and Willis, C.F. (1979). *Race, Crime and Arrests.* Home Office Research Study No.58. London: HMSO.

Tarling, R. (1993). *Analysing Offending: data, models and interpretations.* London: HMSO.

Walker, M, A. (1988). 'The court disposal of young males, by race, in London in 1983'. *British Journal of Criminology,* 28, (4), pp 441-460.

Walker, M.A. (1989). 'The court disposal and remands of White, Afro-Caribbean and Asian men (London, 1983)'. *British Journal of Criminology,* 29, 4, pp.353-367.

Walker, M.A., Jefferson, T. and Seneviratne, M. (1990). *Ethnic Minorities, Young People and the Criminal Justice System.* (Main report). Centre for Criminological and Socio-legal Studies, University of Sheffield.

Whittaker, C. and Mackie, A. with Lewis, R. and Ponikiewski, N. (1997). *Managing Courts Effectively: the reasons for adjournments in magistrates' courts.* Home Office Research Study No. 168. Home Office.

Wilkins, G. and Addicott, C. (1997). *Operation of Certain Police Powers under PACE: England and Wales 1996.* Home Office Statistical Bulletin 27/97. London: Home Office Research and Statistics Directorate.

Williamson, T. (1990). *Strategic Changes in Police Interrogation: an examination of police and suspect behaviour in the Metropolitan Police in order to determine the effects of new legislation, technology and organisational policies.* PhD thesis, Faculty of Social Science, University of Kent at Canterbury. Unpublished.

Willis, C.F. (1983). *The Use, Effectiveness and Impact of Police Stop and Search Powers.* Research and Planning Unit Paper 15. London: Home Office.

Working Group on Pre-Trial Issues. (1992). *Manual of Guidance for the Preparation, Processing and Submission of Files.* Unpublished.

Young, J. (1994). *Policing the Streets: stops and searches in North London.* Centre for Criminology: Middlesex University.

Zander, M. (1979). 'The investigation of crime: a study of contested cases at the Old Bailey'. *Criminal Law Review,* pp 203-219.

Zander, M. and Henderson, P. (1993). *Crown Court Study.* Royal Commission on Criminal Justice Research Study No.19. London: HMSO.

Publications

List of research publications

The most recent research reports published are listed below. A **full** list of publications is available on request from the Research and Statistics Directorate Information and Publications Group.

Home Office Research Studies (HORS)

176. **The perpetrators of racial harassment and racial violence.** Rae Sibbitt. 1997.

177. **Electronic monitoring in practice: the second year of the trials of curfew orders.** Ed Mortimer and Chris May. 1997.

178. **Handling stolen goods and theft: A market reduction approach.** Mike Sutton. 1998.

179. **Attitudes to punishment: findings from the British Crime Survey.** Michael Hough and Julian Roberts. 1998.

180. **Sentencing Practice: an examination of decisions in magistrates' courts and the Crown Court in the mid–1990's.** Claire Flood-Page and Alan Mackie. 1998.

181. **Coroner service survey.** Roger Tarling. 1998.

182. **The prevention of plastic and cheque fraud revisited.** Michael Levi and Jim Handley. 1998.

183. **Drugs and crime: the results of research on drug testing and interviewing arrestees.** Trevor Bennett. 1998.

184. **Remand decisions and offending on bail: evaluation of the Bail Process Project.** Patricia M Morgan and Paul F Henderson. 1998.

187. **Reducing Offending: An assesment of research evidence on ways of dealing with offending behaviour.** Edited by Peter Goldblatt and Chris Lewis. 1998.

Research Findings

52.   **Police cautioning in the 1990s.** Roger Evans and Rachel Ellis. 1997.

53.   **A reconviction study of HMP Grendon Therapeutic Community.** Peter Marshall. 1997.

54.   **Control in category c prisons.** Simon Marshall. 1997.

55.   **The prevalence of convictions for sexual offending.** Peter Marshall. 1997.

56.   **Drug misuse declared in 1996: key results from the British Crime Survey.** Malcolm Ramsay and Josephine Spiller. 1997.

57.   **The 1996 International Crime Victimisation Survey.** Pat Mayhew and Phillip White. 1997.

58.   **The sentencing of women: a section 95 publication.** Carol Hedderman and Lizanne Dowds. 1997.

59.   **Ethnicity and contacts with the police: latest findings from the British Crime Survey.** Tom Bucke. 1997.

60.   **Policing and the public: findings from the 1996 British Crime Survey.** Catriona Mirrlees-Black and Tracy Budd. 1997.

61.   **Changing offenders' attitudes and behaviour: what works?** Julie Vennard, Carol Hedderman and Darren Sugg. 1997.

62.   **Suspects in police custody and the revised PACE codes of practice.** Tom Bucke and David Brown. 1997.

63.   **Neighbourhood watch co-ordinators.** Elizabeth Turner and Banos Alexandrou. 1997.

64.   **Attitudes to punishment: findings from the 1996 British Crime Survey.** Michael Hough and Julian Roberts. 1998.

65.   **The effects of video violence on young offenders.** Kevin Browne and Amanda Pennell. 1998.

66.   **Electronic monitoring of curfew orders: the second year of the trials.** Ed Mortimer and Chris May. 1998.

67. **Public perceptions of drug-related crime in 1997.** Nigel Charles. 1998.

68. **Witness care in magistrates' courts and the youth court.** Joyce Plotnikoff and Richard Woolfson. 1998.

69. **Handling stolen goods and theft: a market reduction approach.** Mike Sutton. 1998.

70. **Drug testing arrestees.** Trevor Bennett. 1998.

71. **Prevention of plastic card fraud.** Michael Levi and Jim Handley. 1998.

72. **Offending on bail and police use of conditional bail.** David Brown. 1998.

73. **Voluntary after-care.** Mike Maguire, Peter Raynor, Maurice Vanstone and Jocelyn Kynch. 1998.

74. **Fast-tracking of persistent young offenders.** John Graham. 1998.

75. **Mandatory drug testing in prisons – an evaluation.** Kimmett Edgar and Ian O'Donnell. 1998.

Occasional Papers

Evaluation of a Home Office initiative to help offenders into employment. Ken Roberts, Alana Barton, Julian Buchanan and Barry Goldson. 1997.

The impact of the national lottery on the horse-race betting levy. Simon Field and James Dunmore. 1997.

The cost of fires. A review of the information available. Donald Roy. 1997.

Monitoring and evaluation of WOLDS remand prison and comparisons with public-sector prisons, in particular HMP Woodhill. A Keith Bottomley, Adrian James, Emma Clare and Alison Liebling. 1997.

Requests for Publications

Home Office Research Studies and Research Findings can be requested from:

Research and Statistics Directorate
Information and Publications Group
Room 201, Home Office
50 Queen Anne's Gate
London SW1H 9AT
Telephone: 0171-273 2084
Fascimile: 0171-222 0211
Internet: http://www.homeoffice.gov.uk/rsd/rsdhome.htm
E-mail: rsd.ho.apollo@gtnet.gov.uk

Occasional Papers can be purchased from:
Home Office
Publications Unit
50 Queen Anne's Gate
London SW1H 9AT
Telephone: 0171-273 2302

HMSO Publications Centre

(Mail, fax and telephone orders only)
PO Box 276, London SW8 5DT
Telephone orders: 0171-873 9090
General enquiries: 0171-873 0011
(queuing system in operation for both numbers)
Fax orders: 0171-873 8200